THE HAPPY SCIENCE

An
Introduction
to
SCHOOLS
OF
CONTEMPORARY
THEOLOGY

by
Randolph Carleton Chalmers

OBSERVER

MATRI
IN MEMORIAM

ISBN: Hardcover 0-919920-00-4
         Paperback 0-919920-01-2

Design by Graeme Armstrong

      Published by
The United Church Observer,
85 St. Clair Ave. E., Toronto M4T 1M8, Canada

in co-operation with
The Ecumenical Foundation of Canada

"Evangelical theology is
concerned with
Immanuel,
God with us!
Having this God for its object,
it can be nothing else
but the most thankful and
happy science."

***

Karl Barth

Contents

Preface

Christian truth has a constant element but it cannot be said to be static in this dynamic age of ferment and change. The contemporary shock created by rapid changes in recent decades has made an impact on both the church and theology as well as on all other aspects of human life. Within this century two world wars, a worldwide economic depression, continuing strife in many lands and the spectre of famine in the Third World have radically altered our view of progess.

Then, too, the rise of the Communist states, the secular view of life, the development of the permissive society, the advances of science and technology, the dawn of the space age, the problems of pollution and poverty, the critical attitude toward institutional religion, the uncertainty and confusion about many matters in both the church and in society — all these are evidence that a present shock has occurred in the life and thought of people in this century. This shock has left its mark on theology. Due in part to the rapidity and variety of change, from which the church is not exempt, various schools of theology have arisen in recent years. They have emphasized one or more aspects of doctrine and it is these schools and their doctrinal position which we will consider in the following pages.

There are no hard and fast divisions between the various schools of theology with which I am concerned in this book. Some of the theologians to whom I refer could be classified in more than one school. However, I hope that by my classification the reader will be able to take note of certain trends in theology and thus clarify his thinking about what has been taking place in the theological field in recent decades.

Wherever possible I have permitted the writers in these

various theological schools to speak for themselves through direct quotation. After setting forth the main emphases of each school, I have given a personal evaluation of them.

This book is written for those who have some knowledge and interest in theology. While the chapters are only brief outlines of the thought of the various schools of theology, I hope they will be of value in introducing students to the many fascinating areas of theology that are current in our time. Theology can still be called "The Queen of the Sciences", not in some medieval sense but in the sense that it is theology that deals with the basic issues of time and eternity.

All the books to which I have referred are listed in the bibliography and they will be of some help to students who wish to pursue further the study of one or more schools of theology.

Unless otherwise stated, the Bible quotations are from the Revised Standard Version.

Thanks are due to many persons: to two former colleagues on the faculty of the Atlantic School of Theology, Halifax — Dr. John B. Corston, who gave a critical reading to the entire manuscript, and Father Thomas Mabey who gave valuable help in making suggestions about Chapter Six; to the chief librarian of the Atlantic School of Theology, Sister Margaret Flahiff, and her assistant, Alice Harrison; to Gail Snarby, library secretary; to Jean Miller, the office secretary who typed most of the manuscript and Judy Cleveland who typed the bibliography. My wife, Evelyn, has given me patient co-operation and understanding as usual throughout this labour of love.

I wish also to thank The United Church Observer and the Ecumenical Foundation, together with Dr. A.C. Forrest and Dr. H.W. Vaughan, for their contributions to the publishing and editing of the manuscript.

R.C. Chalmers.

Lent, 1975
Bathurst, New Brunswick,
Canada.

Introduction

Theology is thinking about God. But it is not thinking about God in abstraction. Theology relates God to his world and to the life of people in the world. In order to be true to the doctrines of Creation, Incarnation and Redemption theology must show the relevance of these doctrines to the concrete situations and conditions of human life, including the influences, intellectual and otherwise, that play upon humanity in society's milieu.

Christianity, arising out of Judaism, has three important figures in its life and religion: the priest, the prophet and the theologian. The third figure has a responsibility to the first two as well as a special task of his own. Theology must give standing ground, focus and perspective to all thought about God and his meaning for human life. Far more than we realize, our theological thought is conditioned by WHERE we do our thinking and WHY we are constrained to think about God and the purpose of our life.

The task of the priest is to lead the people in the worship of God and to offer the sacrifices of the people to God. This task must be based on the priest's concept of both God and persons. Worship, therefore, must have a theological orientation.

The theologian also has the responsibility of assisting the prophet to declare the Word of God to the times in which he lives. The real task of theology in relation to prophecy is to be the critical guide and the illuminating director of the prophetic word which is uttered for the purpose of calling people to be stewards of God's gifts in the world.

In contemporary times, we have witnessed a type of theology that concentrates on the church and her structures, forms and orders, and which may leave the impression that God's only concern is the church. In contrast there has also developed a subjective type of theology which turns one's attention inward upon oneself, concentrating on self-identity and thus becoming absorbed in what Helmut Gollwitzer calls "the abstract ego". Both types of theology by-pass the person in the world and consequently are irrelevant.

Theology must recover the "gritty historicity" (Hans Wolff) of the Old Testament. Theology, in accord with Hebraic thought, must free itself for engagement with the real life of people in their historic setting and thus make them face up to the fundamental questions regarding life's end and goal.

Christian theology should also arise out of an orientation that is based on both Testaments, the Old and the New. These two Testaments belong together. The Old Testament was the bible of Jesus, Paul and the early church. A true interpretation of the theology of the New Testament is founded on a knowledge of the Old Testament. The categories of thought in both Testaments are similar. Unless we see the historical, convenantal and semantic bonds between the two Testaments, our theology will not be a true expression of the christian faith.

We would ask the reader to keep in mind these duties of theology as he reads the following chapters: the need to serve both the priest and the prophet; to be incarnational and historical; and to take into its purview the message of the Word that is derived from both the Old and the New Testament.

It is our purpose in subsequent chapters of this book to show how and in what manner various emphases or schools of theology in recent years have helped, or hindered, both the church and christian disciples in their witness in the world.

Recent and current theological thought owes much of its origin to trends in the philosophy and theology of the nineteenth century. We will trace some of these influences in the first chapter as a background for understanding the various schools of thought.

I

Nineteenth Century Philosophy and Theology

The nineteenth century was "The Great Century" (Latourette) of the church's missionary expansion. It also saw the beginnings of the modern ecumenical movement and the "social gospel" emphasis in Christianity.

But the nineteenth century also witnessed several developments in society which had a subsequent bearing on christian thinking. For example, the industrial revolution, among other things, led to an increase in urbanization with its problems. The 'Copernican Revolution' created by science, especially Darwinism, made for theological difficulties in many quarters. Karl Marx wrote his treatises on Communism, and the seeds of Fascism were sown in Prussian politics and Hegelian philosophy. The methods and findings of science tended to destroy finality, hence the nineteenth century gave new impetus to relativity and a corresponding freedom for what was regarded as human progress in many spheres of life. The gist of these developments produced a tendency for theology to become anthropology (Feuerbach). August Comte's religion of man seemed the inevitable conclusion from these developments and once again there was a wide-spread conviction that "man was the master of things".

Related to, and involved in, these developments in nineteenth century philosophy and theology, there were two religious trends from the eighteenth century which took on added strength in nineteenth century religious thought, namely, pietism and rationalism. Pietism was a revolt against the stratified and ossified dogma of previous generations. It brought warmth into religion. It emphasized a personal life of devotion in which repentance, conversion and prayer played a major part. Many of its contributions were positive, although its somewhat exclusive emphasis upon the individual could be viewed as an inadequate basis for a christian faith.

Rationalism, which was a resurgence of Hellenic and Rennaissance thought, was related to Deism. Deism conceived of God as distant from his world. God was the giant clock-maker who had made the world, set it going, and then absented himself from it. This meant that God no longer mattered in the life of persons. However, man was endowed with reason (nous) and this, for the rationalist, was the final court of appeal in religion as in all other things. All ideas concerning revelation were unnecessary and irrelevant. The source of truth was human reason.

When rationalism was united with an optimistic view of man and his progress, as in the Enlightenment (Aufklaerung) in Germany, there developed a philosophy of life which had no place for either sin or redemption. Man could save himself by cultivating his rational capacities. The authority of reason supplanted the authority of the Bible.

In order to see these developments in nineteenth century philosophy and theology, we will turn our attention to the teachings of four thinkers whose influence in philosophy was very great: Kant, Schleiermacher, Hegel and Kierkegaard.

<u>IMMANUEL KANT</u>
(1724 — 1804)

"The man who was decisive for the theology of the nineteenth century ... is Kant."[1] This Koenigsberg philosopher, who never travelled more than fifty miles from his home, has influenced the world of human thought to an extent that is beyond calculation. Dr. H.P. Van Dusen writes "it is a truism that any discussion of nineteenth century thought, whether philosophical or theological, must make its start from Immanuel Kant. Completing his work

4

just as the century was dawning, he bequeathed the issues, and the terms for their discussion, which have largely dominated intellectual controversy since." [2]

Among the many influences on Kant's thinking were four of special significance. First, there was the pietism of his home that gave him a profound ethical consciousness but which blinded him to the value of religious institutions. In adult life he rebelled against the emotionalism of pietism. Secondly, the rationalism of the eighteenth century led him to believe that all philosophical thinking must begin with an analysis of one's own thought and not with sense experience. It has been said "Kant was a rationalist by education, temperament and conviction." [3] The third influence on Kant's thought was the scepticism of David Hume. He said that Hume awakened him from his "dogmatic slumbers", but, as Bertrand Russell avers, "the awakening was only temporary, and he soon invented a soporific which enabled him to sleep again." [4] Rationalist that Kant was, nevertheless he was led by Hume to cast doubt on the rationalistic approach to truth. Consequently all his life Kant was torn between belief in reason and scepticism regarding the truth which reason gives. Kant also came under the influence of the science of Isaac Newton which made him wonder whether science was the way to find the truth. Should he substitute science and its method for an analysis of his own consciousness? Thus a tension was created in his mind between science and subjective idealism, between empiricism stemming from Locke and idealism coming from Berkeley, both of which were overshadowed by the scepticism derived from Hume.

Kant's thinking centered around three questions: What can I know? What must I do? and What may I hope? In wrestling with these questions he wrote four books: *The Critique of Pure Reason* (Epistemology), *The Critique of the Practical Reason* (Ethics), *The Critique of Judgment* (Aesthetics) and *Religion within the Limits of Reason Alone.*

Knowledge

What can I know? asked Kant. He had faith in the capacity of reason to find the truth and yet he was sceptical regarding absolute truth. He realized that man was a finite creature as well as one that was corruptible. Yet he believed in the incorruptibility of reason. By means of reason Kant came to believe that we only know appearances, not reality itself. By means of mathematics and science we can know the world of appearances but we cannot know things as they really are in themselves. The mind receives the "raw" material and then "cooks" it, that is, transforms it, so that we never know, for example, WHAT a table is, only THAT it is.

This led Kant to distinguish in dualistic fashion between the world of phenomena and the world of noumena, between appearance and reality. Our knowledge is restricted to phenomena which we derive through sense experience (empiricism). But we can know nothing of the world of reality, the realm of truth, values and faith by means of reason. So we have arising a dualism between fact and value, science and faith, reason and truth. Religion for Kant, because of his presuppositions, had to be within "the bounds of Reason Alone". He became the progenitor of the Enlightenment because of his free use of reason and, following Rousseau, he believed in the all-sufficiency of man which made him a child of the Renaissance.

By means of reason Kant proceeded to dismiss the classic arguments for the existence of God, though he held the teleological argument in high regard and paid this tribute to it: "This proof always deserves to be mentioned with respect. It is the oldest, the clearest and the most accordant with the common reason of mankind." [5] From the rational standpoint this would be the only valid argument for God's existence, according to Kant. Yet he could come to no conclusion about God on this ground alone.

Ethics

It is when we turn to the practical reason, or ethics, that Kant believes we can find a valid argument for the existence of God. Ethics is the key to reality. Reason does not lead us to a knowledge of God but by means of the will we can know God. "Nothing is good except a goodwill." The way to God is by means of the "categorical imperative", the intuition of conscience which cannot be confounded or confuted. "I ought, therefore I am." Obedience to the moral law as made known to conscience is the road to reality. "Two things fill the mind with wonder and awe," wrote Kant: "the starry heavens above and the moral law within." The realm of "oughtness" unveils the truth of "isness". So we must "act in such a way that the maxim of our (my) will(s) can at the same time hold good as a principle of universal law." Partly because of the influence of pietism in his early life, and as a consequence of his conclusions about the moral imperative, it could be said that for Kant religion was reduced to morality. Duties must be regarded as divine commands. Man must be treated as an end in himself and never as a means to an end.

The three postulates or axioms of the practical reason, according to Kant, were God, freedom and immortality. He reasoned in this manner: God alone could be the source of the categorical imperative; an act to be moral must be a free decision of the will; and because the good life did not receive its equivalent of desserts in this world, there must be another world in which one would receive his due compensations.

Evaluation

At least the first two of Kant's postulates of the moral conscience still have validity. Dostoyevsky has one of his characters in The Brothers Karamazov say "Anything is permitted, if there is no God." A coerced action is immoral.

7

There is no doubt that Kant's emphasis on the moral law has its background in prophetic religion. We are also indebted to him for bringing out so clearly the finiteness of man and his reason with respect to life and truth.

On the debit side of the ledger, however, there are negative features in Kant's philosophy which have left to the modern age an unhealthy legacy in matters of faith. "It is hardly an exaggeration", writes Dr. Van Dusen, "that the influences which have followed from Kant have strangled and cursed the religious thought of our times." [6] For example, the legacy of a dualism between appearance and reality has had unhappy consequences. Since this seems to imply that the only dependable knowledge we can have is derived from the world of science and that things are only what their outward appearance suggests, then ultimate reality is forever unknowable. Much of current confusion in matters of religion stems from the critical, sceptical outlook left us by Kant. Again, by reducing religion and faith to the realm of morality, he brought in a "suffocating fog of moralism" which is far short of the world of values that Christianity opens up to the faithful. Kant seemed unaware of the fact that religion was not a matter of man striving after God in a moralistic manner, but of man's response to God who is ever seeking man. His deistic and moralistic idea of God left no room for the concept of God as Father, seeking the lost in love. And the social, corporate idea of the church was absent from his individualistic views of faith which, for Kant, was not the Pauline idea of faith but a "practical work-a-day relationship to things and people".

Another negative legacy from Kantian thought is his scepticism regarding the value of metaphysics. Since reason could not lead man to know the truth, the value of natural theology was undermined. Karl Barth was a student of Kant's philosophy in his early days and there is no doubt that his scepticism about the value of natural theology and metaphysics came from the influence of Kant on his thought. William Nicholls has Barth and his followers in mind when he writes: "When we find theologians of the

German tradition decrying metaphysics, while asserting that God is a transcendent person known only by faith, we can detect the influence of Kant. It is a commonplace of this tradition, right up to the present day, to follow Hume and Kant, ignoring the irony of the former, in believing that the destruction of metaphysics is a benefit to faith, and hence to theology." [7]

Someone has observed that "the roots of the present lie buried deep in the past" and that those "who deny history are bound to repeat it." So it is with Kant. The legalistic moralism, scientific scepticism, narrow individualism in religion, the dualism between faith and reason and the making of worship an elective in the school of religion—all these and much more have their origin, in part, in the thought of this bachelor of Koenigsberg.

FRIEDRICH SCHLEIERMACHER
(1768—1834)

This German theologian of the Reformed Church, who was a professor of theology, first at Halle and later at Berlin, has been called "the father of modern protestant theology." [8] H.R. Mackintosh writes "Romanticism, which is more a mood or temper than a creed, was a reaction against the predominance of classical norms in literature and art, as well as a revolt against the arid intellectuality of eighteenth-century rationalism. It may be defined as an impassioned return to natural instincts, to life, to freedom, to individual predilection, to the spontaneity of creative fancy ... 'Be thyself' was its insistent call ... Schleiermacher—without reservations—made himself the champion in the religious field." [9]

What Bishop Butler found in eighteenth century England among the intellectuals, namely, that religion was a matter for laughter, Schleiermacher discovered among the intellectuals in Germany, with their rationalistic approach to life. The first book Schleiermacher wrote shows how he attempted to meet this religious scepticism. The title read: *On Religion, Speeches addressed to its Cultured Despisers*. William Nicholls claims that Schleiermacher's aim "was to vindicate religion, considered as something distinct from the rational activity of philosophy and science, on the one hand, and from morality on the other. In thus distinguishing religion as something sui generis he did not wish to cut it off from either reason or morality, both of which followed from religion, in his view". [10]

Instead of arguing with the rationalists on their own ground, Schleiermacher attempted to deal with religion on another level entirely, that of the feelings. Religion was interpreted as a "feeling of dependence", by which he meant a non-cognitive relation to reality that had cognitive implications. Religious experience became the predominant factor in his thinking, not creeds or revelation. His greatest book, *The Christian Faith*, which has been called "the most influential dogmatic work to which evangelical Protestantism can point," gives a detailed exposition of this "feeling of dependence" in relation to Christian beliefs.

Feeling to Schleiermacher is not really subjective emotion, but "the impact of the universe upon us in the depths of our being, which transcends subject and object." [11] It is an apprehension or awareness of spiritual things. Sometimes he refers to intuition, by which he means a direct perception of the meaning of an object which confronts one's mind. "As often as I turn my gaze inward upon my inmost self," writes Schleiermacher, "I am at once within the domain of eternity." [12] At times he describes this feeling as "a taste and sense of the infinite". Religion for Schleiermacher finds its center in man, not in God. For him all religion begins in the soul of man. Christian dogmas are ways of stating or giving an account of the religious affections. He has a kinship with Feuerbach who turned theology into anthropology, as well as with pantheism as it was handed down from Spinoza.

As Kant was the father of modern liberalism by his stress on reason, so Schleiermacher helped in the development of liberalism by his revolt against orthodoxy and tradition. For him Christianity was not a matter of belief in dogmas but of the experience of faith in the depths of one's being.

Because of his centralizing of experience in religion, Schleiermacher has been called the father of the modern psychology of religion, of modern pietism, of sentimental religion that looks to an inward experience for truth, rather than to objective revelation.

Christian Teaching

How did Schleiermacher interpret the christian faith?

1. *Revelation.* Every communication of the UNIVERSE which brings inspiration and leads to freedom is revelation. The attributes of God have no objective reference but refer to ways in which the feeling of absolute dependence is conceived. To Schleiermacher "doctrines about God are no more than descriptions of our own feeling. They indicate something specific, not in God but in us ... Holiness, wisdom, love are but distinguishable shades of modifications in our God-consciousness or awareness of God."[13] God is now made in man's image. There is—and can be—no revelation in the traditional sense of God's initiative in speaking to and seeking man. Religion as such has nothing to do with a personal God outside the world.[14] Schleiermacher had a tendency to pantheism all his life, for to him God was only a subjective presence.

2. *Trinity.* Because of his emphasis on the feeling of dependence in the soul, Schleiermacher was at a loss to find any feelings corresponding to the triune nature of Deity. Because he also eliminated belief in a transcendent, personal God, there could be no "I-Thou" relationship established with God. Jesus Christ was not the second Person of the Trinity and the best he could say about the Holy Spirit was that he was the spirit of the community, or the church, whose fellowship meant much to Schleiermacher.

11

3. *Jesus.* He loves Jesus as the true Saviour, but in a rather sentimental manner. He is the representative man, sinless and perfect. He is known only in and through the Church. We can call him 'Saviour' because he imparts a God-consciousness to others, but he is not the Word of God become flesh. He disbelieved in Christ's resurrection. His picture of Jesus has docetic ear-marks, because Jesus was not really tempted and tried. He had no real struggles in his earthly life.

On other Christian doctrines Schleiermacher shows the weaknesses of a religion of experience. Sin is not rebellion against God but a conflict between flesh and spirit. Consequently his teaching on atonement and redemption is quite unbiblical. The biblical doctrine of grace as divine love for the undeserving sinner is overlooked. The Old Testament he considered to be a book of legalism, containing very little that was of spiritual value.

Evaluation

In his time Schleiermacher provided an alternative to rationalism in the field of religion. He also showed that religion need not be dependent on science or anything else for its validation. He claimed that the roots of religion lie deeper in human life than that which can be proven by empirical means. And the large place he gave to the corporate fellowship of the church was an antidote to individualistic tendencies in religion in his time.

But the fact is that Schleiermacher turned the christian faith upside down by discarding the divine initiative in revelation, and substituting the soul's experience of some vague, subjective reality called 'feeling'. Schleiermacher's 'feeling of absolute dependence' was a soul state, with no objective ground to support or validate it. His 'feeling' for Jesus was so largely sentimental that it produced a Christology which was docetic and anti-historical.

In his revolt against Kantian rationalism and moralism

Schleiermacher went to other extremes and thus tended to become anti-rational and anti-moral. He went so far as to say that "ideas and principles are foreign to religion." In this way he tried to bypass the arguments of the rationalists. His anti-moralistic statements would lead one into a morass of ethical confusion.

With others in the Romantic movement in theology, Schleiermacher gave such a large place to freedom of expression in matters of faith and life that the believer, so he thought, would be free from dogma, from principles and any restrictions whatever. He did not conceive of freedom as 'freedom for', or in terms of being free in order to be responsible. Thus Schleiermacher became one of the forerunners of modern permissiveness in morals and of some of the 'free' interpretations associated with situation ethics.

The weakness of Schleiermacher's theology is that its centre is man, not God. There is really nothing distinctive about the christian faith, according to Schleiermacher, because when that faith is interpreted in terms of religious experience instead of objective truth, there is nothing to distinguish this faith from the faith of a Muslim, a Hindu, or a Jain. We then find ourselves in a bog of syncretism which G.K. Chesterton described as "religion gone to pot". What Schleiermacher did not see was that religion vaporizes unless it is rooted in history, unless it has an objective and transcendent ground in reality, and unless that reality has made himself personally known in his self-revelation through faith. "For by grace you have been saved through faith (not experience); and that is not your own doing, it is the gift of God" (Ephesians 2:8). It is this matter of faith being a "gift" which Schleiermacher overlooked to the detriment of his theology.

G.W. FRIEDRICH HEGEL
(1770—1831)

This German idealist taught philosophy in the University of Berlin at the same time as Schleiermacher.

Hegel was a philosophical monist who, desirous of creating a new synthesis, subsumed all of life under IDEA or MIND. All things were unified into a synthesis under one mind. Plurality was therefore an illusion.

To Hegel the rational was the real and the real was the rational. Unlike Kant in some of his teaching, he was, nevertheless, a noted rationalist, without that element of scepticism which permeated the rationalism of Kant. To Hegel reason is the final court of appeal. He developed a philosophical system of speculative rationalism in which reason is absolute and thereby set free from all limitations whether of finiteness or sin. Reason is the source of strength, dignity and value.

While Hegel's system of thought is anthropocentric, like that of Schleiermacher, yet his point of view is the very opposite of Schleiermacher concerning the source of truth. For Schleiermacher feeling was all-important. Hegel considered feeling the lowest form of consciousness. According to him reason must prevail over feeling.

God

"God is God," wrote Hegel, "only in so far as he knows Himself; His self-knowledge is His self-consciousness in man" because, according to Hegel, the Absolute Mind is the essence of all finite minds, not another mind. Dr. Mackintosh comments: "Thus, it would appear, the Absolute has reality only in the thought of those who believe in Him." [15]

14

Dynamic View of Life

Contrary to the static categories in the thought of Kant's rationalistic view of life, Hegel conceived of the Idea and all of life in very dynamic terms. The world is in the process of becoming. The Spirit or Idea is always seeking to express itself. This expression must come chiefly through persons who embody the idea. In each generation there are special persons and groups who can express this idea in very significant ways.

This supreme spirit uses the method of dialectic to express itself in human life. This is not a dialectic of question and answer, as in Plato. It is the dialectic of thesis, antithesis and synthesis. In other words, at the heart of Hegel's dialectic are strife and conflict which seem to be the very law of life. Truth is found in opposites—light and darkness, heat and cold, external and internal, freedom and authority, capitalism and socialism. Out of the synthesis there arises something new which again becomes a thesis for a new antithesis. So the striving and the struggle go on through the whole of life. Karl Marx carried this dialectic into the economic realm, substituting matter for Idea, and expressed in theoretical, later practical, terms the struggle of socialism against capitalism.

The State

This struggle and conflict of Hegel's dialectic found its best expression through the state. Some states are better manifestations of this struggle than others. In his day, Hegel believed, and so did Bismarck and German militarists, that Prussia could best express the supreme Spirit in the world. It, therefore, had the right to conquer other states. "The state is the divine Idea as it exists on earth," wrote Hegel. "It is the fullest expression of the immanent activity of the divine Spirit." [16] In this glorification of the state, he singled out military leaders like

15

Alexander, Caesar and Napoleon as persons who made ideal leaders. His praise of Machiavelli and the German military spirit indicates how he values conflict and war. Bertrand Russell points out that Hegel sees a positive moral value in war. "War has the higher significance that through it the moral health of peoples is preserved in their indifference towards the stabilizing of finite determinations," writes Hegel. Therefore, comments Russell, "peace is ossification ... because a family of States needs an enemy. Conflicts of States can only be decided by war; States being towards each other in a state of nature, their relations are not legal or moral. Their rights have their reality in their particular wills, and the interest of each State is its own highest law. There is no contrast of morals and politics, because States are not subject to ordinary moral laws." [17] This is the philosophy of tyranny.

Evaluation

The whole totalitarian movement of the modern era owes much to the philosophy of Hegel. Both Communism and Fascism have their roots in Hegelian dialectic.

Karl Barth claims that Hegelianism is "the philosophy of self-confidence." In Hegel "we have a man who absolutely and undeviatingly believes in himself, who can doubt everything because he does not for a moment doubt himself, and who knows everything for the simple reason that he has complete trust in his own self-knowledge." [18] Barth also affirms that Hegel's philosophy "is not at all the accidental discovery of one particular, gifted individual but the mighty and impressive voice of an entire era, the voice of modern man, or of the man who, from 1700 to 1914, was called modern man." [19] "It is Titanism of the highest degree." It led to Nietzsche's Superman, the one who identified God with himself. In Hegel's view man is supreme and the tyrant or dictator rules the herd. In Hegel's theory we discern the truth of William Penn's words: "Man will be ruled either by tyrants or by God." Hegel's rule is ultimately the rule of the tyrant.

In Hegel's teaching the great doctrines of the christian faith are dissolved by the acids of speculative and rationalistic thinking. Instead of christian dogma, with its affirmations of truth, we are introduced to a fog of abstractions. Man has taken the place of God on the throne of the world and consequently man has unmanned himself.

SOREN KIERKEGAARD
(1813—1855)

This "melancholy Dane" said that while people did not give serious attention to what he had to write during his lifetime, yet the time would come when men and women would pay attention to his ideas. That prophecy has come true in the twentieth century. Kierkegaard has 'come into his own' in recent decades. As the father of existentialism, both religious and non-religious, his influence is widespread. As a precursor of Karl Barth he has had a large influence on the development of neo-orthodoxy. Barth wrote in his early days: "If I have a system, it consists in this, that always as far as possible I keep in mind what Kierkegaard spoke of as the infinite qualitative difference between time and eternity, alike in its negative and positive meaning. God is in heaven, you are on earth." [20]

Existential thinking is decisive thinking in which not only the intellect but the whole of one's existence is deeply involved. It is the opposite of purely academic or theoretical thought. It calls for commitment on the great issues in which, ultimately, life and death are involved.

Two experiences in early life helped to produce the melancholia which afflicted Soren. One happened when he was out on the moor with his father, and as a boy of tender conscience, heard his father curse God. He thought his father had committed the unpardonable sin. The other was his love affair with Regine Olsen. He could not make up his mind to marry her and finally broke off the engagement. This made him a more solitary and morose figure than before.

Kierkegaard studied theology but refrained from ordination in the Lutheran Church. In fact, he became the great critic of the Church in later years and the epithet, "the accusing angel", was well deserved when we consider his attacks on Christendom.

Approach to Religion

Kierkegaard's approach to religion was through an attack on Hegelianism which he described as "the howling madness of the higher lunacy". He had no place in his thinking for "the bloodless categories" of Hegel's system. It was too logical, too abstract, too universal for Soren. It failed to deal with the vital issues confronting man in the everyday world. Its rationalism, with its stress on reason alone as supreme in life, left no room for the transcendent God with whom we have to do. Hegelianism dissolved the issues of life into vague abstractions, according to Kierkegaard, and bypassed the challenges of the gospel in its concern for a philosophical system based on pure speculation.

Life's Three Stages

Kierkegaard believed that life for the individual passed through three stages. The first was the AESTHETIC stage in which one skips along, like a stone that is thrown over the surface of the water. In this stage the person enjoys life, tasting a bit of everything, taking nothing very seriously. Whatever meaning is found in life is discovered in external events. But soon, like the stone that finally sinks, the individual is overtaken by boredom. Frantically, he turns either to excessive work or loses himself in amusements, sometimes of an unprofitable nature. But this boredom can also lead him to the second stage, the ETHICAL.

In this stage the personal is subordinated to the legal and the social. The individual is now determined to fulfil the letter of the law, to obey the categorical imperative and to become righteous in his own legalistic eyes. But this stage soon proves also to be unsatisfactory. He sees that work-righteousness is also not the way to meaningful living. He realizes that "purity of heart is to will one thing, and one thing only," but he cannot achieve this purity by the powers of his own volition. His inner life becomes a sort of civil war and he cannot reconcile this inner conflict himself. Like St. Paul, he cries, "Wretched man that I am! who will deliver me from this body of death?" (Romans 7:24). Thus his wretchedness leads him into the third stage, the RELIGIOUS.

Man has been driven to despair. But in this instance man's extremity becomes God's opportunity. Man by any logical or human means cannot deliver himself from despair, but God can. This is what Kierkegaard means by the absurdity of faith. Man cannot 'think' himself into faith. He must make the 'leap' of faith, a full commitment, an absolute trust in God. Intellectual beliefs and well-formulated doctrines are of little value now. Faith is the eternal moment of decision, initiated by God at life's crossroads. In faith he finds that God accepts him, though unacceptable, and his despair is turned to joy. It is by faith that man is able to get out of the human predicament of despair which is his sin. The example of Abraham willing to offer his son Isaac as a sacrifice, as set forth in his book, *Fear and Trembling*, is the best example of what Kierkegaard means by the leap of faith. Abraham believed God would give him back his son. This is the full trust that faith involves.

Anxiety

Despair is the consequence of anxiety which is "the

dizziness of freedom". Man was made to be free. Yet he is bound. His freedom gives him the dreadful choice of maintaining kinship with God or with the Nihil—nothing. When he chooses the Nihil his life becomes filled with anxiety. He sins because he rejects God. He is guilty and he feels guilty. In his book, *The Concept of Dread*, Kierkegaard deals with this subject of anxiety, guilt and despair. Only by the leap of faith, initiated by God, when we let God take over our lives, can guilt be overcome and the individual enjoy the suffering and bliss of true life.

This anxiety Kierkegaard writes about is not that sort which arises from some external condition of possible poverty or pain or disappointment. It lies deeper in 'the fall of man', in his existential predicament as a finite subject who is confronted by the infinite God who makes demands on the individual that he cannot fulfil. He endeavours to fulfil these demands by his own will. He 'rebels' against God. But he falls, and by his own powers he cannot rise again. Then there comes the moment of the Divine-human encounter, the 'I-Thou' experience of personal faith, when a man, in the leap of faith, says that by GRACE, "I will". This leap of faith involves his whole being, for ultimate truth is apprehended in passion, not in cold objectivity. There is suffering here but there is also bliss beyond compare. There is a cross but there is also a resurrection.

Objectivity and Subjectivity

Kierkegaard is opposed to objectivity on two grounds: (i) There is the objectivity of speculative philosophy, such as is found in the rationalism of Kant and Hegel. Such objectivity has no place for a personal faith that involves one in the issues of life. His life is void of commitment because he may see so many points of view that he is unable to make up his mind as to the choice he should make. Since the rationalist has little place for God in his thinking the will of God does not enter into his patterns of thought. (ii) There is the objectivity of those who do not wish to become involved. Such a person avoids life's challenges by first avoiding God's call to decision in life's throng and press. This denial of God's call is his sin, so for Kierkegaard, "man is always in the wrong before God".

"Truth is subjectivity and subjectivity is truth," according to Kierkegaard. Faith is a subjective commitment to the objective will of God. It is a deeply personal appropriation of divinely revealed truth in Christ, a truth that is beyond us because Christ is beyond us. Faith brings home to us subjectively the grace of the transcendent God Who became incarnate in Christ "for us men and our salvation".

Some Doctrines

(i) *Sin and Redemption.* Sin is universal because anxiety, guilt and despair are common to all men. Thus all have sinned and come short of God's glory. There is a 'break' between God and man because God is so utterly transcendent. God is infinite and man if finite. But there is also the more serious 'break' caused by man's sin. By the 'fall' the imago dei in man has been broken and only God can repair the break by his grace through faith. This means that man needs redemption. It is this need that drives a man to God. "Take away the alarmed conscience," writes Kierkegaard, "and you may close the churches and turn them into dancing halls." [21]

(ii) *Jesus Christ.* Kierkegaard believed that Jesus was an historical person but it is as the contemporary Christ, apprehended by faith, that we see his significance. Reading the historical facts about the life of Jesus, or giving attention to theological concepts regarding his person, are of little value. Like Bultmann in the twentieth century, Kierkegaard claims that paying attention to the Jesus of history of nineteen centuries ago (eighteen to S.K.) we discover that he is of less importance than the neighbour. It is only as the contemporary Christ, who in the moment of decision challenges us in the demand of faith, that we comprehend who he is. This contemporary Christ presents us with a cross. If we bear this cross voluntarily we are Christians indeed. Such cross-bearing contradicts all reasonable living, for man should avoid crosses and look for comfort. But Christ came not to send peace but a sword. This again is the absurd element in the gospel.

(iii) *The church.* Kierkegaard's tombstone epitaph is "that individual". He was an individualist from first to last. He had no real place in his thinking for the church, the corporate fellowship of believers, which he attacked unmercifully, especially in his later years as he became more solitary and segregated from society. His book, *Attack on Christendom*, is a satire on the state church of Denmark and its clergy. He would not accept the sacrament on his last illness, even from a Lutheran clergyman who had befriended him. His charge against the church was that it had domesticated Jesus Christ and made the offense of the cross to cease. The clergy had become sanctimonious humbugs. Theology had been reduced to forms of rationalistic propositions and consequently had little or no relationship to vital faith.

Evaluation

Kierkegaard was "a corrective" theologian, a critic of both society and the church. We ought not to expect critics to be well balanced in their point of view. They often exaggerate for the sake of proving a point. Such a critic was Kierkegaard. He recalled men to the deeper realities of life before God. Beneath the supposed progress of western civilization he saw social and spiritual disintegration. In the age of the mass man, he saw the individual being depersonalized, losing his identity in the collective mob and he recalled men to the life of commitment in faith which he believed would preserve that identity. Much of his criticism of the church is searching and relevant. Over against the type of liberalism that makes God into a "chummy pal", S.K.'s stress on God's transcendence has value for the religious soul. He is the opponent of all anthropocentric and utilitarian views of religion, whether of the rationalistic or pragmatic kind. God cannot be enclosed in systems of human ideas; nor can we 'use' God to bolster our ego or the social order.

Kierkegaard is one-sided in many of his 'corrective' statements about the church and society. In attacking philosophy as found in Hegelianism he failed to see that some other metaphysic might be developed that had little to do with Hegel. His attack on the rational element in human life and the 'absurdity' of faith made him one of the anti-intellectuals of his time. His criticism of the church made him more than ever a solitary individual who needed the church's fellowship and faith. He failed to see the good side of institutional religion. So the primary value of his teachings is as an antidote to several trends in the society and church of his time which called for correction. "In his profound distrust of all mediatorial agencies except Christ himself, he (S.K.) manifests the best in Protestantism," writes David E. Roberts. "But in assuming that the establishment of an 'I-Thou' relationship with God requires a deep break with communal ties, he manifests the worst in Protestantism." [22]

Not without reason, Kierkegaard believed he had been a great sufferer. Consequently he welcomed death at the age of forty-one. Something of his whole teaching is seen in his last words: "Greet all men, I have loved them all: and say to them that my life has been a great suffering, unknown to them; everything looked like pride and vanity, but it was not. I have not been at all better than others. . . . I was the exception." [23]

1. Paul Tillich, *Perspectives on 19th and 20th Century Protestant Theology.* P.64. Harper & Row, New York. 1967.
2. H.P. Van Dusen, *The Vindication of Liberal Theology.* P.163. Charles Scribner's Sons, New York. 1963.
3. Ibid, P.165 (quoted)
4. Bertrand Russell, *A History of Western Philosophy.* P. 704. Simon and Schuster, New York. 1945.
5. Geddes MacGregor, *Introduction to Religious Philosophy.* P.117 (quoted). MacMillan & Co. Limited. London. 1964.
6. H.P. Van Dusen, Op. Cit., P.171f.
7. William Nicholls, *The Pelican Guide to Modern Theology.* Volume 1, Systematic and Philosophical Theology. P.50. Penguin Books Ltd., Middlesex, England. 1969.
8. Tillich, Op. Cit., P.91.
9. H.R. Mackintosh, *Types of Modern Theology.* P. 33n. Nisbet and Co. Ltd. London. 1937.
10. Nicholls, Op.Cit., P.63.
11. Tillich, Op.Cit., P.96
12. Mackintosh, Op.Cit., P.62. (quoted)
13. Mackintosh, Op.Cit., P.75
14. Op.Cit., P.51
15. Op.Cit., P.103.
16. Russell, Op.Cit., P.740 (quoted).
17. Op.Cit., P.741.
18. Karl Barth, *From Rousseau to Ritschl,* P.275. S.C.M. Press Limited, London. 1959.
19. Ibid., P.281.
20. Mackintosh, Op.Cit., P.219 (quoted).
21. Mackintosh, Op.Cit., P.238 (quoted).
22. David E. Roberts, *Existentialism and Religious Belief.* P.90. Oxford University Press. New York 1957.
23. G.O. Griffith, *Interpreters of Man.* P.41 (quoted). Lutterworth Press, London. 1943.

II

Liberal Theology

Several contemporary theological commentators have been telling us recently that we are in the midst of a theological renaissance.[1] Christians are rethinking their faith and its implications in new and startling ways in order to face the challenges of the age. We realize that if theology is to be something other than a "museum of antiquated ideas", it must be able to respond to the demands of changing life. It has to be able to give some answers to questions of why? whence? and whither? which people ask in every generation.

One of the most prominent schools of theology which endeavours to answer these recurring and fundamental questions is known as Liberalism. Among its basic convictions is the fact that truth may be constant but is not static. On the contrary, its very nature is dynamic. Liberalism believes that the truth of the gospel must be related to the newspaper accounts of what is happening in our world. Its aim is to relate theology to the cultural milieu and make men aware of the relevance of Christianity.

Essential Elements in Liberalism

Walter Horton has written that "the characteristic liberal approach to the knowledge of God is through experience."[2] He refers to Schleiermacher as "the father of liberal theology" because he based theology on experience. However Dr. Horton also mentions another type of liberal theology, much less mystical, which stresses "the moral and social rather than the mystical experience."

Liberalism is to be distinguished from, though related to, modernism. Liberalism is largely a point of view, an twentieth century was Walter Rauschenbusch, though this social emphasis had its beginnings in the nineteenth attitude to life and religion. Modernism is a method which is characterized by a critical, historical and scientific approach to religion and more especially to the bible.

In a book published in 1942, *Liberal Theology: An Appraisal*, which consists of a collection of essays in honour of Eugene William Lyman, a former professor in Union Seminary, New York, Dr. Walter Horton, writes the introductory essay in which he summarizes the essential elements in the liberal outlook of Dr. Lyman as follows:[3]

"1. The maintenance of a close and vital relation between faith and reason.

"2. The union of the transcendence and immanence of God.

"3. The insistence upon the centrality of the historical personality of Jesus Christ for our faith and for salvation.

"4. The close and vital relation between the religious and the ethical in the Christian way of life."

The liberal man is the 'free' (Latin liber) man. He is free in his manners, in his giving and his thinking. He is free to investigate, to pursue his own interests and to follow truth wherever it may lead. He is exploratory in nature, ready to experiment, and willing to consider other points of view than his own. "Openness to truth" is a liberal stance in theology as in other areas of human life. David E. Roberts[4] writes that "openmindedness, a respect for any man's sincere convictions, and a willingness to accept truth from whatever quarter it may come" is the mark of the liberal spirit. This does not necessarily mean that the liberal person is lacking in personal conviction. Nor does he hold that one opinion is as good as another. He may have principles and convictions on which he can stand at all times. But he is a man who respects the conscience of another and who may have much to teach others in the search for truth.

Finally there was the ideology of progress. Originating in

the nineteenth century and closely related to certain interpretations of the Darwinian theory of evolution, some thinkers like Herbert Spencer were convinced that progress was "inevitable".

Some Factors abetting the rise of Liberalism

Among a large number of trends and influences which helped to produce what is called 'liberal theology' there are four which I wish simply to list and describe briefly.

First of all, there were the philosophical and theological developments of the nineteenth century. These would include Kantian rationalism with its tinge of scepticism; Schleiermacher's religion founded upon experience in which the transcendence of God tends to be eliminated; Hegelian dialectic and its attendant religious speculation which has almost no place for biblical revelation; and Kierkegaard's existentialism which places a premium upon an individualistic understanding of religion. The whole rational approach to religious truth has had a great influence on liberal thinking. It tends to minimize the self-revelation of God, replacing it with a revelation whose validity, if not its origin, must be tested by human reason. In that tradition the centre of religion becomes man and his finite mind.

A second contributing factor is to be found in the development of science. It is no accident that the rapid development of science and the corresponding growth of liberal theology are closely identified. Not only were their paths parallel but on the side of many liberal theologians there was the conviction that the new outlook on life provided by science must be translated into theology. For them, the functional, objective, experiential, exploratory and inductive features of science belong in the realm of theology.

A third influence in the development of liberalism was the rise of what became described as 'the social gospel'. The great prophet of social Christianity in the early part of the century in the writings of Marx, F.D. Maurice, Ritschl and others. The economic depression of the fourth decade of this century, however, gave added weight to the social gospel and the need for the church to be seriously concerned about the economic and political structures of society. True, there were certain back-eddies in the on-going progress of life but the over-all picture was that man was going on to better and greater things, especially in a materialistic sense. This idea of progress had its roots in a very optimistic view of human nature and society, about which serious questions were raised by the First World War and the economic depression later on. For some the experience of World War II shattered that idea.

The tenets of Liberalism

Because of its pervasive influence, I now propose to set forth in summary eight basic tenets apparent in most theology which can be characterized by the use of the adjective 'liberal'.

Firstly there is the basic affinity between God and man. Man is made in the image of God. This implies a correspondence between man and his Maker from the point of view of creation. The image can be marred by sin but it cannot be broken entirely. Because of the imago dei the thought that there is a total separation between God and man must be ruled out. The distinction must remain but there must be no separation between the two. Consequently there is a continuity between faith and reason, revelation and human insight.

This belief in the affinity between God and man leads the liberal to make two affirmations about the nature of man. The first is that man is a rational being. God is MIND and man, who has been given a mind by God, is capable of 'thinking God's thoughts after Him'. John C. Bennett writes: "Man is a rational being, who asks questions without limit, who is capable of understanding to an

28

amazing degree the universe which he inhabits and to some degree himself. . . .Man is a creative person."[5] The second is that man is basically good. The liberal does not deny that man is also a sinner. But it is man's goodness that is of more significance, whether actual or potential. This leads the liberal to take an optimistic view of man. This optimism is expressed in the words of a strong critic of liberalism, Reinhold Niebuhr: "Though there are minor dissonances the whole course of modern culture learned to sing the new song of hope in remarkable harmony. The redemption of mankind, by whatever means, was assured for the future."[6] This assurance was founded on the belief in the goodness of human nature.

A second characteristic is found in a tendency to accommodate theology to contemporary culture.

If theology is to be meaningful, it is necessary to relate it to the culture of the age. This has been done by liberalism. But when the culture is permitted to predominate over christian teaching, watering-down this teaching in order to make it more acceptable to a secular culture, we have a different condition of affairs. This has often happened with respect to liberal theology in relation to culture. It has accommodated christian truth to the latest affirmations of psychology, science and technology. In such an adjustment theologians often lost sight of the christian teaching they ought to have held in stewardship. The result was a dilution of gospel truth, leading one writer to say that liberalism came to have "a passionate faith in the Great Whatever". Vagueness in belief was the consequence of this accommodation to culture.

The third tenet to be noted is an emphasis on natural theology.

This follows from the place accorded reason in liberalism. L. Harold DeWolf defines natural theology as "the learning of some truth about God or about man's rightful destiny from considerations logically independent of the biblical revelation and of a prior commitment to christian faith."[7] Under the heading of natural theology we include Plato's evidences of God's wisdom in the orderliness of nature; the Thomist arguments for the existence of God; and the ideas of many people in all ages that have given mankind indications of a divine being in nature, in history and in the heart of man. Calvin claimed that the very idea of God was "naturally engraved on the hearts of men".

Dr. DeWolf points out that natural theology is necessary to form a "bridge" between dogma and knowledge in other fields of interest, such as science. It can also serve as a corrective to errors that can arise, and have arisen, in theology. It is natural theology, in part, that enables Christians to discuss, plan and evaluate ideas and ideologies with respect to such matters as human rights, the religions of mankind and the ideas of those who do not believe in deity. Dr. DeWolf concludes that "A christian theology that includes the conviction that all natural theology must be rejected is cut off from effective participation in such important christian ministries of reconciliation and understanding".[8]

A fourth emphasis in liberalism might be stated as a proposition, namely, tradition must give place to the contemporary.

This does not necessarily mean that the liberal discards tradition. But the chief interest of the liberal is with the contemporary world and its life, with its problems and its promises. The NOW syndrome is part and parcel of liberalism. At best tradition may serve as an aid to abundant living, but not as a base or guide, according to liberalism.

A fifth characteristic lies in its conviction about the scientific method of induction as a guide to truth.

Science has become the guide to thought in many areas of life in this century. Some writers have referred to the fact that in the recent past some Christians discarded the idea of, or belief in, miracles because they appeared to be impossible from the standpoint of science.

What does the scientific method mean for the liberal in theology? It means we must always be alert to new developments in science which may displace old beliefs. It means we must always be factual and objective giving little place to the emotional and the more deeply personal elements in human life. It suggests that truths are to be held tentatively and that all knowledge is relative.

Dr. Van Dusen, himself an exponent of liberalism, is critical of much of this modern dependence on science and the scientific method. "Modern scientific civilization," he writes, "has tended to shut man off from living contact with his parent, the world of nature—its immensities, its grandeurs, its austere indifference to him and his petty achievements, its beauties, its benefactions, its fascination; no longer can the 'starry heavens above' give him their message. . . .It has fixed his attention upon the amassing of things, the multiplications of accoutrements, the perfecting of appliances and conveniences. It has persuaded him that plumbing is more important than poetry, facts than understanding, the latest than the best. . .success than life. Its net result has been very materially to dull the modern man's awareness of religious reality, and to dissolve from his life the sense of need for religious certainty." [9]

In the sixth place one should note that religious experience supplants the primacy of religious truth. The stress of liberalism is on "abiding experiences in religious categories." The "events" of the christian revelation, the mighty acts of God recorded in scripture must give place to how we think or feel about a subject, how we communicate with, or respond to, a person. The bible is no longer what Luther called it, "the cradle in which Christ lies," or the book which conveys to us the word of God, but simply an aid, a resource book, which may or may not be referred to, depending on the situation in which we are involved. The chief questions for the liberal are: how do we grow spiritually? how do we relate to others? how do we feel about certain matters and problems?

The zenith of this "experience" type of religion would appear to have been reached in a definition of christian education given in 1929 by Dr. George A. Coe, professor of

Christian Education in the Union Seminary, New York. At the end of the book, *"What is Christian Education?"*, he has a special page in which he summarizes his answer to the question of the title in these words:

> "It (Christian Education) is the systematic critical examination and reconstruction of relations between persons, guided by Jesus' assumption that persons are of infinite worth, and by the hypothesis of the existence of God, the Great Valuer of Persons." [10]

Seventh, there is here a mild stress on the sinfulness of man. "The easy conscience of modern man", about which Reinhold Niebuhr had much to say, is derived, in part, from the liberal school of theology from the nineteenth and early twentieth century. Because man's goodness was emphasized by liberals, it seemed contrary to such a belief to say that man was a sinner in any deep sense of the word. Sin was explained very often as a lack or the result of social influences. It could be attributed to environmental factors such as an unfortunate home influence or pre-natal problems.

This 'going soft' on man's sinfulness meant, on the other hand, that atonement, except in its moral influence theory, was abandoned, that redemption should be treated rather mildly and that judgment was eliminated, or nearly so. It was this sort of liberal stance concerning sin, judgment and redemption which led Dr. H. Richard Niebuhr to write that liberal theology speaks of "a God without wrath (who) brought men without sin into a kingdom without judgment through the ministrations of a Christ without a cross". [11]

It is important for us to note also that liberalism is the avowed enemy of docetism. D.M. Baillie reminds us that one of the good contributions of modern liberalism to theology is that it brought "an end to docetism," [12] that heretical view of our Lord which regarded him as less than human, or other than a real historical person of flesh and blood, thus denying the statement of the Nicene creed, "And was made man".

All liberals give special place to Jesus as a real historical figure. Dr. Van Dusen severely criticizes the school of Form Criticism for positing a Christ of faith who has little reference to the Jesus of history. He quotes Dr. Baillie and other scholars in support of his contention that the historical Jesus is the source of any knowledge we have of the Christ of faith. Dr. Van Dusen goes so far as to say that if the sceptical conclusions of men of the school of Form Critics, like Rudolf Bultmann (who tells us that we know very little about a person called Jesus of Nazareth, and "that it is not important that we should") should finally prevail, then "both intellectual honesty and ethical integrity would compel me not merely to renounce the christian ministry and resign from membership in the church, but to surrender adherence to christian faith." It is the historical person of Jesus that is the foundation of the gospel according to the liberal tradition. In this connection Dr. Van Dusen underscores the words of Gerhard Kittel that "the Christ of faith has no existence, is mere noise and smoke, apart from the reality of the Jesus of history." [13] Jesus is consubstantial with humanity as well as with deity.

Finally, let us consider the need for tolerance which this position emphasizes. The liberal believes that tolerance is the hallmark of a mature person. Such tolerance must extend to conservatives and to others who may be in opposition to the liberal's own position. He holds that no one person or group has a monopoly on truth and that he must look for the truth wherever it is evident. The true liberal, therefore, must be patient with people of differing points of view, with persons holding other religious opinions and with those whose political, economic or cultural stance may be very different from his own. The liberal maintains that in a democratic civilization tolerance must be upheld at all costs.

Evaluation

The influence of liberalism has been widespread within this century in religion, especially on the North American continent. The strong conservative reaction against liberalism indicates that the latter has played a leading role in christian circles.

On the positive side there are many things in liberalism that we find worthy of praise. The "essential elements" of liberalism set forth previously in this chapter by Dr. Walter M. Horton have much to commend them providing, for instance, that God's transcendence and immanence are held in proper proportion. There is no doubt also that the liberal emphasis has freed many in the church from obscurantist beliefs and crude superstitions which often follow in the footsteps of religious faith. While some liberals have become rationalists, thereby making reason autonomous in the religious sphere, nevertheless they have not been characteristic of liberalism in recent years.

Following on the large place that the liberal gives to reason, we should note that the open-mindedness for which the liberal contends, with its subsequent emphasis on freedom of thought, is a boon for both the liberal and the conservative and all other shades of religious belief. There can be no real discussion of important questions, theological or otherwise, nor any reconciling of ideas that appear at variance with one another, without this openness to truth which the liberal affirms.

The liberal also has much to teach the church concerning a positive attitude toward science. In the past the church has often been found in the wrong in opposing new scientific theories and discoveries. It has opposed geology with Genesis, evolution with the garden of Eden. But it has been the church liberal, with his open-mindedness to truth, who called on the church to be critically receptive of those scientific developments which advance human welfare and which release mankind from outworn dogmas regarding the universe.

Then too, the liberal believes that we must exercise our christian discipleship on this plane of history because history matters to God who became incarnate in history in Jesus Christ. The liberal emphasis on the historical Jesus, which opposes docetism in all its forms, is an inspiration and incentive to liberals and others to be involved in the field of social service and to call for the reformation of society along more humane and just lines. Such an emphasis is a real gain for the whole church as well as society in general.

There are some points, however, on the negative side of which we must be aware when we consider liberal theology. The liberal stress on openness to truth has often led to an erroneous view of tolerance. This has left the impression that one opinion is as accurate and good as another; that one religion is as acceptable as another, that one creed is as valid as another. This has made for confusion in religion and in Christianity it has made for a dilution of the faith. When such a weak view of tolerance comes into the church, christian theology loses its cutting edge. The will to witness to the faith arises out of strong convictions about the truth of the faith. When such convictions are undermined by a waffling type of tolerance, the faith itself is weakened. Christian tolerance gives Christ himself the central place in one's belief and from him we are able to discern the truth and appreciate it wherever it is found.

The liberal also must take some responsibility for 'the easy conscience of modern man'. Liberalism in the recent past has gone 'soft' on sin. The element of judgment on sin in the gospel has not been stressed in liberalism and consequently the mercy of God has been sentimentalized. The greatness of God's mercy must be seen over against the heinousness of man's sin. The liberal must remember that it is 'with mercy and with judgment' that God weaves the pattern of human life.

Liberalism must also be criticized for its "acculturation" of religion; that adaptation to the culture of the age to such a degree that the strong, prophetic spirit in the faith becomes domesticated and tamed. The christian faith then

35

is 'watered down' and the gospel urgency has been lost. It is valuable for the liberal to teach the Christian to be involved in the world. The disciple of Christ must live in the world but he must not be of the world.

Dr. Walter Horton claimed that one of the "essential elements" in the liberal outlook was "the union of the transcendence and immanence of God." But liberalism has not held to this union, nor has it kept a balance between these two aspects of deity. It became associated largely with God's immanence—in nature, in history and in human life. Much of liberalism in the twentieth century was little more than a pantheistic or humanistic belief about God. Hegelianism, with its rationalistic standpoint, seemed to make persons the real deity to be adored. Man and not God appeared to be the master of things. Jesus was regarded as the ideal man and little more. To this humanistic and naturalistic trend in liberalism there was bound to be a reaction. And it came in Neo-Orthodoxy.

Some liberal emphases will always have to be retained in the church. But if liberalism is to make a worthy contribution to the furtherance of the gospel, it must free itself from those expressions of its thought which have hindered the truth from being set forth in its pristine glory.

1. D.D. Williams, *What Present Day Theologians Are Thinking.* P.17 Harper & Row, Chapel Books. Third Edition. 1967.
2. Walter M. Horton, *Christian Theology: An Ecumenical Approach.* P.67. Harper & Brothers, New York. 1955
3. D.E. Roberts & H.P. Van Dusen, Ed's, *Liberal Theology: An Appraisal.* P.8. Charles Scribner's Sons, New York. 1942.
4. Ibid., P.179
5. Ibid., P.196
6. Reinhold Niebuhr, *Faith and History.* P.6. Charles Scribner's Sons, New York. 1949.
7. L. Harold DeWolf, *The Case For Theology In Liberal Perspective.* P.19. The Westminster Press, Philadelphia. 1959.
8. Ibid., P.33
9. Henry P. Van Dusen, *The Vindication of Liberal Theology.* P.68.
10. George A. Coe, *What is Christian Education?* P.296. Charles Scribner's Sons, New York. 1929.
11. H. Richard Niebuhr, *Quoted in 20th Century Religious Thought,* John MacQuarrie. P.347. S.C.M. Press Ltd. London, 1971.
12. D.M. Baillie, *God Was In Christ.* P.11f. Faber and Faber Limited, London. 1948.
13. H.P. Van Dusen, Op.Cit., P.128ff.

III

Neo-Orthodox Theology

Karl Barth, the chief exponent of Neo-Orthodox theology, informs us that having been educated in the theological liberalism of Germany, it was the experience of reading one day early in August, 1914, that 93 German intellectuals had issued a proclamation supporting the war aims of Kaiser Wilhelm II that made him see that liberalism was bankrupt morally. For "among these intellectuals," says Barth, "I discovered to my horror almost all of my theological teachers whom I had greatly venerated. In despair over what this indicated about the signs of the time, I suddenly realized that I could not any longer follow either their ethics and dogmatics or their understanding of the bible and history."[1] Henceforth, Barth became the critic of liberalism. He returned to the bible and the theology of the protestant reformers to discover anew the meaning of the gospel for modern man.

Various other descriptions have been given of Neo-Orthodoxy, such as "A New Reformation Theology", "Theology of the Word", "Dialectical Theology", "Theology of Paradox", all of which refer to certain emphases upheld by this school of theologians. And while the theologians to whom we shall refer in this chapter have differences on some theological points, they can all be said to be opposed to rationalism, humanism, liberalism, immanentism and psychologism. Neo-Orthodoxy is a 'corrective' theology in that it attempts to correct some of the tendencies in liberal theology in the twentieth century.

We select the following emphases as being indicative of the Neo-Orthodox school of theology.

The primacy of revelation

Barth believes that the only way for man to know God is for God to make himself known to man. "In thy light do we see light" (Psalm 36:9). This means that man must entirely depend on God's self-revelation for a true knowledge of God.

Revelation is God's self-disclosure of himself through his word. In biblical parlance a word also indicates an act, so that when God speaks his word something happens, an event takes place.

The word of God has three forms: [2] there is the word as preached, the written word of God in scripture and the revealed word of God in Jesus Christ. All three forms are a unity in relation to the one God.

It is revelation through God's word that led Bonhoeffer, following Barth, to write about "religionless Christianity". Barth believed that God's self-revelation meant "the abolition of religion". [3] What Barth and Bonhoeffer meant by religion was man's search for God, which, they claimed, ended in man making God in his own image. Barth affirmed that the god (s) of religion were idols, or "wish-beings", as Feuerbach had said they were.

The Niebuhr brothers have been called American Neo-Orthodox theologians and if we read *The Meaning of Revelation* by H. Richard Niebuhr we can detect an emphasis, not so sharp, yet still of a similar kind to Barth's meaning of revelation. To Dr. Niebuhr Christianity is a religion of revelation. On his own "man conceives and brings forth the gods in his own image in order that his image of himself may be protected". [4] But it is only by means of the divine self-disclosure that man can know God. Such a revelation creates a revolution in our lives, according to Dr. Niebuhr. [5]

In his revelation God is free to act where and when he wills. "The wind blows where it wills. . . .so it is with everyone who is born of the spirit" (John 3:8). Man cannot decide beforehand just how God will manifest himself. We

38

must not attempt to "crib, cabin and confine" the Lord of life.

This freedom of God is to be seen in his electing grace. It is of his free grace that we have been chosen in Jesus Christ, the elect person who is our redeemer. William Hordern writes: "We are saved by God's free grace, and a most important aspect of this grace is that God reveals himself freely where, and only where, he chooses. In revelation the initiative is always with God."[6]

Man receives God's self-revelation through faith, which is also God's gift. No reasoning or argument or willing can create faith. Neither can they destroy it. For faith is commitment, a response which is inspired by God himself. Such a concept of faith is not opposed to reason, but reason is subservient to faith. Faith makes use of reason to utter forth the oracles of God, to witness to his claim on human life. With Augustine and Anselm (some claim that Barth's best work is on Anselm), Barth says that faith seeks understanding. Reason must always operate within the context of some faith given by one's perspective on life. "Christian faith. . . .is a perspective of reason like any other in so far as it is constituted by an evaluation of significance. . . .it finds decisive significance. . . .in the concrete goodness which Jesus Christ lived and further revealed on the Cross."[7]

A disparagement of natural theology

Barth is the most extreme of the neo-orthodox theologians on this point. The Thomist analogia entis has no place in his thought. He substitutes for this analogy of being between God and man an analogia fidei, an analogy of faith. Barth claims that the analogia entis leaves the door open for man-made religion, in which man by his own reasoning and thinking can know God. This he denies. And even though in his later years he gave more place to what he called "The Humanity of God", through the Incarnation, nevertheless his early criticism of natural theology still remained.

In his controversy with Barth over this matter of natural theology (see *Nein*), Emil Brunner feels that even Karl Barth has left the door ajar for natural theology to have a rightful place in man's understanding of God. Reinhold Niebuhr would give a large place to natural theology. But all neo-orthodox theologians give primacy to revelation and are opposed to that type of rationalism which they believe goes hand in hand with the Thomistic two-storey structure of revelation. It is not reason, for example, to which Brunner is so strongly opposed but to autonomous reason. That is, reason that is not the handmaid of faith. He believes that man is theonomous and is totally dependent on God. Therefore the self-sufficient mind of man that is often implied when natural theology is interpreted by some as giving knowledge of God is ruled out by these theologians.

The deity of God

This is sometimes referred to as the Godness of God. Neo-Orthodox theologians give a prominent place in their theology to God's transcendence. The vertical dimension in faith, over against the horizontal dimension in liberalism, is of primary importance. "The infinite qualitative difference" between God and man is set forth in the phrase, the deity of God. "For my thoughts are not your thoughts, neither are your ways my ways, says the Lord" (Isaiah 55:9).

The deity of God reminds us of God's "otherness" or "apartness". Barth, especially in his early writings, wrote of God as "wholly other". As we shall see later on, Barth has been severely criticized for using this phrase to describe God because it leaves the impression that God has nothing to do with the world. Similarly Barth, in relation to God's "otherness", referred to God's revelation as "hidden" even in revelation. This too, has meant that Barth left some misunderstanding as to his meaning, for while the nature of God is unfathomable, God is not unknowable. In his self-revelation God has 'unveiled' himself to man, though in

40

this self-revelation there are depths of meaning which even faith cannot plumb.

The sinfulness of man

Reinhold Niebuhr, in his Gifford Lectures, says that "man is a sinner. His sin is defined as rebellion against God. The christian estimate of human evil is so serious precisely because it places evil at the very centre of human personality: in the will. . . .Sin is occasioned precisely by the fact that man refuses his 'creatureliness'. . . .He pretends to be more than he is."[8] His predicament is a form of titanism. Sin is not so much a defect as a self-contradiction, a misuse of freedom in which man says 'no' to God. This biblical view of sin "issues inevitably in the religious expression of an uneasy conscience".

Sin expresses itself in many forms of pride, according to Niebuhr—pride of intellect, of race, of class, or religion. Niebuhr believed that the American faith in progress was an expression of pride, based on a too optimistic view of human nature. He claimed that the errors of liberalism were the result of this "erroneous" view of man.

Sin is always considered in relation to God. It is a 'break' in this relationship that is caused by man's 'godalmightiness'. As William Hordern writes: "Man sins because his high place in creation tempts him to forget that he is a creature, and so he longs to be equal to the Creator. Instead of allowing God to be at the centre of life, man attempts to put himself at the centre." And this is his "original sin". Hordern says that this term, "despite its misuses, must be retained. It points up the fact that all man's sins stem from his original sin, the sin that is logically first. Man sins because he is a sinner in the wrong relationship with God; he sins because he has tried to place himself, his concerns, his insights, at the centre of his life, where God ought to be. It is also original in the sense that it describes a situation that we inherit. . . .Sin is something that has somehow got its

41

hold upon the human race as a whole."[9] From sin as an inner contradiction in a person's life come sins, acts or attitudes that are evil and morally wrong. Neo-Orthodoxy has served to 'correct' the naive and overly optimistic view of human nature propounded by the liberals by giving prominence to man's sinfulness in its theology.

Sola gratia, sola fide

"Faith, which appropriates God's self-revelation in His Word," writes Emil Brunner, "is an event, and that a two-sided act—an act of God and an act of man. An encounter takes place between God and man. While God is coming to meet man He also makes possible man's going to meet Him."[10] The initiative of faith is in the grace of God. Such faith is not first belief in propositions but personal trust and obedience. It is an 'I-Thou' encounter between God and man.

Both Barth and Brunner place a great emphasis on freedom by faith under the grace of God. This is a freedom that is united with "complete dependence" on God. Freedom in grace is not freedom to do as one likes but to obey as one ought. This is why, paradoxically, freedom is linked with dependence.

Because of the priority given to grace and faith by Neo-Orthodox theologians and the correlative of freedom, ethics is regarded as a part of dogmatics. Barth will not separate ethics from dogmatics. "Theology must have ethical consequences, including political ones, and correspondingly ethics must never be divorced from theology,"[11] for this would imply that man can act ethically "on his own". He is always and everywhere under the command of God in faith, though, it is this command that is the source of his freedom. "Make me a captive, Lord, And then I shall be free" is at the very heart of true freedom. We find freedom through dependence on God's grace, through faith, and in no other way. This is the path of redemption.

The authority of scripture

This is the new reformation emphasis in Neo-Orthodoxy. "The source and norm of all christian theology is the bible," writes Brunner. [12] Barth found "a strange new world" in the bible. "It is not the right human thoughts about God which form the content of the bible, but the right divine thoughts about men. The bible tells us not how we should talk with God but what he says to us. . . .the word of God is within the bible." [13]

The story of the bible is that of God seeking man

The bible is not to be thought of as containing infallible propositional statements which are to be believed, but the historical record of a people, a person and a church, which sets before us the great moments of revelation, the events in which God has acted and spoken to men. The bible is not to be read in an impersonal manner, an 'I-it' fashion, but as if God himself were speaking to us in a very personal manner. "When God's revelation (in the bible) comes to us, it does not come as propositions to subdue the mind; it comes as a challenge to the 'heart'; it appeals to the whole man." [14] In this way the bible will be found to have a living message for a living people.

Eschatology

Neo-Orthodoxy has brought a new prominence to eschatology. According to Barth, any theology that is not altogether eschatological is not in accord with the gospel of Jesus Christ. It is eschatology that gives Christianity a purpose and goal—the Kingdom of God.

Biblical religion is oriented toward the future. The golden age of the bible is not in the past. It is still to come when there will be a new heaven and a new earth—and in that order. It is an end that comes down from God out of heaven and is not the result of human works. Because of the coming consummation of the kingdom, the church continues to pray, "Come, Lord Jesus" (Rev.22:20).

Christianity possesses a great hope based on the resurrection of Jesus Christ and oriented toward his parousia or second coming. There is a sense in which we can say that the 'last days' or the 'end time' has already arrived because Christ is risen. Between 'now' and 'then' we have the time of the church's mission, when proclamation in word and deed of the mighty acts of God is the church's task. The church must busy herself about the things of the kingdom because "the kingdom is coming. . . .In this light all our church action is allowed and in fact commended. So the church, waiting and hurrying, goes to meet the coming of the Lord." [15]

Barth referred to theology as "the happy science". One reason, among others, for this happiness is that this profound hope of the coming of the kingdom in its fulness and power lies at the very heart of the church's message. Sursum corda!

Evaluation

In making an evaluation of Neo-Orthodox theology we must place first, on the positive side, the contribution that this school has made to the recovery of the importance of theology in the church as well as its value for society. Neo-Orthodoxy has put theology in the front window of modern thought so that secular magazines have often carried articles on doctrines, and writings by theologians, and this school has helped to make religion 'popular' in the good sense of this term.

Neo-Orthodoxy has also based its theology on the biblical revelation. It has helped people to see 'the strange new world of the bible', with its emphasis on the activity of God in human life. If there has been, as we believe, a recovery of biblical study in our time it is due, in no small part, to the influence of Neo-Orthodoxy.

Secular and liberal influences have sometimes made God appear to be little more than 'a good fellow'; a 'grandfather' in heaven or close at hand; some sentimental pal who is easy-going in his attitude to people. Neo-Orthodoxy brought God's judgment to bear on such an attitude. It has made men believe again in the great God of creation, transcendent of his world, its judge and lord. The God of Neo-Orthodoxy has made us recover the sense of sin in human life, the falling short of the divine intention for us, and made us realize that "it is a fearful thing" to fall into the hands of the living God and an even more fearful experience to fall out of his hands.

Neo-Orthodoxy has been referred to as the New Reformation theology. While there is no "mimicking" of Calvinism or Lutheranism among modern Neo-Orthodox theologians, nevertheless, their teachings help to recover much of the heritage of the Protestant Reformation of the sixteenth century. Neo-Orthodoxy has made us aware once more of this great inheritance of truth and demonstrated how the recovery of its central doctrines can bring life and health to the church in our time.

On the negative side there are those who take issue with Neo-Orthodoxy because it gives exclusive claim to the biblical revelation as the only source of a true knowledge of God. Allied with this criticism is the disparagement of natural theology and the place of reason in religion by the Neo-Orthodox theologians, especially Barth. This means that we must ignore much research that is being done in the fields of anthropology, science and comparative religion and bypass the relationship that has prevailed in the church in previous ages between philosophy and theology.

Has Neo-Orthodoxy given so much place to God in theology that man becomes a robot? This criticism must be taken seriously, for so much emphasis in this school of theology is given to God's activity that it seems to rob man of his true freedom under God. Of course writers like Barth and Niebuhr lay stress on man's freedom. But how free is man in divine election? Is man's freedom real or illusory?

In the prominent Neo-Orthodox theologians, such as Barth and Brunner, one cannot escape the feeling that there is a dualism between God and man in their writings which is not warranted in the light of the gospel. Man is seen as 'over against' God, not intimately related to God in either judgment or in mercy. God's transcendence is thought of as so great that man does not seem to be able to be his child, even in faith. The relationship seems more like that of a lord toward his slave than of a father toward his son.

Because of the anti-rationalist bias in these same two theologians there is a latent scepticism regarding the value of reason in their writings. In the case of Barth we believe that this scepticism is related to the influence of Kantian scepticism on his thinking. What Barth, for instance, fails to see is that while reason must never be taken as a test of revelation it is, nevertheless, by means of reason that we are able to identify revelation, to sift genuine revelation from superstition, to elucidate revelation, respond to it and serve it in the name of the Revealer who has given man reason to be used for his sake. We believe that these Neo-Orthodox theologians have not given sufficient significance to human reason as the servant of the word of God in their theology. Because of this fact scepticism has arisen in the minds of some who were formerly followers of Barth and who later came to make an 'about turn' in theology, taking the position of the 'death-of-God' theologians. All of which ought to make us aware of the danger of dismissing reason as the servant of faith.

1. Karl Barth, *The Humanity of God*, P.14. John Knox Press. Richmond, Va. 1960.
2. Karl Barth, *Church Dogmatics*. 1/1 Pp. 98-140. T. & T. Clark, Edinburgh, 1963.
3. Karl Barth, *Church Dogmatics*, 1/2 P.280f. T.&T. Clark, Edinburgh, 1963.

4.   H. Richard Neibuhr, *The Meaning of Revelation.* P.181. The MacMillan Company, New York. 1941.
5.   Ibid., P.183f.
6.   William Hordern, *A New Reformation Theology.* P.77. The Westminster Press, Philadelphia 1959.
7.   E.T. Ramsdell, *The Christian Perspective.* P.41. Abingdon-Cokesbury Press, New York. 1950.
8.   Reinhold Niebuhr, *The Nature and Deity of Man.* Volume 1, P.16, Charles Scribner's Sons. New York. 1942.
9.   William Hordern, Op.Cit., P.130.
10.   Emil Brunner, *The Divine-Human Encounter.* P.74. The Westminster Press, Philadelphia. 1943.
11.   William Nicholls, Op.Cit., P.132f
12.   Emil Brunner, Op.Cit., P.45.
13.   Karl Barth, *The Word of God and the Word of Man.* P.43. Harper and Brothers, New York. 1957.
14.   William Hordern, Op.Cit., P.63.
15.   Karl Barth, *Dogmatics in Outline.* P.148. Philosophical Library. New York. 1949.

IV

Post-Liberalism

This school of theology is a sort of half-way house between Liberalism and Neo-Orthodoxy. We have accepted John MacQuarrie's designation of the theologians who are prominent in this school as 'post liberals'. Macquarrie [1] believes that "a new synthesis is clearly needed" between the Neo-Orthodox and the Liberals and it would appear that theologians like the Baillie brothers, John and Donald, for example, would supply this synthesis and unite the best elements in both of the former schools of theology that we have mentioned.

We select the following points as indicative of the emphases of this school, all of which refer to a new synthesis.

The transcendence and the immanence of God

The Liberals stressed God's immanence, the Neo-Orthodox God's transcendence. The Post-Liberals try to hold a proper balance between the two, a sort of via media between clashing theologies. For example, D.M. Baillie criticises Karl Barth [2] for maintaining that God's self-revelation in Christ is hidden (deus absconditus) as well as revealed (deus revelatus).

Baillie comments: "While the revelation of God to us men on earth must always continue to be in some sense and measure a 'veiled' revelation, surely to Christian faith it is LESS veiled at that point of the Incarnation, than anywhere else; which is precisely what we mean when we speak of that as God's supreme 'unveiling' or revelation."

What Barth means, probably, by speaking of God's

revelation as 'hidden' is that there are depths in that revelation which are unfathomable. However, his bold manner of stating this leaves something to be desired and Baillie has corrected this. Difficulty also arises regarding Barth's use of the term "wholly other" when speaking of God. This phrase, describing God's transcendence, could be interpreted as meaning that God was so separated from man that he had 'no dealings' with man.

This, too, has been 'corrected' by the post-liberals. They claim that since God came to us in Jesus Christ, the word incarnate, God cannot be "wholly other". In addition, we should take to heart this other criticism of "wholly other" concerning God from the pen of John Baillie:[3] "When God is spoken of. . .as being wholly other than man, part of the meaning almost always seems to be that he is wholly unlike man. But, since it is ground common to all theologians to affirm that man was originally made in God's image and likeness, his alleged total unlikeness to God can be due only to the total destruction of the original likeness through sin and the Fall." This latter view Baillie and others will not accept.

In another section of his book, *Our Knowledge of God*, John Baillie shows how both transcendence and immanence, as opposed to God as "wholly other", is an experience of every day life. He writes: "The reason why it is difficult to regard the relation of man to God as merely a relationship between two beings who stand over against each other (and are in that sense wholly other) is that God appears in some sort to be present on both sides of the relationship. When I respond to God's call, the call is God's and the response is mine; and yet the response is God's too; for not only does he call me in his grace, but also by his grace brings the response to birth within my soul. His holy spirit is the real author and originator, not only of his address to me, but of my address to him."[4]

It is St. Paul who shows us this mysterious and paradoxical relationship between divine grace and human freedom when he writes: "I have been crucified with Christ;

it is no longer I who live, but Christ who lives in me; and the life I now live in the flesh I live by faith in the son of God, who loved me and gave himself for me" (Gal. 2:20). "I live, yet not I, but Christ. . ." This is the formula in which the Christian expresses God's transcendence and immanence in religious experience. Revelation, faith and reason.

Dr. Leonard Hodgson affirms that "all man's discovery of truth is by the interaction of divine revelation and human reason."[5] Man becomes aware of revelation by faith but faith must employ reason to sift the 'wheat from the chaff' in what is purported to be revelation, in making revelation understood and in communicating the truth of revelation to others.

What God gives in revelation is not information but himself in intimate communion with man. He makes his presence known through the work of the Holy Spirit. He impresses his reality and nature on the heart of the recipient.

To the post-liberals reason does not 'solve' the element of mystery in revelation. It still remains mysterious. John Baillie, in explaining St. Paul's use of the term mystery, says that "for him (Paul) the mystery becomes a mystery only in being disclosed, while at the same time, if it were fully disclosed, it would cease to be a mystery."[6] This mysterious element in revelation which human reason cannot comprehend is due to the unfathomable and infinite nature of God.

Revelation comes to man through faith. Our knowledge of God is, therefore, faith-knowledge which must be distinguished from other kinds of knowledge. There are, basically, two kinds of knowledge: one is the knowledge given to our intellects—facts, information and the like. The other is the knowledge of experience, sometimes referred to as knowledge of appreciation. The latter is very personal, sort of 'heart to heart'. Other terms used to describe these two types of knowledge are: knowledge of description and knowledge of acquaintance. Faith knowledge is of this second kind.

Faith is a manner of seeing, of seeing the presence of God who is revealing himself to the seeking soul. Faith interprets this revelation through 'the mind of Christ', that is, a Christ-inspired attitude and outlook. "The claim of the christian faith," writes Dr. Hodgson, "to be based on revealed truth includes the claim that a certain understanding of historical events, this seeing with the eye of faith, is itself part of the God-given revelation."[7]

The post-liberals, because of the place they give to reason in theology, open the door of their lives for the entrance of natural theology to give them some knowledge of God along with revelation, but such natural theology is not natural in the sense that it is unrelated to God and independent of him. It is, rather, a distinction between the revelation which God the Creator gives through nature, including human nature, and the revelation which God gives as redeemer in Jesus Christ. Dr. Hodgson says that the Christian revelation dovetails "into a hypothesis of natural theology. . .logically both have the same character. The one is the interpretation by human reason of the appearance of human beings and their history in the evolutionary process; the other is the interpretation by human reason of the appearance within that history of the events to which the bible bears witness."[8] Thus revelation, faith, reason and natural theology all take part, according to the post-liberals, in bringing the believer to a knowledge of God.

Revelation carries with it, in its call to obedience, a challenge to service and dedication of one's life to God and man. William Temple says that "every revelation of God is a demand".[9] John Baillie, in his book on Revelation to which we have already referred, has a chapter on "The Response to Revelation". He says that sometimes we are "conveniently deaf towards God". We do not desire to heed his call but it is through "the claims and needs of our neighbours that God makes his own claim heard."[10] Dr. Baillie refers to the story in the Gospels (Matthew 19:22f) of the rich young ruler who came to Jesus and asked what he must do to inherit eternal life. Jesus told him to sell all his possessions.

But he refused and went away sorrowful. Dr. Baillie's final comment on this story is that the rich young ruler "could never again complain of the lack of revelation."[11]

The deity and the humanity of Jesus Christ

The liberal placed emphasis on the humanity of Jesus and the Neo-Orthodox on his deity. Like the definition of Chalcedon, these two emphases must be held together in any true view of our Lord. D.M. Baillie criticizes the early writings of Barth for having so little to say about the earthly life of Jesus and his teaching. His emphasis was on the exalted Christ. [12] Rudolf Bultmann is unconcerned about Jesus' historical life about which, he believes, we know very little. [13]

The post-liberals lay stress on both the deity and the humanity of Jesus Christ. There is a paradox in the incarnation, God becoming man. But it is this paradox that the church has maintained in her creeds since early days, and to which the Chalcedon definition bears witness. Roger Hazelton says that while we no longer talk about the "two natures" doctrine of the person of Christ as Chalcedon did, yet we maintain the truth of Chalcedon by referring to such a paradox as "something which goes beyond or passes belief. . .a paradox always signials mystery". Dr. Hazelton continues: "It is not the perfect, certainly not the only form for setting forth what is mysterious, but it is especially valuable in alerting us to the very limited capacities of words and thoughts in expressing whatever is insistently real. . .when a paradox is ventured, this amounts to saying that we are at our wits' end and know it."[14]

But in presenting Jesus Christ as the God-man there is something other than a paradox involved. What the church is saying is that in Jesus Christ, God entered into time and in so doing redeemed time from insignificance, from "the boredom of mere recurrence," from the emptiness of mere change that has lost its meaning. By the eternal God entering human life in the incarnation, our lives have been taken up into his and now we live 'in Christ' and that is life with high significance. All this is involved in saying, with the creeds related to Nicea and Constantinople, "God of God. . .and was made man".

The love of God

The love of God for sinful man takes first place in the minds of these theologians of post-liberalism. We say this in no exclusive sense. All Christian theologians make mention of God's love. But among the group we are considering we believe it has special prominence. This love is supremely revealed in Jesus Christ, a love that is sacrificial and redemptive, the love of the 'Suffering Servant' who has atoned for the sin of man.

Dr. F.W. Dillistone in the final chapter of his book on The Christian Understanding of Atonement, deals with the reality of human alienation in the modern world. "It is scarcely possible to take up any interpretation of the human situation, scientific or artistic, without soon encountering the concept of alienation." This implies that man needs redemption. Whether he admits it or not, he craves for fellowship with God and man. Man needs to be reconciled to God. From the christian standpoint this reconciliation takes place at the cross, "the cross-roads of the world's history", where God and man are reconciled as "the Son of God takes upon himself the full rage of the world's sin. God was in Christ reconciling the world unto himself".[15] Through Christ's atonement man is reconciled to God.

John McIntyre, after criticizing liberalism for having very little to say about eschatology, goes on to state that "it is not surprising that Neo-Orthodox eschatology should have little place for the doctrine of the love of God." The Neo-Orthodox have been so eschatological in their point of view that they have not paid sufficient attention to life here and now and the need for love. McIntyre says that too many post-war theologians have not given the doctrine of God's love the primacy it deserves in theology. "The concept of the love of God has not disappeared," he observes, "but it has been relegated to the background."[16] He affirms that this doctrine in its strong moral sense must be restored to a place of centrality in Christian doctrine. "It is not love-in-general which they saw in Jesus Christ," writes McIntyre "but love-as-commitment."[17]

This writer regards Jesus' baptism as not only an act of identification with us as sinners in their penitence; "it is a sacrifice unto death" for us men and our salvation. The First Epistle of John declares: "To us, the greatest demonstration of God's love for us has been his sending his only Son into the world to give us life through him. We see real love, not in the fact that we loved God but that he loved us and sent his Son to make personal atonement for our sins. If God loved us as much as that, surely we, in our turn, should love each other" (1 John 4:10. J.B. Phillips).

Social concern

In his book *What Is Christian Civilization?* John Baillie says that "the imminent danger" of the church giving up on social concern "is that by allowing the political and economic order to take care of itself, the church of Christ will tragically fall short of its duty of bringing the light of the gospel to bear upon every activity of the common life."[18] And if the spiritual bank account that has been built up in civilization by the church in past centuries becomes depleted, then society will drift into paganism. "In proportion as society relaxes its hold upon the eternal, it ensures the corruption of the temporal."[19]

The Christian must, therefore, strive for an ideal life in community but he must never give that community his unconditional loyalty. That belongs to God alone.

In a book published by a Committee of the Church of Scotland at the close of World War II, (John Baillie, chairman) we are told that when ideals are detached from their rootage in christian doctrine they are "in danger of losing their power of conviction and their hold over men's minds. All moral standards were originally given in close association with a background of religious belief, and it is doubtful how long they will continue to be accepted after this link has been broken." [20] To maintain this connection between faith and morals in society is a social concern of every Christian. Furthermore, when ideals are detached from christian belief "they suffer inevitable change and deterioration". As an example, the motto of the French Revolution, "liberty, equality and fraternity," words which have a direct religious ground, turn out to be something else entirely. This is so because liberty is rooted in an ultimate bondage by faith in God. We are equal because we are made in God's image. And a secularized ideal of fraternity misses the power and the meaning such a term can have when it is fraternity under the fatherhood of God and the elder-brotherhood of Christ. This, too, means that the Christian has the responsibility of upholding the christian message in order to make social ideals become part and parcel of the ethos of our civilization.

The Christian must become involved in social affairs because God in Christ became involved—in the world of religion, of politics ("crucified under Pontius Pilate") of everyday life. The social world is the world of persons, the good and the bad, people whom God loves, people for whom Christ died. It is this challenge that the post-liberals to whom we have referred, as well as others, present to us very forcibly in their theology.

Grace and gratitude

This is the title of the second last chapter in John Baillie's Gifford Lectures, *The Sense of the Presence of God*. These two words, grace and gratitude, should hold a place of great significance in the vocabulary and the life of every

Christian. It is not, therefore, in any exclusive sense in relation to the post-liberals that we refer to these words here but simply because of the prominence given to these words by members of this school of theology.

"We are saved," writes John Baillie, "not by anything we ourselves can do, but only by the grace of God."[21] This is basic New Testament teaching. We have been taught to sing and to believe that

> "every virtue we possess,
>   And every victory won,
> And every thought of holiness
>   Are His alone."

Grace is God's love reaching out, undeservedly, to the unworthy sinner. It is love in action for the sake of our redemption. "In this is love, not that we loved God but that he loved us, and sent his son to be the expiation for our sins" (1 John 4:10).

For what God has done for us, especially for our salvation in Jesus Christ, the Christian must express his gratitude. Not to be grateful is to sin. To accept God's gifts and not return thanks in word and life is unchristian. "Were not ten cleansed?" asked Jesus, "Where are the nine?" (Luke 17:17). In turn it is gratitude that motivates christian action. Gratitude is the spur to generous giving and generous living. It provides an inspiration to service for others.

But gratitude, springing out of belief in God's grace, depends in turn on living in the presence of God. The life of prayer and devotion, the way of communion and service, the path of dedication and praise—it is by these means of grace that we come to realize our great indebtedness to Christ. Then we realize that we are not our own; we are "bought with a price" (1 Cor. 6:19, 20).

In a sermon on "The Spiritual Life", John Baillie ends with these words: "We cannot be in any doubt as to the kind of spiritual discipline to which we should subject ourselves. It has all been worked out through long ages by the prophets and apostles, by the saints and martyrs. The regular practice of prayer, daily reading of Scripture, the corporate worship of God, and the reception of the Blessed Sacrament—that is the way marked out for us by the experience of the ages. There is no other way." [22]

It is from the practice of the presence of God that the Christian understands the meaning of grace and its significance in his own life. And when a man accepts God's grace and realizes what God has given him, he must be grateful. Grace and gratitude, as well as the life of christian devotion from which they spring, are the very seedbed of christian theology.

Evaluation

In a statement of characteristic Scottish 'humility', John MacQuarrie, in his chapter on the post-liberals, says that "the most distinguished representatives of post-liberal Scottish theology have tempered continental extravagances" by a more balanced view of truth. [23]

We are very sympathetic to the point of view set forth by the post-liberals. We believe, with John Baillie and others, that there must be a place for natural theology within the framework of Christian thought. It must be a place of secondary significance because Christ the Word is the primary revelation. We also believe that the post-liberals have done a service for theology in keeping it related to the world and the culture of the times. It is a positive contribution of this School of theology that while it has steered clear of the Scylla of liberal humanism, it has also avoided the Charybdis of Neo-Orthodox transcendentalism.

Some questions remain, however, and they must be put to all post-liberals. Since post-liberalism is a via media in theology, like all via medias, will it blunt its 'cutting edge?' Has its vital theological thrust been lost in its attempt to achieve a more balanced theology? Then, too, is there not a noticeable danger, at least among some of the writers of this school of theology, to give so much place to natural theology and the power of human reason that the major revelation of God in Christ, recorded in scripture, is lessened in importance? Last of all, is it sufficient to speak about revelation as evident in 'the mighty acts of God' and omit reference to "the saving words of God" spoken by prophets and apostles, and more especially by Jesus himself? Must not words and events be considered together in reference to God's self-revelation? A dualism between words and events cannot be constructive for theology. These, it seems to us, are some of the main questions which must be asked of the post-liberals who have nevertheless, made a major contribution to theological thought in the twentieth century.

1. John MacQuarrie, Op.Cit., P.349
2. D.M. Baillie, Op.Cit., P.49f
3. John Baillie, *Our Knowledge of God*, P.229.
4. John Baillie, Ibid., P.233f
5. Leonard Hodgson, *For Faith and Freedom*. Volume 11, Christian Theology, P.3. Basil Blackwell, Oxford. 1957.
6. John Baillie, *The Idea of Revelation in Recent Thought*. P.59, Columbia University Press, New York. 1956.
7. Leonard Hodgson, Op.Cit., P.26f
8. Leonard Hodgson, Ibid., P.63
9. William Temple (quoted) in John Baillie, Ibid. P.84.
10. John Baillie, Op.Cit., P.142
11. John Baillie, Op.Cit., P.141.
12. D.M. Baillie, Op.Cit., P.16ff, 53.
13. D.M. Baillie, Op.Cit., P.37 (reference).
14. Roger Hazelton, *Christ and Ourselves*. P.12f Harper & Row, New York. 1965
15. F.W. Dillistone, *The Christian Understanding of Atonement*, P.400ff., James Nisbet & Co. Ltd. Didswell Place, England. 1968.
16. John McIntyre, *On The Love of God*. P.26, Collins, London. 1962.
17. John McIntyre, Ibid., P.67.
18. John Baillie, *What is Christian Civilization?* P.54. Charles Scribner's Sons, New York. 1945.
19. John Baillie, Ibid., P.59.
20. *God's Will for Church and Nation*, P.25f. S.C.M. Press, London. 1946.
21. John Baillie, *The Sense of the Presence of God*. P.242. University Press, London, Oxford. 1962.
22. John Baillie, *Christian Devotion*. P.42. Charles Scribner's Sons, New York. 1962.
23. John MacQuarrie, Op.Cit., P.339.

V

Conservative Theology

The beginnings of this school of theology go back to the fundamentalist-modernist controversy in the early part of this century, especially in the third decade. But there was too much obscurantism and negativism in fundamentalism for it to endure. It was too anti-scientific and anti-intellectual to have a base from which to proclaim the gospel. Among thinking people it tended to lose caste.

Out of fundamentalism there developed a conservative, or Neo-conservative, school of theology sometimes referred to as the school of "Orthodox" Theology or "Conservative Evangelical" Theology. By Orthodox, E.J. Carnell says he means "that branch of Christianity which limits the ground of religious authority to the bible." [1]

It is rather strange that in John MacQuarrie's book, *20th Century Religious Thought*, in which the author presents brief surveys of the varied spectrum of religious thinking in this century, he makes no mention of theologians whom we could classify in this school. This is all the more strange because some of the most outstanding scholars in the Christian Church, including the Anglican Church of which Dr. MacQuarrie is a priest, belong to this school. We have only to mention names like F.F. Bruce of Manchester University, J.I. Packer of Oxford University, G.W. Bromiley, a translator of Barth's Dogmatics, Carl Henry, former editor of *Christianity Today*, to note how serious is such an omission. These, and others in biblical and theological studies, are scholars of the highest rank.

Today conservative evangelical scholars, such as those mentioned, are under criticism both from the right and the left theologically, both from fundamentalist and liberal theologians, though the former do not have many scholars of any intellectual weight.

The emphases of this school of conservative theology are:

A strong attack on theological liberalism

Cornelius Van Til finds that even Barth's Neo-Orthodoxy is only "The New Modernism", or liberalism in a new dress, especially Barth's view of the bible. Carl Henry would not go along with Van Til but he is also critical of Barth, especially for his attack on rational theology.

Conservatism continues its criticism of liberalism and modernism because these latter movements, so conservatives believe, have come under the influence of the scepticism, humanism and scientism of the culture of our day. Conservatives state that liberals have done away with the supernatural character of the gospel and have therefore diluted its divine message.

Contrary to many liberals, conservatives maintain that Christ did perform miracles. They are "seals" of his work. They believe in miracles because they have an open view of nature that is under God's control. They do not believe that God is a prisoner in his own world. The American Science Affiliation, whose members must have a doctorate in some science, are men and women who pledge themselves to maintain faith in an infallible bible whose teachings cannot contradict modern science.[2] The conservative says that the liberal, in his denial of miracle, is tied to outworn rigid scientific views that are associated with Newtonian physics.

Conservatives also attack liberalism for its social gospel outlook which, they claim, is more social than gospel, more political than Christian, more interested in changing the social order than in changing men and women who can create a new order, more influenced by Karl Marx than by Saint Mark.

However, in its opposition to liberalism we must not think of conservatism as only reacting negatively. Dr. Carnell says that this was the error of fundamentalism—it attacked liberalism and when the attack waned it had no vital gospel of its own to proclaim. It partook of all the weakness of negativism. The conservatives do have a positive gospel which they believe is in accord with the truth of scripture.

The bible as the infallible rule of faith and life

At the outset we should note what is meant by conservatives in referring to the bible as infallible:

"It is unfair to charge the conservative with being a literalist. He is not required to lop off his right hand or pluck out his eye because Jesus told men to do this. The conservative understands that the bible sometimes speaks in poetic or allegorical language. He does not follow the literal words of scripture: he follows the 'natural' meaning." [3]

Conservatives do not mean by infallibility that all scripture is on the same level of truth; for example, that the gentle cynicism of Ecclesiastes is on a par theologically with the sermon on the mount.

Conservatives do not believe that the bible is a book that is infallible in science—it is infallible for faith and life. E.J. Carnell even sets forth a doctrine of Threshold Evolution which he finds compatible with bible teaching. [4]

Conservatives also believe in "progressive revelation." "revelation is not complete all at once. If the light with which it starts is dim, it grows clearer as the ages advance. . . .revelation has to take up man as He finds him, with his crude conceptions, his childlike modes of thought and expression, his defective moral ideas and social institutions, and has to make the best of him it can." [5]

Conservatives do not maintain that an infallible bible is free from all errors. Copyists made errors. The original text, which was free from error, has been lost. Whatever errors may now appear in the bible do not hinder man from finding there the word of God for his salvation.

Conservatives maintain that the bible is infallible because

it presents the word of God, whether this be in story, parable, narrative, poetry, prose or allegory. Above all, it is infallible because it presents the infallible person, Jesus Christ the Lord. The bible is the "written Christ." All scripture should be interpreted in the light of his person, teaching and work.

There are five rules for the interpretation of scripture:[6]

First, the New Testament interprets the Old Testament.
Secondly, the Epistles interpret the Gospels.
Thirdly, systematic passages interpret the incidental.
Fourthly, universal passages interpret the local.
Fifthly, didactic passages interpret the symbolic.

There is a human as well as a divine element in scripture. But no human errors have imperilled the gospel of salvation which is to be found in scripture.

In a general way there are two theories of the inspiration of scripture found within the conservative ranks: one was set forth by Benjamin Warfield and the other by James Orr. The first is very rigid, bordering on a form of doctrinal literalism; the other is inspiration in terms of life. The bible is a life-giving book. Through the internal testimony of the Holy Spirit, the word comes alive in the believer's heart.

The bible contains its own principle of interpretation. There is a norm of interpretation within the bible. For Luther this norm was justification by faith. J.I. Packer writes: "We look to scripture itself to teach us the rules for its own interpretation, and to the Holy Spirit, the church's only infallible teacher, to guide us into its meaning, and we measure all human pronouncements on scripture by scripture's own statements."[7]

The conservative places great importance on doctrine

The conservative says that the liberal and the neo-orthodox, in stressing revelation through events but not through words, have drastically limited the significance of doctrine. One writer says "the God of most contemporary theologians can act but does not speak." There is no 'thus saith the Lord' in liberal teaching, according to conservatives.

Of course the conservative would be ready to say that we are justified by faith, not by doctrine. He even refers to the fact that St. Paul never asked the church to exclude a person from its fellowship for heresy — only for immoral conduct.

However, this school is bringing back the importance of truth in words and as vehicles of revelation. It claims that doctrinal teaching is one of the great needs of the hour in the church. "Liberals are obscurantists because they disparage the teaching of doctrine. The liberal says that he is only interested in applying Christianity to life. But. . . .how can you apply something unless you know what it is. . . .The liberal disdain for theology is an excuse for shallow thinking or, worse still, for no thinking."[8]

Conservatives place great emphasis on such doctrines as the virgin birth of Christ, his substitutionary atoning work on the cross, his bodily resurrection and his second coming. They will not accept merely symbolic interpretations of the great creedal statements concerning Jesus Christ.

Because of this emphasis on doctrine, conservatives have an important place for preaching, especially biblical and doctrinal preaching. They remind us "that Jesus came preaching" and that his people must do likewise. "How are they to hear without a preacher?" (Rom. 10:14). The gospel must be proclaimed in words as well as in deeds.

The historical basis of Christianity

To some degree the conservatives agree with the liberals on this point of the historical basis of Christianity. But they go farther than the liberals. They assert that the virgin birth, the resurrection and the ascension are not symbols but rather objective, historical events.

F.F. Bruce and other conservatives are very critical of the Form-Critical school of biblical scholarship of which Rudolf Bultmann is the most prominent. Dr. Bruce disagrees with "the excessively skeptical evaluation of the gospel history which marks the work of Rudolf Bultmann". He goes on to quote his predecessor at Manchester, T.W. Manson: "Professor Bultmann's *History of the Synoptic Tradition* is an account not of how the life of Jesus produced the tradition, but of how the tradition produced the life of Jesus. And when the work of the tradition has been undone, there is very little of Jesus left." And Dr. Manson concludes with a plea for "a return to the study of the gospels as historical documents concerning Jesus of Nazareth, rather than as psychological case material concerning the early Christians". [9]

Conservatives believe that to segregate the gospel from history is to lead men into a new kind of Gnosticism which can have little to say to people in this historical setting when they are wrestling with the temptations and problems, the trials and vicissitudes of everyday living. In this sense the gospel is earth-bound, though its source is in heaven.

Conservatives stress evangelism

"Evangelism," declares J.I. Packer, "is just preaching the gospel, the evangel. It is a work of communication in which Christians make themselves mouthpieces for God's message of mercy to sinners. . . .the delivering of it (the message) involves the summoning of one's hearers to conversion. . . If you are not. . . .seeking to bring about conversions, you are not evangelizing. . . But the way to tell whether in fact you are evangelizing is not to ask whether conversions are known to have resulted from your witness. It is to ask whether you are faithfully making known the gospel message." [10]

At the heart of evangelism is the belief that "all have

sinned and fall short of the glory of God." (Rom. 3:23). Man is a sinner in need of salvation. This salvation is offered to people in the gospel of the atoning saviour, who died for the sins of mankind. It is the responsibility of the evangelist—in the pulpit, in conversation, in groups or elsewhere—to herald this message that men and women may believe and be saved. This is what conservatives mean by evangelism.

Conservative theologians, including those within highly liturgical churches, such as the Anglican, would affirm that evangelism is the first priority of the church. Liturgies, fellowship groups, sacraments all have their rightful and necessary place in the church, but always as supporting and directing the church toward its main goal, namely that of evangelizing people in the name of God so that by his grace they may come to a knowledge of the truth as it is in Jesus Christ.

Evaluation

There is no doubt that conservative evangelicals hold to the essentials of the christian faith. Some might say, 'yes, and they believe in a lot more than the essentials'. Be that as it may. They are devout, believing Christians.

Conservative theologians like Bruce and Packer, as well as others, have done much to restore the bible to its central place in the church and the hearts of believers. To this school the bible is something other than a 'resource book'. It is the living word of God.

It should be a judgment of much of church life that such important matters as the study of doctrine, the practice of prayer, the preaching of the word and the responsibility to evangelize do not find sufficient emphasis in many ecclesiastical circles. But it is these very things that conservatives emphasize. In this we ought to give heed to them.

Conservative theologians have not dropped the message of sin and salvation from their proclamation, as has happened in many liberal pulpits. The secular culture has not robbed them of the call to repent and become new creatures in Christ Jesus.

But there are also questions to raise and criticisms to make concerning conservative evangelicals. For instance, how should Christians think of inspiration? The two theories mentioned above seem unsatisfactory. Too much is left to the individual. And what of the locus of biblical authority? To say that the bible is infallible and authoritative is insufficient because many christian groups from Mormons to Jehovah's Witnesses, say the same thing. But their interpretation of scripture varies in spite of the authority and infallibility.

E.J. Carnell says there is always the danger of conservatism becoming a cult, which he says is what happened to fundamentalism. [11] Cultic groups usually have separatist tendencies and in some instances present a 'holier-than-thou' attitude to the world. This cultic tendency is further abetted by the fissiparous trends in Protestantism.

Then, too, as Dr. Carnell points out, because of their cultic tendencies conservatives are often not very strong churchmen. The conservative's authority appears to be an individualistic matter. "Contemporary orthodoxy," writes Dr. Carnell, "is a curious blend of classical and cultic elements, for whereas it claims to be true to general biblical doctrine, it defends a separatist view of the church. Behind this inconsistency is the familiar error of thinking that possession of truth is the same thing as possession of virtue. As long as orthodoxy is comforted by this error, it imagines that it is sufficiently virtuous to decide who are, and who are not, members of the church." [12] In this connection Dr. Carnell says that orthodoxy tends to glorify church divisions, creating a "caste system" which is a denial of christian brotherhood.

Last of all, the conservative can learn—and he is learning—that the gospel has something to say not only to the individual but also to society. Here he should take a leaf out of the book of liberalism. Poverty, racism, injustice, war—these are evils that rob people of their rightful inheritance under God, people whom God loves and for whom Christ died. For conservatives to say that we should not involve the church in politics and economics is as much as declaring that the church should isolate itself from man's everyday life and shut up its gospel from "the world's ignoble strife". The church today cannot do this, even if it would. The world is pressing in on the church as never before and the church should be prepared to face the world, not on the world's terms but on gospel terms, declaring to all men: "This is the way, walk in it, when you turn to the right or when you turn to the left" (Isaiah 30:21).

1. E.J. Carnell, *The Case For Orthodox Theology.* P.13. The Westminster Press, Philadelphia. 1959.
2. William E. Hordern, *A Layman's Guide to Protestant Theology*, P.69. The MacMillan Company, New York. 1968. Revised Edition.
3. William E. Hordern, Ibid., P.63.
4. E.J. Carnell, Op.Cit., P.94f
5. E.J. Carnell, Op.Cit., P.52
6. E.J. Carnell, Op.Cit., P.53ff
7. J.I. Packer, *Contemporary Views of Revelation in Interpreting Religion*, Donald Walhout, Editor. P.315. Prentice-Hall Inc., Englewood Cliffs, N.J. 1963.
8. William E. Hordern, Op.Cit., P.67.
9. Ed. Carl F.H. Henry, *Jesus of Nazareth: Saviour and Lord.* P.92f. *History and the Gospel.* F.F. Bruce. William B. Eerdmans Publishing House, Grand Rapids, Michigan, 1966.
10. J.I. Packer, *Evangelism and the Sovereignty of God.* P.41. Inter-Varsity Fellowship, London. 1961.
11. E.J. Carnell, Op.Cit., P.113f.
12. E.J. Carnell, Op.Cit., P.132f.

VI

Neo-Thomist Theology

It was in 1879 that Pope Leo XIII, in his encyclical
Aeterni Patris, commended the philosophical-theological
system of St. Thomas Aquinas to the faithful for study and
guidance in matters of faith. While most Roman Catholic
theologians look to Aquinas for some direction in
theologizing, nevertheless they do not look to his teaching
for a list of propositions which they simply reiterate in
modern form. Rather, it is St. Thomas' method and outlook,
the manner in which he dealt with nature and grace, faith
and reason, for example, which can have a bearing on the
life of man today—it is this which modern Neo-Thomists
find to be valuable in the writings of this "Angelic doctor".

While most of the Neo-Thomist writers are to be found
within the Roman Catholic church, there are also many
thinkers within this church who could not be classified as
Neo-Thomists, such as Hans Kung, Leslie Dewart and
others. On the other hand, there are theologians outside the
Roman Catholic church, especially Anglicans, such as E. L.
Mascall and A. M. Farrer, who definitely belong to the
tradition of Thomism.

The following points are selected to show some of the
main emphases in Neo-Thomist theology.

The relation of nature and grace

A famous statement of St. Thomas is that "grace does not
abolish nature but perfects it." Whatever we experience of
ourselves apart from divine revelation can be considered as
belonging to the world of nature in the Thomistic
understanding of this term. "Grace is God himself, his
communication, in which he gives himself to us as the

68

divinizing loving kindness which is himself." [1] This grace brings nature to completion, to fulfillment and in so doing gives illumination to men. Natural law participates, therefore, in the eternal law which is its source and ground. There is a complementarity between the divine and the human, between God and nature which is created.

In Thomism there is the assertion that since God is the creator of nature, there is a grace in creation as well as in redemption. E. Gilson writes of this grace in nature as "universal grace whereby all things are what they are." Then there is also the grace given to us through Jesus Christ which Gilson declares is the "grace which saves nature." [2]

According to Thomism there is an analogy of being (analogia entis) between God and man and this refers to a continuity between nature and the supernatural world of grace. The natural knowledge of God is a 'bridge' to the supernatural. "It is analogy alone," writes Dr. Gilson, "which enables our intelligence to arrive at a transcendent God from sensible things. It is analogy, too, which alone permits us to say that the universe has its existence from a transcendental principle and yet is neither confused with it nor added to it." [3]

When we speak of grace in nature or a natural grace we must not think of such grace as being unrelated to God. It too is from God. It is that knowledge of the divine which man discerns by means of his God-given capacity to think and understand. "Who is to say that the voice heard in earthly philosophy," writes Karl Rahner, "even in non-christian and pre-christian philosophy, is the voice of nature alone and also the groaning of the creature, who is already moved in secret by the Holy Spirit of grace, and longs without realizing it for the glory of the children of God?" [4] In Neo-Thomism as in the teaching of St. Thomas the supernatural is not held to be in opposition to the natural but it is that which pervades the natural "as its constitutive principle and completes nature as its final consummation." [5]

Reason and faith

What we have been saying about the Neo-Thomist view of nature and grace applies also to the relation of reason and faith. Reason is God's gift to the natural man by his creation. Faith, which presumes revelation, is the gift of God's supernatural grace. Faith and reason are, therefore, not contrary to each other as in the writings of Tertullian who asked, "What has Athens to do with Jerusalem?"— philosophy with theology? On Thomistic principles reason and faith are inter-related as divine gifts on different levels of life.

Jacques Maritain [6] points out that there are three major degrees of knowledge: scientific knowledge, or knowledge of facts; metaphysical knowledge, or knowledge of being; and supernatural knowledge which is the knowledge of revelation received through faith. In the first two kinds of knowledge reason predominates. But it is faith alone which gives us real knowledge of God. Metaphysical knowledge, such as the kind presupposed by St. Thomas' five arguments or proofs for the existence of God, can tell us that there is a God, a divine transcendent being who is supreme and the First Cause of all things. Then, like a second storey to the house of knowledge, there is given to man through revelation the supernatural knowledge that God is triune, that his providence controls all things in love, that Jesus Christ is the son of God who rose from the dead and that the church is the divinely instituted organism in the world for the propagation of the truth. All this is received by faith. "Thomism combines great confidence in the power of reason with an emphasis on the need for faith. It holds that philosophy is, in principle, independent of faith in revelation; yet they complement each other, for that part of philosophy which deals with God—natural theology— prepares the way for faith." [7]

Thomism assures us that the truths of reason and revelation cannot contradict each other because both reason and faith have their source in God.

True humanism

Jacques Maritain has written a book under the title, *True Humanism*, in which he maintains the necessity of developing this type of christian humanism in the modern world. He claims that there has been a spiritual and moral degeneration, full of divisive trends, due to the fact that there is no common ethos to guide our western culture. He believes that the dichotomy between man and his world which has developed since the breakdown of the medieval synthesis must be repaired. Unity must be restored to the body of humanity. This can only come about by the humanism which recognizes God as the father of all mankind. According to Maritain, what we have today is a secularized humanism, of which Communism and Fascism are the end results.

Following St. Thomas, Neo-Thomists today stress the unity of body and soul in the constitution of human nature which is basic to true humanism. Man is no longer, in Platonic fashion, a soul inhabiting a body, with its consequent dualism, but the soul is the form of the body. Soul as well as body has substance. This view unites the soul to the body in such a manner as to give high value not only to the soul, as many previous thinkers had done, but also to the body. Man's sensate and bodily life is related to God as well as the soul. It was because of this belief that St. Thomas treated all human knowledge as sensory in origin. "There is nothing in the intellect," he wrote, "which has not first been in the senses." Hence also the dualism between the sensory and the intelligible disappeared in Thomistic metaphysics.

Professor Gilson holds Descartes responsible for the rise of some forms of modern dualism. He points out that Descartes wished to give "a mathematical demonstration of the spirituality of the soul. The better to do it, he had begun by turning the old scholastic soul as the form of the body into a disembodied mind."[8] The result was that the mind of man was considered as a mere machine and the true spirituality was lost.

Professor Gilson, considering the constitution of man, sees that reason has a place of great significance. It forms the "specific difference" between man and the lower creatures. "Man is best described as a rational animal; deprive man of reason, and what is left is not man, but animal. . . ." [9] It is this belief in the primacy of reason that is at the base of western culture and the only conceivable foundation for a rational system of ethics. "It is proper that a beast should act as a beast, that is, according to its own nature; but it is totally unfitting for a man to act as a beast, because that means the complete oblivion of his own nature, and hence his final destruction." [10] The nature of man, therefore, is basically rational and this implies that "by his very nature, man is a metaphysical animal." [11] All of which would be supported by Gilson's master, St. Thomas Aquinas.

In relation to his teaching on true humanism, Maritain calls for a new kind of saint, one who is dedicated to God in secular callings, and one who does not shirk the work of living and helping the 'last, the least, and the lost', like Mother Teresa or Jean Vanier. Catholic action for Maritain is nothing less than the consecration of the secular life to God. "All this means that the church," writes Maritain, "must work for a christian order, howsoever it may be otherwise: that the creature should be truly respected in his connection with God and because he is totally dependent on him; humanism indeed, but a theocentric humanism, rooted in what is radical (root) in man: integral humanism, the humanism of the incarnation." [12]

In this concept of true humanism there is a basic optimism that is involved in spite of the problem of evil. This optimism is founded first on the doctrine of creation. Gilson writes: "The basic principle on which christian optimism. . . has always rested" is "the capital fact of creation, and the creator himself, contemplating his work has made it good. And then, on the evening of the sixth day, casting a comprehensive glance over all his work, he gives for the last time a similar testimony, proclaiming his creation very good ...There ... we have the unshakable foundation for christian optimism." [13] In other words, the ground of christian optimism about man and his world is rooted in God, the creator who is good and who created the universe out of his own goodness.

Neo-Thomists would also claim that another ground for christian optimism, and one that is in accord with that of creation because "salvation is from the Jews" (John 4:22), is the doctrine of the incarnation. It is only because creation is from God that Christ, the Messiah, could be born a man in this world. There could be no incarnation on the basis of a metaphysic that posited a dualism between spirit and matter.

Since Christ has come as a human being, God incarnate, all human life has been dignified. Every person is one for whom Christ lived and died. Human life is precious in God's sight because Christ was human as well as divine. The social relevance of this teaching is far-reaching and shows Neo-Thomism to be both a humanising and humanitarian force of great significance in the world.

Sacramentalism

A sacrament is "an outward and visible sign of an inward and spiritual grace, given to us by Christ himself, as a means whereby we receive this grace, and a pledge to assure us thereof" (Anglican Catechism). Sacraments according to Neo-Thomists bring to the faithful the grace of Christ's redemption. Christ himself is present in the sacrament. Christ is the chief minister in the sacrament and the objectivity of his grace is set forth in the Roman Catholic teaching of transubstantiation.

Sacraments are visible signs of the presence of God in the world. God became visible to man in Jesus Christ, and Christ himself has given signs that he is with his people. The inward reality is always in need of a material

73

manifestation in this material world in which we live and move and have our being. This too is in accord with Thomist teaching about the nature of man being a unity of body and soul. We are not angels, beings of pure spirit. We are men and women living in physical bodies and our spiritual longings and expressions must be in and through these bodies. Consequently sacraments are both suitable and necessary for the nature of man in his relation to God.

The Roman Catholic church believes in seven sacraments within the church. But Neo-Thomists and other theologians believe that there are two sacraments prior to any of these seven, Christ being first, and the church his body, second, though these two are inseparable.

Christ is the supreme sacrament because he is the embodiment of God in human life, the enfleshment of the divine in mankind. All christian living is 'in Christ' and all christian speech and action is related to his mind and will.

The church is Christ's body. He is enthroned at the right hand of the Father in heaven. But through the Holy Spirit he is present in his church on earth to the end of time. All reference to the spirit of Christ indwelling people apart from his corporate body would appear to be without foundation. "Where Christ is, there is his church," said St. Cyprian—and Calvin after him. "There is one body and one spirit" (Eph.4:4). The New Testament knows nothing of a disembodied spirit in this material world. In this connection Father Schillebeeckx sees the church, among other things, as "a Sacrament of Dialogue", that is, of dialogue with the world casting off its exclusiveness and its isolation and entering into real communication with man in his everyday life. He goes on to state that "the idea of the church as the sacramentum mundi" is basic to this teaching that the church must be in dialogue with the world. [14]

We should also see that the sacramental principle is in accord with the doctrine of creation as set forth in Genesis 1 where we read that God created the world in goodness. In creation matter and spirit were united, the material becoming the vehicle of spirit, the means whereby spiritual reality is made visible in the world. This is high, biblical doctrine promulgated by Neo-Thomists and is substantiated by Thomist teaching on nature and grace.

It is in relation to the Roman Catholic church's teaching of the church being sacramental in nature that we should view the doctrine of revelation. Because the church as Christ's body in the world manifests the spirit of God and is sustained and guided by his spirit, tradition as well as scripture has a place in revelation. Revelation is a continuing process, under the spirit's guidance, and as the centuries pass "God has more light and truth to break forth from his holy word" which the church has the duty of declaring to men in the form of dogmas which may, or may not, have a biblical foundation.

Does this mean that in the Roman Catholic view of revelation scripture and tradition may be at variance with one another? Not so. Scripture and tradition, according to this teaching, "flow from the same well-spring, in a certain way merge into a unity and tend toward the same end. . . . Sacred tradition and sacred scripture form one sacred deposit of the word of God, which is committed to the church." [15] Both tradition and scripture have their origin in the one tradition, the gospel itself, whose centre is Jesus Christ. This leads Father Avery Dulles to declare that "these reflections on scripture and tradition . . . are not really two separate sources, but two facets of a single source. The bible is not revelation unless it is read in the light of church tradition; the tradition is not revelation unless grounded in the bible. The one channel by which revelation is available today is scripture enveloped in the atmosphehre of living tradition." [16] But for the proper interpretation of both scripture and tradition the church in its teaching office, focusing in the Papacy, is of supreme authority. In fact, scripture, tradition and the church's teaching authority form a unity and "are so linked and joined together that one cannot stand without the others." [17]

When we turn to the 'Document on Revelation' of Vatican II we can see the Thomistic emphasis of linking together reason with the divine disclosure at several points, beginning with the preface: "Hearing the word of God with reverence and proclaiming it confidently ..." [18] The "hearing" brings man's reason into play in understanding revelation. what is heard is the word of God, the objective self-manifestation of God in his church. Human nature and divine grace are thus united in this all-important matter of revelation.

From the above it can be seen that sacramentalism is at the heart of Neo-Thomist teaching. It is inclusive of nature and grace, faith and reason, creation and redemption, man and God. It links together all of life in one comprehensive wholeness (catholic) in which God is seen as the author and source of all who does not eliminate second causes, as Gilson points out, but sustains them. "Those who deny all efficacy to second causes in order to reserve the privilege of causality to God himself do no less injury to God than to things. ... The urge by which certain philosophers are driven to withdraw everything from nature in order to glorify the creator is inspired by a good intention, but a blind one ... to deprive things of actions of their own is to belittle God's goodness." [19] The sacramental principle leaves room for man as God's agent but all is under the Almighty's sovereign command. Thus for the Neo-Thomist, sacramentality is at the heart of the christian faith.

The development of dogma

Cardinal J.H. Newman in the nineteenth century gave expression and substance to the idea of the development of dogma in the church, although the origin of this idea lies far back in the history of the church. The idea is also Neo-Thomist in that it affirms that the spirit will guide the church into further manifestations of the truth that is enshrined in the mystery of Christ.

Father von Balthasar believes that "it is perfectly normal nowadays to speak of the development of dogma, meaning

76

thereby the unfolding of 'all the hidden treasures of wisdom and knowledge' (Col.2:3) lying in the church's heritage of revelation, which she can bring forth through contemplation under the light and guidance of the Holy Spirit." [20] 'Hidden treasures' in St. Paul's writings refer to the mystery of God's truth which he makes known to the faithful through his spirit in the corporate body of the church.

Karl Adam has pointed out that truths are usually wrapped up in "the forms of the times" in which they were first given as dogmas and they have to be freed from these ancient forms and put in new forms for the new age. "The wrappings" in which truth can become encased are conditional and contextual and these can be changed. "The seed of revealed truth is a living and organic thing" and "it requires for its progressive growth a fertile field of maternal soil, which may foster the seed committed to it and bring it to maturity. The living community is the fertile field." In other words, the church is "the fertile field." [21] Thus the church, speaking through the teaching authority of the magisterium and under the power of the Holy Spirit who guides the church, is able to develop dogma and bring out of the treasures of heavenly wisdom things new as well as old.

This belief in the development of dogma does not mean that the church is able to change her basic faith. There is a faith "once for all delivered to the saints"; a deposit of faith which must be handed on from generation to generation in the church. This is an important aspect of the teaching authority and ministry of the church. Nor does the development of dogma simply mean the adaptation of the dogmatic formulations of the faith to meet changes in conditions and language. It means, rather, that because God is the living God and his spirit is continually at work in his church bringing fresh revelation out of his holy word, the church has the responsibility to give expression to this revealed truth in new formulations of the faith which have been there since the beginning but which are not seen in the fullness of truth. In the New Testament revelation and mystery are conjoined. St. Paul even speaks of "the revelation of the mystery which was kept secret for long ages, but is now disclosed" (Rom. 16:25). And the concept of the development of dogma informs us that from the depths of the mystery of revelation there is disclosed to the church from time to time further light on the supreme revelation which has been given to us through Jesus Christ.

This teaching of the development of dogma is connected with the sacramental view of the church which we have previously discussed. Von Balthasar, in referring to the church as the "general sacrament", says that "as the sacrament of the redeemed cosmos, the light of Christ that progressively illumines all the world's darkness", the church is under obligation to bring the light of truth to bear on all of life. He makes much of Jesus' words: "You are the light of the world" (Matt.5:14). [22] This implies that the light of God's mystery will shine more and more unto the perfect day as the truth is unveiled and the mystery revealed, even though it remains unfathomable to human understanding.

Yves Congar, whose book on The Mystery of the Church shows the strong sacramental principle which undergirds his doctrine of the church, in writing that a Neo-Thomist does not give "strict adherence to the letter of Aquinas, as though no new thought had been conceived since 1274" but follows the spirit of St. Thomas, goes on to state that this means a true Neo-Thomist is one whose "mind is open to reality". [23] Thus there is an openness to truth, a seeking, a searching after truth. And when God discloses more of his light and truth to his church there is, of necessity, a development of dogma.

The development of dogma is one of the doctrinal strengths of both Neo-Thomist theology and the Roman Catholic church. It means that truth is not static but dynamic; that the living God keeps faith alive in his church; that new light can be shed on ancient truth and that it can also disclose new insight into eternal truth; that the dogmas of the one faith can be related to new situations through new disclosures of this faith. The development of dogma lends freshness to faith and new vitality to the church. Above all, it can be a spur to new forms of the liturgy and make a new appeal to the people of God in their devotional life.

Evaluation

Neo-Thomism is one of the most impressive and all-embracing systems of thought that the world has known. Its ability to unite a variety of factors within its compass with the truth of the christian gospel is an achievement of high merit. The synthesis it attempts to make of different aspects of human culture with divine revelation creates a strong appeal to a multitude of people.

Neo-Thomism is not only a metaphysic and a theology. It is also a culture in that it is so comprehensive as to include all phases of religious, social and personal life within its purview. The religious dimension remains predominant in such a culture but it is religion that is related to every area of human concern. This is part of the strength of Neo-Thomism which has enduring value.

The emphasis on the development of dogma in Neo-Thomism, which has taken on a new vitality in recent years and which is in part due to the influence of Vatican Council 11, shows that this type of theology is always able to be renewed and bring forth a fresh approach to truth. Because this is so Neo-Thomism opposes all static and pedestrian ideas concerning the truth and the application of truth to the human scene. It was because of this openness to truth which was based on the deposit of faith, that Karl Barth in the early sixties of this century, seeing what was happening in the Roman Catholic church at Vatican 11 and elsewhere, claimed that it was this church which was showing more of the real intent of the Reformation formula, ecclesia semper reformanda, than the church of Protestantism. For this development of dogma is not confined to dogma. Dogma in Neo-Thomism is related to worship and to life. And the manner in which the liturgy of the Roman Catholic church has been reformed, as well as the deeper interest the faithful have shown in social matters, is indicative of concern for the spiritual and material welfare of people.

Because of its stress on the doctrine of creation Neo-Thomism has a special appeal in the scientific age in which we are living. It can easily relate to new discoveries and achievements and bring all scientific truth within the range of God's self-disclosure to man. The world of nature, so vast and interesting today, can be related to the world of grace in a new and larger way.

Today man must take an interest in ecological problems. Again the emphasis on God, the Creator, who has given us this earth as our home, makes Neo-Thomism a system of thought with special value for our times. It enables us to see that we have a responsibility to God as well as the generations to come to preserve life on this planet and to manifest a real concern for the material things in creation.

The Neo-Thomist appeal to reason as well as revelation is also a strong point in this system. Without a place for reason in religion there will likely develop a superstitious approach to faith, or else a dualism will arise between reason and faith which is detrimental to the rational aspect of human life as well as the faith of a Christian.

On the other hand, there are some serious questions that we must raise about the Neo-Thomist system of metaphysics and theology. For instance, does Neo-Thomism take seriously the doctrine of original sin? If reason is corruptible, should we think only of grace perfecting nature? Must not grace also redeem nature? It would appear that a true system of theology, which takes into consideration the implications of the doctrine of redemption, must stress discontinuity as well as continuity in a paradoxical manner. Man was created good but he has sinned and come short of the glory of God. This sinning does not have to go all the way with Karl Barth and other extreme Neo-Orthodox theologians who affirm that by sin the imago dei has been blotted out in order to affirm that reason can be tainted by sin. But the imago has been corrupted and must be redeemed. Because this is so we must beware of thinking only of continuity between nature and grace, reason and faith. Here is where Barth's criticism of St. Thomas' analogia entis must be taken seriously in any consideration of the system of Neo-Thomism. Here we believe substitution of the analogia fidei for the analogia entis has much to commend it.

Protestants have learned much in ecumenical gatherings in recent years about the place and value of tradition in Christianity. The sola scriptura formula which has heretofore dominated much of Protestantism is open to serious questioning when we realize that scripture itself arose out of the early christian tradition and that the churches have developed their own traditions in succeeding centuries.

However, the very large place which Roman Catholics gave to tradition which when united with the belief in the development of dogma leads to the formulation of dogmas which have little or no relation to the word of God written in scripture, raises serious questions for Protestants. We believe, with Luther, that the bible is "the written Christ", that scripture contains "all doctrine necessary for salvation". To formulate doctrines, therefore, which appear to arise out of other sources than scripture appears to many to be unwarranted. The Holy Spirit testifies of Christ (John 15:26). The Holy Spirit, we believe, also guides his church. Will the Spirit, then, give some other testimony than that which is to be found in Christ? We do not believe this to be so.

The danger of departing from scripture in doctrine is that over the course of centuries ideas, beliefs, notions and assumed needs of people will often present the church with apparently "significant truths", while in reality they may be contrary to the truth as it is in Jesus. The departure from scripture can permit people to bring forth all sorts of theosophical ideas which corrupt the christian faith. This

81

has happened from time to time in Protestantism, though the 'main line churches' have endeavoured to keep free from such heresy.

We believe that this danger is also implicit, if not already realized, within Roman Catholicism. For instance, the unscriptural dogma of the bodily assumption of the Virgin Mary into Heaven is, according to our view, a denial of the truth that the Holy Spirit, the guide and guardian of the church, always bears witness to Jesus Christ. Such a dogma we believe, is derogatory of the centrality of Christ in Christianity.

Does not the comprehensiveness of Neo-Thomism, akin to the comprehensiveness of Hinduism though from a very different base, lend itself to the formulation of dogmas which arise out of human piety rather than from divine revelation? And is not this also the result of an emphasis on continuity between nature and grace in Neo-Thomism? Neo-Thomism, like the seamless robe of Christ, is of one piece, woven from the top throughout. And the promulgation of new dogmas of the faith would appear to be part and parcel of the Thomist system of thought. Consequently, from a Protestant point of view we must raise some serious questions about new dogmas of the faith being given under the authority of the papacy.

Again, the sacramental view of life, arising first from the doctrine of creation, must be subject to the prophetic criticism of the word of God. "What to me is the multitude of your sacrifices (or masses)? says the Lord; . . . Bring no more vain offerings; incense is an abomination unto me . . . Wash yourselves; make yourselves clean; remove the evil of your doings from before my eyes . . ." (Isa. 1:11,13,16). Without this prophetic approach to reality sacramentalism can degenerate into vain repetition. And so can other forms of religion, including protestant preaching which lacks the prophetic fire. But to accept the sacramental approach to religion uncritically would be to do a disservice to true religion.

Another question: does not the comprehensiveness of

Neo-Thomism, good as it is, leave little room for the 'cutting edge' of certain other vital doctrines? For example, the Lutheran stress on justification by faith has been a source of strength in Lutheranism. This is the 'cutting edge' of Lutheran religion. Would this be lost in a more comprehensive system of theology which could be so inclusive that no one element in the faith was given priority? No dogmatic reply can be given but we believe this is a question that requires serious consideration, not least of all by Neo-Thomists.

Then, too, must not the christian optimism of Neo-Thomism, based on the doctrine of creation to which we have previously referred, be always countered by a christian pessimism about man as he is? It is this 'counter' which makes necessary the christian doctrine of redemption in order to restore the first creation. Man needs redemption. With Athanasius and the fathers of the church, we believe that it is only the God-man, Jesus Christ, who can redeem mankind. We realize that Neo-Thomism would affirm this also but we believe it must take seriously the depth of human sinfulness and the spiritual power of God's redemptive grace.

However, Neo-Thomism is a theological system of great weight and value. Its view of life commends it to many people. Its strength lies in its inclusiveness and the relation of the totality of life to the divine creator. As such, it will continue to make an appeal to the mind of man.

1. Karl Rahner, *Nature and Grace*, P.24. Sheed and Ward, London, 1963.
2. E. Gilson, *The Spirit of Mediaeval Philosophy.* P.379. Sheed & Ward, London. 1936.
3. E. Gilson, *The Christian Philosophy of St. Thomas Aquinas*, P.360. Victor Gollancz Ltd. London. 1961.
4. Karl Rahner, Op.Cit., P.42.
5. E.E. Aubrey, *Present Theological Tendencies*, P.137. Harper & Brothers, New York. 1936.

6.   Jacques Maritain, *In 20th Century Religious Thought*, John MacQuarrie, P.284. S.C.M. Press, London. 1971.
7.   *Handbook of Christian Theology*, P.362. Meridian Books, New York. 1958.
8.   E. Gilson, *The Unity of Philosophical Experience*, P.173. Charles Scribner's Sons, New York. 1937.
9.   Ibid., P.274.
10.   Ibid., P.274.
11.   Ibid., P.307.
12.   Jacques Maritain, *True Humanism*, P.65, Geoffrey Bles: The Centenary Press, London, 1938.
13.   E. Gilson, *The Spirit of Mediaeval Philosophy*, P.109f.
14.   Edward Schillebeeckx, O.P. *God and the Future of Man*, P.121f. Sheed & Ward, Ltd. London. 1969.
15.   Walter J. Abbott, S.J. Editor. *The Documents of Vatican 11*, P.113. Guild Press, New York. 1966.
16.   Avery Dulles, *Revelation and the Quest for Unity*, P.80. Corpus Books, Washington, D.C. 1968.
17.   The Documents of Vatican 11, Op.Cit., P.117f.
18.   Ibid., P.14.
19.   E. Gilson, *The Christian Philosophy of St. Thomas Aquinas*, P.181f.
20.   Hans Urs von Balthasar, *A Theology of History*, P.136. Sheed & Ward, London. 1964.
21.   Karl Adam, *The Spirit of Catholicism*, P.153ff. Sheed & Ward, London. 1934.
22.   Leonhard Reinisch, Ed., *Theologians of our Time*. Hans Urs Von Balthasar, P.162. The University of Notre Dame Press, Indiana, 1964.
23.   Yves Congar, Ibid., P.166.

VII

Process Theology

Nearly fifty years ago A.N. Whitehead wrote: "Today there is but one religious dogma in debate: what do you mean by God? and in this respect today is like all its yesterdays. This is the fundamental religious dogma and all other dogmas are subsidiary to it." [1]

While many religious ideas must be taken into account when we consider the teaching of the School of Process Theology it is, nevertheless, with this question, "What do you mean by God?" that most of the discussion must be concerned.

We have singled out the following emphases as being of special importance to the process theologians.

God and creation are in continuous process

This process type of theology owes much to A. N. Whitehead. Some would say that he is the real originator of this school in this century. While Whitehead was primarily a metaphysician, his metaphysics have had a very large influence in the field of theology.

According to Whitehead's point of view, the world is in continual process and change is going on all the time. The world is an organic whole and God is inextricably involved in the process of change. God, the finite reality, who is both living and personal, "is no remote deity. He is in the world; or we might even say that the world is in him . . . God is operative in the whole creation, at every level of existence; he moves through it, works upon it, accomplishes his good will in it." [2]

The process theologians stress God's immanence. But

they also have room for a special view of God's transcendence. But this term transcendence does not mean 'otherness' or 'beyondness' but 'superiority' to other beings. He is the One who "surpasses everything", according to Charles Hartshorne, a disciple of Whitehead. [3] God is the self-consistent One, "the unexhausted and unexhaustible reality," who is "closer than breathing, nearer than hands or feet."

Process theologians refrain from speaking of God as supernatural. They are afraid that this term leaves the impression that God is above creation, apart from it, and consequently cannot be constantly involved in the organic whole of creation.

The world is the body of God, [4] although God is "more" than the world in the sense that a man is "more" than his body. But at no point must we think of God as being separated from the world. He is the world's very life. He is as bound to the world as the world is bound to him. As Whitehead [5] has expressed it: "It is as true to say that the world is immanent in God, as that God is immanent in the world. It is as true to say that God transcends the world, as that the world transcends God. It is as true to say that God creates the world, as that the world creates God." God and the world are so united in an organic wholeness that it would appear to be impossible to think of the one without the other.

This last statement of Whitehead's about creation would lead one to ask: in process theology is God the creator? If we think of creator as a God 'outside' his world then process theologians do not believe in him as creator. And taking, for instance, as Hartshorne does, the organic-social analogy of man and his body, then God is not the creator, any more than a man can 'create' his bones. [6] However, we do know that mind has an influence over bodily growth and what happens imperfectly in human life can happen between the perfection of God and the world uniquely. So if by 'creation' is meant the 'supreme influence upon growth', then we can speak of God as creator. But Hartshorne has much hesitation about thinking of God the creator in terms of 'ex nihilo', which has been the traditional way in which christian theology has thought of God 'making' the world 'out of nothing'.

This view of God has been greatly influenced by the developments of modern science. Theologians of this school will have nothing to do with God as an 'unmoved mover', a static, unchangeable God. So great has been the influence of science on modern man that, according to Whitehead, the "quick growth of science has practically recoloured our mentality so that modes of thought which in former times were exceptional, are now broadly spread through the educated world. . . .The new mentality is more important even than the new science and the new technology." [7] This makes it imperative, according to the process theologians, for christian man to re-think all his theological concepts, beginning with his concept of God. And because science now thinks of the world, not as a machine but as an organism, we must view all life in organic terms, including the life of God. God is he who is both behind and within the "principle of life, order and growth" in the universe. He is "the principle of concretion", the "upholding principle of the whole scheme of creation" (Col. 1:17, J.B. Phillips).

To the thinkers in this school the world is "the garment of the living God". God is the dynamic power within the world, creating, sustaining and promoting all goodness and love, even in the material earth. Teilhard de Chardin dedicated his book, *Le Milieu Divin*, to "those who love the world." [8] He sees God in the world of matter. "The Mass on the World" [9] is one of the most spiritual of de Chardin's writings. He tells of a Mass performed in an Asian desert when he had "neither bread, nor wine, nor altar" and when he made "the whole earth" his altar. De Chardin sees that through God's incarnation in Christ "all matter is henceforth incarnate". Near the end of this discourse he writes: "For me, my God, all joy and all achievement, the very purpose of my being and all my love of life, all depend on this one basic vision of the union between yourself and the universe . . . I have no desire, I have no ability, to proclaim anything except the innumerable prolongations of your incarnate Being in the world of matter." [10] God is here conceived as the dynamic, living ground of all creation.

Though de Chardin seems to have been unacquainted with Whitehead's writings, their point of view is very similar regarding the relation of God to the world of nature, including human nature. Following our references to de Chardin, it is interesting to study for a moment Tennyson's "Flower in the Crannied Wall" in the light of Whitehead's views on nature. Tennyson wrote:

> "Flower in the crannied wall,
> I pluck you out of the crannies,
> I hold you here, root and all, in my hand,
> Little flower—but if I could understand
> What you are, root and all, and all in all,
> I should know what God and man is."

What Tennyson is saying is that the totality of all being is involved in the existence of the flower. Both the life of God and man are related intimately to the flower. "The flower prehends all being; the universe is concreted in the flower."

This is not pantheism, according to Whitehead, because God is not the equivalent of the whole of the universe. He is, rather, the one sustaining, all-pervading character which the universe displays of goodness, beauty, and love, a point of view that has a Platonic background as Whitehead pointed out in his lectures on *Process and Reality*.

God as primordial and consequent

Primordial and consequent are two terms which Whitehead used to describe two aspects of the nature of God and which other process theologians make use of to elucidate their view of God.

When they speak of God as primordial they are referring to the aspect of God's nature of mutual adjustment, mutual helpfulness, mutual support. It is primordial because it is the one order that always was and ever will be. Without this primordial order all would be chaos or nothing. Primordial refers to the constant and unchanging aspect of deity. This aspect of deity reminds us that his life sustains all values. He exercises a qualitative power in the universe that upholds goodness, truth, and beauty. "This is the aspect that makes God God, namely, what is common to God in all his states. This is also the basis of the unity of God by which he is not reduced merely to relative states. . . . God will EXIST regardless of what happens; he depends for his existence on no particular world or process." [11]

But if God is so 'bound up' with the life of the world that it would seem they are in fact inseparable, and if, as we are aware, the world itself is perishing, will not God perish also? Not so, reply the process theologians because "the primordial nature of God is eternal. This means that it is wholly unaffected by time or by process in any other sense. The primordial nature of God affects the world but is unaffected by it. For it, before and after are strictly irrelevent categories." [12] This seems to be in contradiction to Whitehead's statement we have quoted above that "it is as true to say that the world is immanent in God, as that God is immanent in the world." How God can be "unaffected" in such a view of the organic relation between God and the world we fail to understand.

They also speak of God as consequent. This has been likened to an added "dome" or "spire" to the cathedral of God's primordial nature. Whitehead introduced this aspect of God into his total concept of deity in order to deal, in part, with the problem of evil.

"Time is a perpetual perishing." Will values perish also? We see heroism and sacrifice. Will they all eventually go for nothing? Creation itself seems to be a perishing entity. But, as John B. Cobb, Jr., points out, "there is no perishing in God. . . . This means that every achievement of value in the temporal world is preserved everlastingly in God's consequent nature." [13] Therefore nothing of the past that is valuable is ever lost. "There will never be one lost good," wrote Robert Browning. Whitehead expressed this thought at the close of his Gifford Lectures in this way: "The kingdom of heaven is with us today. . . . What is done in the world is transformed into a reality in heaven, and the reality in heaven passes back into the world. By reason of this reciprocal relation, the love in the world passes into the love in heaven, and floods back again into the world. In this sense, God is the great companion—the fellow-sufferer who understands." [14] Nothing of value is ever lost because of God's consequent nature. "Whatever enters into the consequent nature of God remains there forever," writes Dr. Cobb, "but new elements are constantly added." [15]

This school of Process Theology makes all of us aware of the need to develop a christian theology of nature, or a christian natural theology, freed from medieval concepts with their static background, and conceptualized in forms and images more in accord with the dynamic, organic world that we live in today.

Up until recent times theologians conceived of God 'breaking into' his world from outside, as in the case of miracles. This left the impression that God was not in his world, though he remained its governor. But this concept of God's relation to the world can no longer be held by thinking people. And it is because theology has not given us new concepts of God and his relation to the world to suit the new age that many people have become naturalists, viewing the world without any belief in God. Whatever criticisms we may offer of process theology, we should agree that one thing it is making all theologians do is re-think their theological concepts in a new way for this scientific age. In other words, we must no longer think of God as a workman operating a machine, but as the spiritual power in an organic world. The world is "in the making still". Creation is a continuous process and we are in the midst of it and so is God. God, as de Chardin says, is "the within" of things.

The Australian christian biologist, L. Charles Birch,

writes in opposition to the mechanistic view of the world which thinks of God as the controller of a machine. [16] This view of God makes people into automata. When Darwin came on the scene in the last century, he points out, it was essentially a deistic view of God that was held by most theologians. But in Darwin's century there were theologians of whom Charles Kingsley was an example, who saw that the new view of nature must lead to a new concept of God. Kingsley wrote: "Now that they (scientists) have got rid of an interfering God—a master-magician as I call it—they have to choose between the absolute empire of accident and a living, immanent, every-working God." [17]

Dietrich Bonhoeffer in a Nazi prison read Weizacker's book, *The World-View of Physics*, after which he wrote that we must cease thinking of the "stop-gap" God, as if all that we did not know about the universe were to be left to God. He wrote: "We are to find God in what we know, not in what we don't know. . . ." Again God is no "stop-gap" in the sense that we turn to him when "we are at the end of our resources". God "must be recognized at the centre of life." [18] It is this thought, beautifully expressed, that C.A. Coulson gives us in the final words of his book, Science and Christian Belief. He writes: "All life is sacramental; All nature is needed that Christ should be understood. Christ is needed that all nature should be seen as holy; that amid all its turbulance and tumult God's perfection might grow; and our hearts be filled with wonder at the significance of the least of all this work." And Professor Coulson ends by quoting from Alfred Noyes' poem, The Forest of Wild Thyme:

> "What does it take to make a rose
>   Mother mine?
>
> It takes the world's eternal wars,
> It takes the moon and all the stars,
> It takes the might of heaven and hell,
> And the everlasting love as well,
>   Little child." [19]

All thinkers in this school of theology believe that life shows there are different levels of creation. C. Lloyd Morgan in his Emergent Evolution [20] sees the development of life involving "leaps to new levels of being." He sees three distinct levels in the evolutionary process: The physico-chemical level, the vital level, and the mental level. William Temple, in his sacramental view of the universe, sees these levels as being matter, life, mind and spirit. [21] De Chardin writes of the biosphere, the noosphere and the christosphere. And in this developing creation these writers remind us that life progresses from the lower to the higher, while it is in the higher that we see the true meaning of the lower. The natural world is the outward and visible sign of an inward and spiritual life. It is this mental and spiritual factor which de Chardin has in mind when he writes about "the within of the earth," which he says, denotes "the 'psychic' face of that portion of the stuff on the cosmos enclosed from the begining of time within the narrow scope of the early earth." [22]

This on-going creation, developing from lower to higher, shows the Christian that life has a purpose, that we live in a meaningful world that has a goal. De Chardin calls it Omega point. The New Testament calls it the kingdom of God.

In order not to accept the accusation frequently levelled at them that they are pantheists, many process theologians struggle to differentiate their view of God from that of pantheism; they do so by employing a new word 'panentheism'.

The Oxford dictionary of the Christian church defines panentheism as "the belief that the being of God includes and penetrates the whole universe, so that every part of it exists in him, but (as against pantheism), that his being is more than, and is not exhausted by, the universe." According to Bishop J.A.T. Robinson this implies that "there is a co-inherence between God and the universe which overcomes the duality without denying the diversity." [23]

Bishop Robinson points out that panentheism is a term

which in meaning is closer to theism than it is to pantheism because it desires to avoid the impersonal factor in pantheism and to retain the personal element in both God and man. In panentheism there is no thought of the person being absorbed in some speculative absolute.

Bishop Robinson does not like using the word 'and' in the phrase "God and the world" as if God were someone who was joined to the world. He maintains that panentheism avoids such a duality because it affirms that God and the world are united, yet different. God is in the world and the world is in God, as Whitehead has stated. God is thus "the fullness of him who fills all in all" (Eph.1:23).

Let us also take a brief look at the problem of evil for the process theologian. "The most serious problem confronting the organic analogy," writes Charles Hartshorne of the process view of creation, "is that of evil. How can there be conflict, disorder, defects in the body of God?" [24]

The process theologians do not avoid this problem of evil but they regard it as a 'defect' in an evolving universe, the result of man's freedom, a deviation from the path man should take, a "failure to participate in the purposes of love." [25]

De Chardin has been accused of avoiding the problem of evil and Henri de Lubac [26] attempts to answer these charges against his fellow Jesuit. De Chardin himself writes an appendix to his, *The Phenomenon of Man*, to deal with this accusation. He also refers to the problem of evil, including sin, in several of his books. What does he say in reply?

De Chardin believed that he was correct in setting forth the positive side of his evolutionary theology, namely, that the universe lends support to progress in goodness. Consequently he did not dwell on the negative, evil aspects of life.

De Chardin was a stretcher-bearer in World War I. He saw suffering at first hand. It touched him deeply, as one can see from reading his war-time correspondence. Basically he believed, with St. Paul, that evil was a mystery. He wrestled with the problem of evil.

Listen to him raising profound questions: "Whence did the universe acquire its original stain? Why are we obliged in some way to identify evil and matter, evil and determinisms .... Is it only because, in relation to our souls, the lower zones of the universe and of union are a country that has been left behind .... to fall back into which is to be corrupted?"[27] He seems to equate evil with the forces of disunity against which God himself is struggling. "At every degree of evolution, we find evil always and everywhere, forming and reforming implacably in us and around us." He believed that evil is necessarily involved with growth and change in an evolving world. There is no progress without pain, no salvation without sacrifice. "The human epic resembles nothing as much as a way of the Cross."[28] But he knew from personal experience that it was by bearing his cross that a person is sanctified.

De Chardin has contributed significantly to the process theology vocabulary by coining the term hominisation. By it he means "the individual and instantaneous leap from instinct to thought, but it is also, in a wider sense, the progressive phyletic spiritualization in human civilization of all the forces contained in the animal world."[29] He goes on to say that "with hominisation .... we have the beginning of a new age. The earth gets 'a new skin'. Better still, it finds its soul." Hominisation informs us that in the noosphere (reason) which man has attained, he has 'come into his own', into a stage of special human responsibility and development.

In man, evolution has become conscious of itself. But evolution need not stop with man as we know him to be. Personal evolution can go on, and will go on, according to de Chardin, because of God. But in the future progress will depend largely on man's conscious willingness to advance. Great possibilities in the personal sphere are before mankind. The birth of reflective thought has marked a new emergent in the course of life. Now life can be transformed in depth. In man and his thought processes, we see the very interiorization of the forces of the universe itself. Man is the microcosm; the universe is the macrocosm. Hominisation tells us that man has 'leaped' from instinct to thought. Henceforth there should be an increasing spiritualisation in human life and culture. Man, now conscious of himself and his role in creation, can be joined with the creative will of God in bringing about what de Chardin calls a "Christifying" of the universe. "If the world is convergent and if Christ occupies its centre, then the Christogenesis of St. Paul and St. John is nothing else and nothing less than the extension .... of the noogenesis in which cosmogenesis .... culminates." [30] Such is the tremendous vision of this Jesuit.

The power of persuasive love

In his book, *The Adventures of Ideas*, A. N. Whitehead [31] has an essay entitled, "From Force to Persuasion", in which he writes as follows: "the creation of the world—said Plato—is the victory of persuasion over force". And what Plato divined in theory, Christianity has exhibited in an act of revelation in the person of Jesus Christ. This victory is the power of God's persuasive love.

All writers in this school of process theology, beginning with Whitehead, make much of God's nature as that of redemptive love. "All that is up-building, expressive of love and tenderness .... all of this is the working of the Holy God." [32] God is the "cosmic lover" who is at work in the world, overcoming the obstacles to his purpose of goodness. But one thing is certain: his love will never fail. Even when crucified, it lives again as the truly victorious power in creation. The process theologian can speak of the omnipotence of God, since love is all-powerful in the sense that it is able to overcome evil. It is not possible for any human situation of pain or sin to arise in which love cannot be at work savingly for "in him we live, and move, and have our being" (Acts 17:28).

Norman Pittenger writes: "We are 'made towards the image of God' who is love, the cosmic love or lover, who grounds our human striving and gives to it meaning which is enriching, enabling, ennobling, and in the long run able to win the victory over everything that is hateful, ugly, mean, selfish, and wrong." Here is "the victory that overcomes the world". In our faith that such is indeed the case, "human existence is redeemed from triviality, futility and absurdity". [33]

These theologians affirm that love is the ruling power of the world. God's persuasive love is the very foundation of the universe. Only in the unity of love can the world 'hang together'. One writer claims that inherent in de Chardin's theology of the universe, which finds its order and unity in Christ, is the ecumenical spirit which is at the heart of the world. Love makes for unity. Hate makes for disunity. But, praise be to God, His love is "above all and through all and in all' (Eph. 4:6). "Love alone is capable of uniting living beings," writes de Chardin, "in such a way as to complete and fulfil them, for it alone takes them and joins them by what is deepest in themselves." [34] To this writer "love is energy", love is power, love is completeness, love is the instinct of the heart that leads us toward unity. The rationale of all this, the only explanation for it, is that God is love.

These process writers stress the fact that a religion that is lacking in love has really separated itself from God, for God is love. It may have orthodox liturgies, carefully drafted propositions of faith, but these are no substitutes for love in action. "He who does not love does not know God . . . . No man has ever seen God; if we love one another, God abides in us and his love is perfected in us . . . . God is love, and he who abides in love, abides in God, and God abides in him" (1 John 4:8, 12, 16). These words of St. John are at the very heart of the profession of a process theologian for he affirms that there can be no theology worthy of the name Christian unless it is built on the love of God revealed in Jesus Christ.

Evaluation

Process theology has much to commend it. It has delivered us from a static view of deity which is more in accord with Greek, Aristotelian views of God than the living God of the Old and New Testaments. It has made us realize that God is the dynamic power of love at work in his world and this is our basic ground for optimism in the face of the dark clouds of evil that overhang our civilization. Truly, on this view, our hope is in God and in God alone, who never will forsake his world.

This type of theology rescues us from the many dualisms that arise in our life between religion and science, for instance, or faith and the material world. God is so intimately involved in the world that one cannot think of his existence apart from it. This faith redeems us from believing that God is 'over against' the world.

There is no doubt also that this view of God delivers us from materialistic and naturalistic ideas concerning the universe, with its consequent belief in God the great "Onlooker", who appears from time to time in the world he has created. To think of God as the power of love that makes for co-operation, whose soul or life is creative and creating, whose dynamic goodness is all around us and within us seeking for expression—all of this is helpful in thinking about God. It is also more in accord with the scientific view of creation and it relates modern science to faith.

There is no doubt that process theology, with its love of the material world in which God is so involved, will give support to those ecologists who are endeavouring to arouse the conscience of mankind to the preservation of this good earth, with its animal, fish and bird life. It tries to make men alive to the need of taking care of forest and soil, and the necessity of reducing the pollution of the atmosphere, of the seas and rivers and of our total environment. In this respect process theologians, with the call to a sense of stewardship concerning the world, have a worthwhile contribution to make to the life of all mankind. They also may become instruments in maintaining the lower forms of life on this earth.

On the other hand there are some very serious questions to be raised about process theology. We have noted that its view of evil in God's world is rather weak. To regard evil as inevitable in an emerging world is of little help to those who are involved in the evil. The 'mystery of iniquity' appears even more mysterious for process theologians. It is of some value, however, to note that de Chardin places the cross at the heart of this mystery.

A question of major importance for process theology is its view of God as creator. Can God really be called creator in process theology? God and the world are one—everlastingly. The world is 'running down'. Entropy is a reality in the universe. Is God 'running down' also? Can we really say that God is without beginning and end (finis) if we cannot think of him as in some sense having a life of his own, a life in which he is not dependent on the universe for his existence? And in the light of God's inextricable unity with the world, as process theologians declare, is it proper at all to use the term transcendence concerning deity?

We should also be aware that some process theologians, of which Teilhard de Chardin is a notable example, have been accused of being determinists. To de Chardin the world is in process of evolving toward what he designates as Omega point. The world gives evidence of cosmic development or cosmogenesis. De Chardin claims that the process is continuous and apparently nothing can stop this development from achieving its goal. Such a view looks very much like cosmic determinism.

To speak of the world as 'the body of God' appears unbiblical. "Creation in the language of the bible unquestionably connotes origination," writes Dr. George Hendry. It is true that the verb used in Genesis 1, bara, is predicated exclusively of God." This writer points out that there are analogies in the human act of making something that did not previously exist, yet "the divine act of creation

98

is unique and incomparable". This, Dr. Hendry affirms, is "the understanding enshrined in the formula, creatio ex nihilo, which was intended not only to exclude the notion of a pre-existent, unformed matter, or to substitute some mysterious un-matter for it, but to indicate, as Aquinas put it, that the world was made 'after nothing'." [35] Nowhere in the bible do we find any reference to the world as 'the body of God'. This phrase excludes the idea of God as creator who is distinct from his creation, even though he is involved in it.

There are also other theological grounds for questioning this teaching that the world is the body of God. Jesus said, "God is Spirit" (John 4:24). Spirit is manifest in creation but there is a radical distinction between spirit and creation. Spirit is immanent in creation but has an existence of his own that is not dependent on creation.

This questioning of the doctrine that the world is the body of God has support also in St. Paul's epistle to the Philippians. In the kenosis (self-emptying) passage in chapter 2 (vs 5-11) the apostle clearly refers to God becoming incarnate in Christ Jesus, "assuming the nature of a slave" (v. 7. N.E.B.). This fact of the incarnation makes plain to us that "the Word became flesh" (John 1:14). That is, Christ was not simply 'a phase of the universe' but a distinct being who was other than the world, though he came into the world in the form of man. One must conclude that this statement seeing the world as the body of God is entirely unbiblical and contrary to the Christian's thought of God.

Again, can we really speak meaningfully of God changing, growing, developing and fulfilling himself in creation as process theologians do? God, being personal for the process theologians, is not some inert, statuesque being, an unmoved mover. He must respond to man and man must respond to him. But does this mean change and growth? We doubt it very much. His love remains the same yesterday, today and forever. To some degree this is brought to our attention by Whitehead in his religious philosophy of the consequent nature of God. But it appears to be an 'extra' even in Whitehead's teaching, something 'added on' to God's nature in order to deal with the problem of 'perpetual perishing,' and not a vital aspect of God's being. But some other process theologians leave the impression that even God is subject to the law of entropy and that he will perish with his finite creation.

In process theology we see the re-emergence of Hegelianism. Hegel's idea is in process theology that 'phase of the universe' which creates and sustains goodness. God is no longer the great "I AM" but a being who is so bound up with the world that he is inseparable from the world. Like Hegel also, there is a tendency in process theology to depersonalize deity. This must inevitably have repercussions in people's devotional life. Men and women will pray to a THOU. It is doubtful if they will continue to pray to a THAT.

Is God really personal if He is a 'phase of the universe', 'the principle of concretion'? Can we really call him Father? It seems rather difficult, to say the least, to have fellowship with one who is so bound to the created universe that he would appear to be a prisoner of his own natural law. Prayer in relation to such a person would certainly be circumscribed in content and worship unlikely.

Have the process theologians given over too much to scientific theories concerning creation? To be related to the recent scientific theories and to consider them seriously is important for the theologian. But to become the lackeys of the latest scientific views is another thing. Even the theory of evolution which is so prominent in the writings of the process theologians is not the final word about the world. This theory, both cosmic and biological (which we admit to be more than a theory because of the immense array of facts which support it), cannot give us direction in matters of faith, or be the basis from which faith can reach forward to its goal of the kingdom of God.

A final question: is the God of process theologians supported by the bible's vision of God? We have shown cause to doubt this previously. And while some verses of scripture appear to support the view of God maintained by process theologians there are many other passages which seem contrary to their view. The biblical picture of God as the good shepherd, the high tower, the judge, the law-giver and the deity who gives a covenant to his people and elicits from them the obedience of faith—all these pictures of God are almost impossible to reconcile with the view of the deity in process theology. If God is a 'Father in Heaven', one who is very personal and whose being transcends earth in the very word 'heaven', then we have to question seriously the process theologian's description of God as 'the principle of concretion' or some other similar term.

Having made these critical remarks about process theology, we must go on to state that we believe the church owes much to process theology. It has made a contribution to christian thought in its emphasis on the living God. Outside the church we find some intellectuals taking a new interest in theology because of the writings of some process theologians, especially Teilhard de Chardin. Many have also found their faith to be enlightened and their religious views strengthened by the organic philosophy of Whitehead. For this contribuiton of process theology to the living faith of living people we can say sincerely: praise be to God!

1. A.N. Whitehead, *Religion in the Making*, P.67f. MacMillan Company, New York. 1926
2. Norman Pittenger, *God in Process*, P.17. S.C.M. Press, London. 1967.
3. Edward Farley, *The Transcendence of God*, P.154.(Quoted)The Westminster Press, Philadelphia. 1960
4. Edward Farley, Ibid., P.157.
5. A.N. Whitehead, *Process and Reality*, P.492 Cambridge at the University Press. 1929.
6. Charles Hartshorne, *Man's Vision of God*, P.193f. Willett, Clark, and Company, Chicago. 1941
7. A.N. Whitehead, *Science and the Modern World*, P.12 Pelican Books. 1938.
8. Teilhard de Chardin, *Le Milieu Divin*, Dedication page. Collins, Fontana Books. 1964.

9. Teilhard de Chardin, *Hymn of the Universe*, P.19 Collins, Fontana Books. 1970.
10. Ibid. P.38.
11. Edward Farley, *The Transcendence of God*, P.147f.
12. John B. Cobb, Jr., *A Christian Natural Theology*, P.187. The Westminster Press, Philadelphia. 1965.
13. Ibid., P.162.
14. A.N. Whitehead, *Process and Reality*, P.497.
15. Op.Cit., P.187.
16. L. Charles Birch, *Nature and God*, Chapter 1, S.C.M. Press, London. 1965.
17. L. Charles Birch, Ibid., P.52 (quoted).
18. D. Bonhoeffer, *Letters and Papers From Prison*, New Greatly Enlarged Edition, P.311f. The MacMillan Co., New York. 1971.
19. C.A. Coulson, *Science and Christian Belief*, P.118. Oxford University Press, London. 1956.
20. J. MacQuarrie, *20th Century Religious Thought*, P.260 (Quoted)
21. William Temple, *Nature, Man and God*, Chapter XIX, The Sacramental Universe. MacMillan and Co., London. 1951.
22. T. de Chardin, *The Phenomenon of Man*, P.72 Collins, London. 1961.
23. J.A.T. Robinson, *Exploration Into God*, P.84f. S.C.M. Press, London, 1967.
24. Charles Hartshorne, *Man's Vision of God*, P.195
25. N. Pittenger, *A Dictionary of Christian Theology*, Article "Process Theology", P.276 S.C.M. Press, London. 1969.
26. Henri de Lubac, S.L., *The Religion of Teilhard de Chardin*, P.116ff. Desclee Company, New York. 1967.
27. T. de Chardin, *Science and Christ*, P.80 Collins, London. 1965.
28. T. de Chardin, *The Phenomenon of Man*, P.313.
29. Ibid., P.180.
30. Ibid., P.297
31. A.N. Whitehead, *The Adventures of Ideas*, P.103. Penguin Books, 1948.
32. Norman Pittenger, *God in Process*, P.45
33. Norman Pittenger, *The British Weekly*, December 1, 1972
34. T. de Chardin, Op.Cit., P.265.
35. George S. Hendry, "The Eclipse of Creation", Article in *Theology Today*, January, 1972. P.420

VIII

Existential Theology

"Existence precedes essence." This is the motto of existentialism. Life's purpose and meaning, so it affirms, is to be found in contemporary existence and nowhere else.

Paul Tillich says that the word existentialism comes from the Latin, existere, to exist, or to stand out.[1] In terms of existentialism this means "to stand out of one's own non-being." So if we are to think of existentialism as a way of doing philosophy we should remember that this is not philosophy in the Platonic abstract sense which regards existence as lacking in true reality, but as philosophy that takes its cue from everyday living where man is involved in his trials, struggles and temptations.

Platonic philosophy claims that true reality is in the realm of essence, of eternal ideas. This is a type of philosophy which is at the opposite pole of thought from existentialism. "The opposite of existentialist is essentialist. In existential thinking, the object is involved. In non-existential thinking, the object is detached. By its very nature theology is existential; by its very nature, science is non-existential."[2] Thus all speculative philosophy is ruled out of bounds by the existentialist.

We have noted in Chapter One the stance and teaching of Soren Kierkegaard, the father of existentialism. We do not intend to deal further with his teaching in this chapter, but to give consideration to the main emphases of existentialists in this twentieth century. If we regard existentialism as a type of philosophy, we must remember that it is "a type so flexible that it can appear in .... widely differing forms,"[3] all the way from Sartre's atheism to Marcel's Catholicism. However, as we shall see, all existentialists have several common emphases.

We can single out five special emphasis which are current in existentialism:

Revolt Against Rationalism

First it is a **revolt against rationalism.** The turning point in the life of Blaise Pascal came on Monday, November 23, 1654, when he had the experience of "FIRE .... God of Abraham, God of Isaac, God of Jacob, not of the philosophers and scholars. Certitude, certitude, feeling, joy, peace. God of Jesus Christ."[4] This brilliant intellectual had a faith experience that was deeper than reason, one that could not be explained in rational terms. Such an experience was an encounter with objective reality which was total in its personal depth. God was no longer a someone whom Pascal theorized about, studied about or intellectually considered. He was one whom he knew, 'face to face', in a deeply personal manner.

It is this belief that "all real living is meeting" which is presented to us in Martin Buber's use of the term as "I-Thou" relationship. This is a relationship which involves the rational element in human life but which is at the same time suprarational; that is, much more than the rational is included in this person-to-person encounter. This "I-Thou" relation is seen in contrast to the "I-It" relation, that is of a person to a thing. "If I face a human being as my Thou," writes Buber, "and say the primary word I-Thou to him, he is not a thing among things, and does not consist of things."[5] Person to person relation is on a higher plane than person to thing. It is the former relation that involves the total personality on both sides of the relationship.

Existentialists protest against systems of philosophy because they believe that they circumscribe a person's life. The rational approach to life that is made by philosophers is too objective, too detached, to give one a true view of existence, according to existential thinkers. This is why existentialists, following Kierkegaard, believe that "truth is subjectivity and subjectivity is truth." In the citadel of one's soul, where systems no longer prevail, where one experiences a level of truth that is deeper than the intellect — it is there that one knows the meaning of existence.

For believing existentialists this person to person encounter is what is meant by faith. There is a numinous element in it and the rational is only one factor in this experience, maybe not even the dominating factor. In religious faith there is always a 'mysterium tremendum' component which makes us realize that this faith, like the peace of God, passes understanding. God is the supreme thou whom we meet in faith and the element of mystery, which cannot be analyzed by the reason, is part of faith.

A Personal Philosophy

Second, existentialism is a truly **personal philosophy.** Over against speculative metaphysics and philosophy, existentialism, with its stress on the individual and his existence, emphasizes a truly personal philosophy. As existentialism is a protest against reducing life and its meaning to rational elements, so it is a protest also against reducing human life to scientific measurements and explanations. John MacQuarrie says that "existentialism has appeared as a philosophical reaction against the scientific humanism that prevailed in the early part of this century. It denies the claim of that school of thought that the only knowledge is that which can be scientifically verified, and affirms, on the contrary, that scientific knowledge is only one kind of knowledge, not privileged but specialized, and subordinate to the fundamental knowledge, which is knowledge of existence."[6] In other words, true knowledge of existence is so personal that it cannot be weighed and measured, it cannot be calculated and computerized.

Any person's view of life is shaped by the totality of his existence and by the activity of the whole person. Man thinks with his will and emotions as much as with his intellect if we may, for a moment, think of the person in this tripartite fashion. But the fact is that we cannot divide up a person in this threefold manner in real life, and it is real existence, not speculative existence, with which the existentialist is concerned.

What we have said about the existentialist criticism of scientific humanism is not to be taken as a criticisim by them of science itself or of technological developments. They would acknowledge that, in the world of everyday, science and technology have a practical value and their achievements have enhanced human life. But it is in the realm of meaning that existentialists claim that we have to turn from science and technology to the truly personal to discover what life is all about. "The subject of supreme concern to man is his own inner being," according to existentialists, "and this can be understood only as one is personally involved."[7] As Heidegger claims, man's existence is "being-in-the-world" (Dasein). And it is in relation to his existing world that he comes to know who he is.

This modern search for identity is an existentialist approach to life. Who am I? Why am I here? What am I here for? Whither am I going? Questions of this sort remind us how deeply existentialist modes of thought have taken hold of people in our generation. Groups of youth, searching for answers to these existential questions, have forsaken the affluence of our material civilization because they have become convinced that life's purpose is not to be found in the abundance of things which one possesses. They believe that the world of things leads to unauthentic existence. The world of persons leads to authentic existence.

Luther used to say that all vital religion was summed up in personal pronouns. "The Lord is MY Shepherd. I shall not want. I know whom I have believed." Only a religion that is truly personal is real. It is only then that a person encounters God who sends him forth into life in reply to the call, "Whom shall I send, and who will go for us"? (Isa. 6:8) God is the one who concerns us ultimately and, according to

Tillich, it is one's ultimate concern that is at the basis of religious faith.

Importance of the Contemporary

Thirdly, existentialism stresses the importance of the **contemporary**. Rudolf Bultmann is an existential theologian of this century who has affirmed that it is faith in the Christ of the kerygma, the Christ that is preached in the Church, the contemporary Christ and not the historical Jesus, that is all-important for the Christian. Bultmann believes that Jesus of Nazareth was a person who lived and taught and died on a cross. But this historical fact is of little significance to men in the twentieth century. The central question, says Bultmann, is what is Christ for me today? Is there a living presence whom I can encounter by faith who will help me to find value in life?

Faith for Bultmann, as for other existentialists, is a matter of decision for God, and the commitment of the will. Bultmann writes: "Faith is the work of God, in so far as the grace which comes from him first makes possible the human decision, so that this decision itself can be understood only as God's gift, without on that account losing its character as decision." [8] Man's decision in faith is real, for man is not an automaton before God. But the decision is, nevertheless, God's gift for God made it possible for man to decide, though the decision is also man's very own.

This matter of commitment to life in the here and now for God (Kierkegaard) is what makes the christian life of faith so very different from uninvolved metaphysical, speculation. The latter, says the existentialist, may become so rooted in past systems of thought that he fails to see the need for decision in the present. And it is in the contemporary world, not in the world of the fifth century B.C. or of the first century A.D., that we are living.

Bultmann claims that while there may have been a prophet who was crucified, the main question is, will I bear

107

my cross today? He thinks of the resurrection of Jesus Christ from the dead as a myth. But again, the facticity of the resurrection is of little concern to him. Rather, the important question is a contemporary one: have we experienced new life by faith today? "For Bultmann as a theologian simply denies that faith can accept as final the picture that Bultmann as a historian has constructed. For faith, the historical explanation is essentially irrelevant. For faith, it is the act of God in Jesus Christ made newly effective for us in its repeated proclamation that alone places us in the position of deciding for or against faith."[9]

Bultmann's reason for demythologizing the New Testament is not because we live in a scientific age that has made many of the biblical myths untenable to modern man, but because the interest of the New Testament is for man to find faith in personal decision. This means that concentrating on history and tradition is of little value.

Listen to Bultmann on Paul. "For Paul ... cross and resurrection are to be understood, not as mere facts of the past, but as they become contemporary for the individual in the baptism which is a dying with Christ and a rising again with him. The whole life of the believer is a being 'crucified with Christ' (Gal. 2:20), 'always carrying in the body the death of Jesus' (2 Cor. 4:10). And since the Christian life is a life of faith, it is at the same time a sharing in Christ's resurrection. The resurrection is not an isolated event in the past; it marks the beginning of new humanity."[10]

For Bultmann, as for other existentialists, an emphasis on tradition, on history, and on the structures of thought of former generations may be one way of escaping from God's call in the present situation. For the emphasis of the existentialist is always this: "Behold, now is the acceptable time; behold, now is the day of salvation" (2 Cor. 6:2).

Concept of Freedom

Fourthly, consider existentialism and the concept of

freedom. All existentialists, in one way or another, give a large place in their teaching to personal freedom. The Orthodox church believer, Nicolas Berdyaev, who left the Communist party in Russia and was finally exiled from his native land, knew at first hand how Communism robbed men of their freedom. "No revolution ever loved freedom," wrote Berdyaev. He remained a socialist but a "personalist" socialist, in contrast to totalitarian thought which is based on "the supremacy of society over personality." Personalist socialism "starts from the supremacy of personality over society."[11]

Berdyaev believes that there is nothing that can be compared to the worth of personality. It is our highest standard of value. And this value is not derived from the state or an economic system but from man's relation to God who is at one and the same time the source of man's value and freedom. It is man's freedom under God which is evidence of man's worth to God. Berdyaev writes: "In order to understand personality it is most important always to remember that personality is defined above all not by its relation to society and the cosmos, not by its relation to the world which is enslaved by objectivization, but by its relation to God, and from this hidden and cherished inward relation it draws strength for its free relation to the world and to man."[12]

In his book, *Freedom and the Spirit*, Berdyaev asserts that "to be free is to have entered upon another order of being which is spiritual in character."[13] To this writer there is no real freedom apart from the spiritual life. This is why he comes round to stating, over and over again in this book, that it is the mystics who have realized true freedom. They are the trained athletes of the spiritual life and have won that freedom which is "to be in possession of oneself" through being possessed by God. "Man is determined from within, from the inmost depths of his being, insofar as the spirit subdues in him the physical and natural elements and the soul is absorbed by the spirit and the spirit enters into the soul. Freedom belongs only to those phenomena of one life of the soul which can be called spiritual."[14]

Berdyaev believes he is affirming his biblical faith of freedom through spirituality. He often supports his affirmations by quoting such scriptural passages as: "You will know the truth, and the truth will make you free" (John 8:32); and "If the Son makes you free, you will be free indeed" (John 8:36); and "the wind blows where it wills, and you hear the sound of it, but you do not know whence it comes, or whither it goes; so it is with every one who is born of the spirit" (John 3:8).

Because of his emphasis on freedom as being a by-product of the spiritual life of communion with God, Berdyaev was a critic of much of liberalism which thought of freedom largely in terms of liberty on the horizontal plane of life. To Berdyaev the liberty of the sons of God was obtained by giving place to the vertical dimension. In other words, man to be free among and with his fellows must first be free in God. In God alone man finds the truth which sets him free for God and man. And he will find this truth not by flying into some metaphysical stratosphere of abstraction but as he obeys God in faith in the daily round and common task. It is in everyday existence that truth comes alive.

The Meaning of Life

Fifthly, look at existentialism and the **meaning of life**. Many authors write of modern man's sense of a loss of meaning. They state that one reason why existentialism has become prominent today is that it takes up the problem of meaning in a serious manner.

Paul Tillich, like a modern Kierkegaard, deals with this problem of meaning, especially in his book, *The Courage To Be*. He says there are three main types of anxiety today: anxiety over death, over emptiness or meaninglessness, and over guilt. The christian doctrine of the Fall points to man's existential predicament, namely, that in his existence he is separated from his essence, he is alienated from the ground of being and the threat of non-being hangs over his head. He becomes anxious (Angst). This is anxiety about life itself and the future. This anxiety creates objects of fear, but in itself it is an anxiety that is not caused by any object but by this tension between essence and existence. "We use the term meaninglessness," writes Tillich, "for the absolute threat of non-being to spiritual self-affirmation, and the term emptiness for the relative threat to it ... in the background of emptiness lies meaninglessness, as death lies in the background of the vicissitudes of fate ... The anxiety of emptiness drives us to the abyss of meaninglessness." [15] Tillich believes that there is an underlying unity between the three types of anxiety mentioned above and all are existential, that is "they are implied in the existence of man as man, his finitude, and his estrangement. They are fulfilled in the situation of despair to which all of them contribute." [16]

What is the way out of the human predicament, with its consequent doubt, anxiety and despair? Tillich says the answer is the new being who is Jesus as the Christ. In a sermon on The New Being he says that if he were asked to sum up "the Christian message for our time in two words, I would say with Paul: it is the message of a new creation." [17] Man, says Paul, finds this new being by union with Christ. "The old has passed away, behold, the new has come" (2 Cor. 5:17). This new being, who is Jesus the Christ, is "essential being under the conditions of existence, conquering the gap between essence and existence." [18]

Tillich sees three basic expressions of the new being in Jesus as the Christ: in his words, in his deeds and in his suffering. By faith in him, that is by trust in him 'in spite of', believing that one is accepted by him, though unacceptable, the estrangement is overcome, anxiety is defeated by one in whom we can have confidence, and despair gives way to hope. Jesus as the Christ has won the victory. By commitment of one's life to him, we too, can triumph. It is in our decision of faith in him that we come to know him as the truth, even the truth that makes us free. Unbelief gives way to faith, and doubt to certitude. This is no longer a case of theoretical affirmation but of existential acceptance by him who accepts us. Where our sin of unbelief abounded, his grace did much more abound. His love can conquer all.

Evaluation

Existentialism is a corrective in religion and theology. Like all correctives it overemphasizes some points of significance. But no one can doubt that existentialism has brought a healthy emphasis on personal religion. The decisiveness of the existentialist faith, as over against a domesticated faith; the call to commitment in contrast to sitting at ease in Zion; the urgency of dealing with the existential condition of man in his interior life, with his loss of meaning—all this provides us with a theological emphasis that is not content with an easy-going attitude in religion but one that must wrestle with problems that confront man today.

In contrast to that prideful intellectualism and scientific humanism which would dismiss religious faith as the equivalent of superstition, existentialism in its religious orientation reminds us that faith in God is a real factor in a life that is concerned with the whole person and not just with man's reason.

In a world of depersonalization it is the existential stress on the unique value of persons as persons that helps to remind us in a materialistic and technological culture that the machine was made for man, not man for the machine; that the state was made for man, not man for the state. Perhaps the greatest threat to civilization now is this one of depersonalization—that people are only numbers, things to be used and manipulated by autocrats—or worse. Existentialists will help to allay this threat and keep before us the fact that is supreme, that people matter!

On the other hand, we must take note of two charges commonly made against existentialism: its subjectivism and its irrationalism. In the case of some existentialists there is an element of truth in these charges. "Existentialism perhaps lends itself to extravagances," writes John MacQuarrie, "but in the hands of its saner practitioners, these are avoided." [19] To these "saner practitioners" the subjectivism which is prominent in their faith is not held in solitary isolation from the world but is deeply involved with existence in the world. And, too, the irrationalism with which existentialists are charged, is not the irrationalism of mere emotionalism as a substitute for reason but of an awareness of God in real situations and the importance these have for our human living.

Of more significance, we believe, as a criticism of existentialism is its lack of historical persepctive, its unawareness of the significance of tradition. We are a part not only of what we have met in our own day, in the NOW, but also a part of what has gone before us. We have been, in part, shaped intellectually and culturally by history and tradition. And it would appear to be the duty of a Christian to weave together his personal, existential experience of the living God with the faith that was once and for all delivered to the saints. To create a dualism between faith as enshrined in Church tradition and a personal living faith is unwarranted and, we believe, is not in accord with the gospel which brings out of the treasure house of faith things new AND old.

Then, too, the existentialist should accord greater respect to institutions and institutional religion. Many existentialists, following Kierkegaard, cast aspersions on institutional religion. They regard it as a 'drag' on their personal faith, which hampers a genuine expression of their experience. Undoubtedly some forms of institutional religion may do that. But it is well to bear in mind that we live an embodied life; that is, that the spirit must express itself through bodies, material manifestations of the inner life of humanity. Consequently we cannot avoid having institutions to promote the working of the spirit and to make known to the world in visible form the spiritual experience of the faithful. Of course the institution may become inert, rigid and the enemy of new expressions of the spirit. Then it becomes demonic. But if the institution can remain what God intended it to be, the servant of spirit, then it can be an instrument for God's glory. This the existentialist must learn if he is to make a worthy contribution to the religious life of society.

We must also observe that some existentialists, chiefly atheistic ones, give emphasis to the concept of freedom in a manner that borders on licence and socially may lead to anarchy. Liberty without discipline, especially self-discipline, such as Christianity offers through being disciplined to the word of God in Christ, is both anti-personal and anti-social. It will lead to personal dehumanization and social rebellion. What the existentialist must learn is that "if the Son makes you free, you will be free indeed" (John 8:16). Freedom from the Christian point of view is not to be able to do as one likes but as Christ requires. In his bondage is perfect freedom.

When existentialists come to see true freedom as freedom in Christ, to regard tradition with respect, to look upon institutions as the bearers of truth, and history as one of the "great storehouses of ends" and at the same time maintain their call to a genuine faith commitment—they will make a more fully rounded contribution to theology.

1. Paul Tillich, *Systematic Theology*, Volume 11, P.20. University of Chicago Press, Chicago. 1957.
2. Ibid., P.26.
3. J. MacQuarrie, *An Existentialist Theology*, P.16. Torchbook, Harper & Row, New York. 1965.
4. David E. Roberts, *Existentialism and Religious Belief*, P.20. Oxford University Press, New York. 1957. (quoted).
5. Martin Buber, *I and Thou*, P.8f., T.&T. Clark, Edinburgh, 1958.
6. Op.Cit., P.5.
7. John B. Cobb, Jr., *Living Options in Protestant Theology*, P.224. The Westminster Press, Philadelphia. 1962.
8. J. MacQuarrie, Op. Cit., P.196 (Quoted).
9. John B. Cobb, Jr., Op. Cit., P.243.

10.   Rudolph Bultmann, *Faith and Understanding*, P.306f. S.C.M. Press, London. 1969.
11.   Nicholas Berdyaev, *Slavery and Freedom*, P.17. Charles Scribner's Sons, New York. 1944.
12.   Ibid., P.44.
13.   Nicolas Berdyaev, *Freedom and the Spirit*, P.121. Geoffrey Bles: The Centenary Press, London. 1935.
14.   Ibid., P.123.
15.   Paul Tillich, *The Courage To Be*, P.54. Collins, The Fontana Library, London. 1970.
16.   Ibid., P.61.
17.   Paul Tillich, *The New Being*, P.15. Charles Scribner's Sons, New York. 1955.
18.   Paul Tillich, *Systematic Theology*, Volume 11, P.118f.
19.   John MacQuarrie, *20th Century Religious Thought*, P.370.

IX

Secular Theology

John MacQuarrie[1] begins his book on God and Secularity
with these words: "God and secularity: these are the poles
between which the contemporary theological discussion
moves ... Nowadays theology has to be done in a
secularized world."

We must begin with a definition of terms. The word
secular means belonging to this world alone, the terrestrial,
horizontal world of everyday life. Secularity is an outlook or
point of view which concerns itself with the affairs of this
world, while secularization is the process of secularity.
Secularism is an ideology, an ersatz religion, a world view
arising out of concentration on secular matters alone.

It has come about that in our culture there has developed
a secular attitude toward not only our world but toward
man himself. Langdon Gilkey[2] says that "the modern spirit
is ... radically this-worldly." He sees four general
characteristics of this secular spirit:

First there is **contingency**. This means that man and his
world are the result of causes "that are neither necessary,
rational, nor purposive." It is a world that looks to science
for guidance, to the world of facts alone for truth, for the
tangible and the material as signposts of what life is all
about. The intangible and the spiritual are unreal. This
comes out clearly in logical analysis, the philosophy of A.J.
Ayer and others, which tells us that unless we find truth
through sense experience we are only talking nonsense.
Thus a term like God is ruled out as nonsensical. We have
only Kant's world of phenomena to deal with, the world of
appearances alone.

Second there is **relativism**. The "panta rei' of Heraclitus
has become prominent again. "All things flow." The only

116

unchanging reality is change. This is a world of becoming, a world in process. Nothing is permanent. The values that we thought were 'fastened down' are coming loose. How can God be unchanging if he is Lord in a changing world? Alvin Toffler writes several chapters on "The Death of Permanence" in his book, Future Shock.[3]

Third, there is **transience**. Gilkey says this is "closely related to relativism." Everything, including humanity, faces mortality. Eternity is a mirage, for nothing abides. It is on this plane of history, and here alone, that man is to find any meaning in his life. There is no far-off divine event to which the whole creation moves. Part Two of Toffler's book deals with this phenomenon. People are today the "new nomads" who belong to a "throw-away society", a society that is always on the move and has a "waster-mind".

Fourth, there is **autonomy**. Man is on his own. He need not look to any God above for help. He helps himself. He has now "come of age" and has no need to rely on any power beyond his own and the world of science and technology. We shall have more to say about this characteristic later on in this chapter.

In the document on "The church in the modern world" of Vatican II we read in the preface that the church "now addresses itself without hesitation, not only to the sons of the church and to all who invoke the name of Christ, but to the whole of humanity . . . Therefore the church focuses its attention on the world of men, the whole human family along with the sum of those realities in the midst of which that family lives."[4] In his response to this document, Robert McAfee Brown says that it shows a new "openness" to the world, a new willingness of the church to learn from the world. This, he believes, is a new departure which argues well for the church in relation to the world. All of which reveals how the secular age is causing the church to take a new stance in her relationship to the culture of our time.

There are certain emphases which are to be found in secular theology and to which we will give our attention.

These emphases are related to the characteristics of secular culture which Langdon Gilkey has brought to our attention, and yet they go far beyond them in their range and influence.

Celebration of the Secular

There is to begin with the celebration of the secular. Instead of condemning the secular age we should 'join it', is the advice of Harvey Cox. "The world has become man's task and man's responsibility . . . the world has become his city . . . The name of the process by which this has come about is secularization."[5]
Secularization simply means that man has turned his gaze away from heaven towards the earth. The religious and the metaphysical ways of understanding life have given place to a secular way of viewing everything. The new human community is called technopolis which signifies "the fusion of technological and political components" in our culture. This, to Cox, implies that man will be liberated from religious and metaphysical guides, enjoy his world and its culture and find the meaning of life through the celebration of the secular.

In his later book, *The Feast of Fools*, Cox explains what he means by celebration. It includes fantasy and festivity, two elements which have been lost in our Western culture and which must be restored. He believes that "the festival . . . affirms the sheer goodness of what is."[6] "Festivity, by breaking routine and opening man to the past, enlarges his experience and reduces his provincialism. Fantasy opens doors that merely empirical calculation ignores. It widens the possibilities for innovation. Together, festivity and fantasy enable man to experience his present in a richer, more joyful, and more creative way."[7]

Both festivity and fantasy are part of what Cox means by celebration. And for Dr. Cox these have deep religious significance. Celebration enables man to see that he is part

118

of a larger whole, a creature with a past and future as well as a present. A term like God has lost its meaning for many people because they do not experience him in real life. "If God returns we may have to meet him first in the dance before we can define him in the doctrine," says Dr. Cox.[8]

The German theologian, Dietrich Bonhoeffer, called for a "holy worldliness" in Christianity. He said that a man should take "life in one's stride". He believed that Christ called people to plunge into the world of culture and politics and become involved, even to the point of suffering. To him this "holy worldliness" was not to be a shallow worldliness "of the enlightened, of the busy, the comfortable or the lascivious"[9] but a worldliness that experiences both death and resurrection. To Bonhoeffer there was no other way of being a christian disciple than by participation in the concrete situations of life where Christ is to be found among the people for whom he lived and died. "It is only by living completely in this world," writes Bonhoeffer from prison, "that one learns to believe."[10] He came to believe profoundly in the "this worldliness" of Christianity. He wrote about a "religionless" Christianity which, to him, meant a narrow, individualistic, metaphysical type of religion, whose God was an idol, whose faith led a person away from the world instead of into the world. "By this-worldliness I mean," writes Bonhoeffer, "living unreservedly in life's duties, problems, successes and failures, experiences and perplexities. In so doing we throw ourselves completely into the arms of God, taking seriously, not our own sufferings, but those of God in the world—watching with Christ in Gethsemane."[11]

While Bonhoeffer is much more 'orthodox' in his Christology and other christian doctrines than many others who would describe themselves as christian secularists, nevertheless, he is one with them in his emphasis that we must take our world seriously, live in it, love it, and die for it if necessary. Escapist religion is not of the gospel.

Secular Theology Gives Glory to Man

There is another aspect of this celebration of the secular to which we should give attention: the affirmation that the secular world of matter is God's creation. He loves it. Christ was incarnate in it. God controls it. "The earth is the Lord's, and the fulness thereof, the world, and those that dwell therein" (Psalm 24:1). Respect for this 'good earth', a sense of stewardship toward God's material gifts—all this is definitely Christian. We have a responsibility to creation and toward other human beings. We find the sacred in the secular, the holy in the house of life.

Furthermore, secular theology gives glory to man. Since God is being more and more "edged" out of the world, according to Bonhoeffer, man is on his own. As we have noted above he is autonomous man. Alexander Pope wrote:

> "Know thyself, presume not God to scan,
> The proper study of mankind is man . . ."

And this is the "proper study" of millions today who have by-passed God.

Eberhard Bethge, writing of Bonhoeffer in prison, in relation to the latter's statement about "the world that is 'come of age' is more godless, and perhaps for that very reason nearer to God," says that this phrase refers to man's maturity, not necessarily that man is growing better. It speaks of man's autonomy but always within a larger theonomy. But there is undoubtedly a new emphasis in Bonhoeffer's prison writing after April, 1944, which Bethge calls "a milestone" in his life because of the change and "different tone" in his letters to Bethge. From then on he uses the term "worldliness" instead of "secularization". He claims that this "worldliness" is a heritage of Christianity, it is "the free responsible attitude of Christianity," writes Bethge regarding Bonhoeffer's new emphasis, "and the secularizers are no longer powerful seducers, but the protagonists and midwives of humanity." [12] The church should, therefore, regard the secular world no longer as the very devel, but as that which God has made for man's life when it is lived in fulness of faith.

The secular theologian also discerns the glory of man in a new emphasis on freedom. In an age when freedom has been lost, or never found, in some countries, especially economic and political freedom, Christians must be concerned to uphold that freedom which Christ gives to the person, the church and ultimately, to the world. This emphasis on freedom lies behind the advances we have made in science and in social progress. Scholarly enquiry depends on freedom to seek for the truth and to express it. Our educational systems are based on the concept of freedom. Our democratic way of life, in government and out of it, emphasizes the importance of free expression. It is certain that the secular emphasis in theology has given support to liberty in the modern world.

Stress on God's Immanence

Again, the secular theologian stresses God's immanence.

It is in the world that we find God, or God finds us. Bonhoeffer says that it is only in the 'concrete situation' that Christ is known. He shies away from the term supernatural regarding God because he believes it seems to say that God is 'apart' from His world. And when he uses the word transcendence it is in a personal way, implying that one person 'transcends' a situation.

J.A.T. Robinson [13] startled some in the theological world in 1963 by telling us that our image of God as 'up there' and 'out there' must be eradicated from our thought of God (We wonder if his image of God 'in depth', 'down there' is any better). He says we have to drop such concepts of God as "supernatural" or "supranatural" because such terms belong to a world of pre-Copernican cosmology, that the idea of transcendence must be radically revised. Because of these changes in terminology concerning deity he entitles a section of his book, *Honest to God*, "The End of Theism?"

121

that is, theism as we have understood it in orthodox christian theology. Basing his views on those of Bultmann, Bonhoeffer and Tillich, he calls for a "worldly holiness" in which Christians are called to see Jesus as "the man for others" (Bonhoeffer).

Bishop Robinson points out that we do not know the God of love whom Jesus has revealed by talking about some supernatural being who came to earth and has returned to heaven. Rather, we know what divine love is in that God in Christ "emptied himself" and thus revealed true love. "For it is in making Himself nothing, in his utter self-surrender to others in love, that he discloses and lays bare the Ground of man's being as Love." [14] In other words it is only in this earthly existence of ours, in this everyday world where Christ lived and died, that we can understand true love.

If God is in the world and not 'above' it, man must witness to God, make him real in life, by giving a renewed emphasis to the social gospel. Since, as Bishop Robinson says, we must start at "the other end", that is with man and not with God, if faith is to be real to modern man, then we have to 'plunge' into the problems and troubles and trials of humanity.

In this connection Harvey Cox says there are three Greek words which inform us about the work and witness of the Church today.

There is the term kerygmatic. This refers to the proclamation of the victory of Christ over all the powers of evil. Man now "has the power and the responsibility to rule over them (evil powers) and use them in responsibility before God." [15] These powers are not evil in themselves but man has turned them into idols that he worships and consequently has perverted the proper use of these powers. This is also a proclamation of freedom, according to Dr. Cox. He writes that "Exodus and Easter remain the two foci of biblical faith . . . the Exodus is the event which sets forth what 'God is doing in history'. He seems to be liberating people from bondage . . .Easter means that the same activity goes on today, and that where such liberating

122

activity occurs, the same Yahweh of Hosts is at work."[16]

There is also the term diakonic. This is the service of healing and helping, of giving health and reconciliation to men. This implies that the task of the church is one of communication in which the purpose is to bring unity and wholeness into human life. This is the church's role as servant.

Then there is koinoniac. This is "the hope made visible" through fellowship. The church must give a "visible demonstration" of what she says in the proclamation and points to in her service. The church is to be God's "avant-garde" of the new society, or, what Karl Barth calls "God's provisional demonstration of his intention for all humanity."[17]

These three terms, as interpreted by Dr. Cox, show us that we start neither with God nor the church to build the new society but with man and his needs, moving upward and outward to God and other people through the church whose function is instrumental. The renewed interest in the study of sociology is further evidence of the rebirth of interest in social problems.

Are social gospel and sociology far off from the thought of God? Not to the secular theologians. They believe that it is in society, in the call to freedom and in the social milieu of our time that God is known. God is immanent in his creation. In the case of some theologians of this school of theology his transcendence is practically eliminated. It is not any wonder, then, that Bishop Robinson agrees with a German thinker to whom he refers who says that Luther's question, "How can I find a gracious God?" must now give way to this question: "How can I find a gracious neighbour?"[18]

Secularism and the Ultimate

We must also observe that secular theologians have very little to say about the ultimate. The concentration of the

123

secular theologian is with the penultimate, the things before the ultimate. Life is a matter of process and change and it is the penultimate or preliminary concerns of everyday which demand man's attention. Questions about the 'why'? of life, its 'whence'? and 'what for'? are pushed into the background of man's thinking. The secular theologian becomes preoccupied with such concerns as what to eat and drink and wear, how to make 'good' in the world, find security, and the like. He shuns the thought of death as best he can because he realizes that this means 'finis' to all his achievements.

There is no doubt that because of the secular theologians casting aside God's transcendence there is a consequent loss of interest in ultimate reality and the things that belong to eternity. It is time, not eternity, that absorbs the attention of the secular-minded person. This world and not the next is our responsibility. The secular theologian holds that if Christianity has a message for modern man it must be for man in this world of space and time because it is the only world he knows and the one that engages him day by day.

Truth Replaced by Function

Moreover, in secular theology truth is replaced by function. This is a pragmatic age which asks, 'what is the use of anything?' 'What is the truth?' is a question seldom asked

Harvey Cox says that two motifs in particular "characterize the style of the secular city. We call them pragmatism and profanity. By pragmatism we mean secular man's concern with the question, 'Will it work'? Secular man does not occupy himself much with mysteries ... He judges ideas ... by the 'results they will achieve in practice'. The world is viewed not as a unified metaphysical system but as a series of problems and projects."[19] Closely related to pragmatism is the term profane which stands for a wholly limited terrestrial view which blots out the horizons of worlds beyond this one.

Colin Williams in his book, *Faith In a Secular Age*,[20] refers to the Dutch sociologist, Cornelius van Peursen, who pictures three periods of history. The first is the period of myth. This is a period when the world is alive "with magical and frightening forces." The second period is the ontological in which man "sought better control of his world by developing a rational understanding of it." Period three he calls the functional period in which the ontological understanding of human life is being discarded. "Man's increasing confidence in his ability to understand and control the forces of life" which he encounters makes him believe that he can live pragmatically in a world in which truth is regarded from the functional point of view. Both Cox and Van Peursen endeavour to defend pragmatism on biblical grounds, including Jesus' emphasis on "Go and do!" Thought must give way to action, reasoning is supplanted by activism.

Evaluation

We should see the rise of secular theology, in part, as a revolt against an other-worldly pietism which developed an escapist mentality and an inward-looking religion about which Bonhoeffer and others became very critical. Secular theology endeavours to correct the balance between concentration on the inner spiritual life and the call to responsibility in the world of human need.

Secular theology also humanizes our faith, bringing the gospel in the arena of man's affairs, avoiding that type of aloofness which seems to say 'I do not care'. It is a caring message, socially oriented, that these theologians present to us under the tutelage of "The Man for Others". He cared!

Secular theology has also made Christians radically revise their concepts of God, even if they do not follow the secularists in this regard. God as an object among other objects; God as a static deity outside his world; God as someone who intervenes now and then—like the process theologians the secular thinkers, too, say this view of God must be cast aside.

This school of theology does good service for the church in stressing the importance of man's earthly and material existence. Man can learn of the significance of the material world from the Old Testament which, in large measure, has a this-worldly reference, though God is thought of as both transcendent and immanent.

On the other hand, we must take note of some negative criticisms of secular theology. For one thing, it is a reductionist theology. It tends to accommodate itself to the culture of the age and thus loses its prophetic vision to challenge that culture. Peter Berger refers [21] to Dean Inge who "once remarked that a man who marries the spirit of the age soon finds himself a widower." And the theologian who wishes to take his cues from the culture of the times may soon find himself a captive to that culture. John MacQuarrie writes: [22] "The Christian faith, properly understood, does not permit itself to be identified with either a thoroughgoing secularism or an escapist religiosity. It cannot allow the sacred to be swallowed up in the secular, but equally it cannot allow the secular to be reduced to the level of the unreal through an exclusive concern for the sacred."

Harvey Cox's appeal is, really, a call for the desacralization of life; that is, that we must no longer confine the sacred to certain areas of life but relate God to life in its totality. However, even if we see virtue in Cox's reminder that we have passed from the era of the tribe and town to that of technopolis, we cannot share his optimism regarding the secular city. Cox's claim that the new city leads to greater freedom, more liberation for people, seems unwarranted. City life in this late twentieth century has ushered in a host of problems which, instead of liberating man, seems to imprison him in welfare systems, slums and poor housing with the consequent loss of personal identity and meaning.

Secular theology is a modern form of Pelagianism. Its emphasis is so humanistic and this-worldly that there is little, if any, room for the grace of God to work in human lives. Archbishop Ramsey claims that "the total dismissal of any concern about prayer and contemplation or the deliberate seeking of God's grace . . . and the encouragement of that activism which has in the past proved spiritually starving, this is the real issue which secular Christianity has thrown into relief. It is not the issue of religion. It is the issue of grace. The dividing line is not a Christianity of religious practice and a Christianity of action. It is whether modern secular man is self-sufficient or whether he still needs in his pride to seek those means of grace which the humble God of the Incarnation brings him."[23]

The loss of transcendence and ultimacy is a serious one because man needs to hear "a rumour of angels", to have the 'lift of the far view', if he is to find the abundant life. "Man must be fed on angels' food," wrote Robert Browning. He needs such food even in the secular city. Man has been granted freedom by God but not from God. He is autonomous but it is an autonomy within a theonomy.[24] We are freed for work in the world through a faith that is free from the world through the acknowledgment of a higher world than that of the secular.

Bishop Leslie Newbigin suggests that "if the mastery which is given to man through the process of secularization is not held within the context of man's responsibility to God the result will be a new slavery."[25] Apart from the vertical dimension to life human existence may become a bagatelle of transient experience, with little light for the road ahead.

How can completely autonomous man accept the Lordship of Jesus Christ? It is the Christian confession of faith that Christ is Lord. But the secularist holds that "no power outside of himself is authoritatively and finally to determine for him his thoughts, his standards, his decision, or to create his meaning. He and his fellows are together 'on their own'."[26] Of course theologians like Bonhoeffer and

Cox are far from believing in the complete autonomy of man, though they do believe his freedom is real. But the tendency among some secular theologians is to speak of freedom in a manner that would leave room for some people to think that they maintained they were free from God.

The meaning of lordship is related to transcendence. The Lord cannot be confined within the secular sphere and remain Lord. "God's lordship manifests itself supremely in his forgiveness of sinners," writes Dr. David Cairns in his book on transcendence, "and here he shows himself free from, and above, his own laws—and able by this self-sacrificing love to win man over to repentance and responding love. And all this without infringing man's freedom."[27]

The secular theologians for the most part are social activists who place much confidence in technological advance to usher in the brave new world of tomorrow. Lewis Mumford is critical of such social optimism. He claims that we need something more than "improved technological facilities" to deal with environmental and human degradation. "Nothing less than a profound re-orientation of our vaunted technological way of life will save this planet from becoming a lifeless desert."[28] This demands a change of desires, habits and ideals which he says will call for "something like a spontaneous religious conversion: one that will replace the mechanical world picture with an organic world picture, and give to the human personality, as the highest known manifestation of life, the precedence it now gives to its machines and computers." Without a vantage point of faith 'above' the world we will be unable to direct life properly in the world. The men who best guide human history have a standing ground in eternity.

The secular stress on pragmatism really presents a low view of human nature. To use man as a means to some functional end is to degrade him. Man himself is, under God, the supreme end of life to which all else must be means. The functional view of man would make him an 'it', not a 'thou'. It would regard him as a 'thing' to be manipulated for some 'higher' purpose. The functional view of man would say that man was made for the state, or for the economy, or something else. The Christian view is the reverse—all these things were made for man.

To consider another point, while many people live, and apparently live happily, without any metaphysical interpretation of life, at least superficially, we wonder whether it is possible to construct a theology without some underlying, perhaps hidden, metaphysic? Even Karl Barth admitted in his latter days that to some degree metaphysic was unavoidable in arriving at a theological position respecting reality.

If these negative criticisms appear to devalue secular theology entirely, we trust that the reader will revise his opinion. The criticisms are pertinent and they remind us of trends in secular theology which are not for the ultimate good of mankind. But we hope that the positive points in our evaluation will not be lost sight of in making a judgment of secular theology. It has made, and is making, a valuable contribution to theological thought in our time.

1. John MacQuarrie, *New Directions in Theology Today*, Volume III, God and Secularity, P.13. The Westminster Press, Philadelphia. 1967.
2. Langdon Gilkey, *Naming the Whirlwind: The Renewal of God-Language.* Pp.39-71. The Bobbs-Merrill Co., New York. 1969.
3. Alvin Toffler, *Future Shock.* Parts One and Two. Random House, New York. 1971.
4. The Documents of Vatican II, P.200.
5. Harvey Cox, *The Secular City*, P.1. The MacMillan Company, New York. 1965.
6. Harvey Cox, *The Feast of Fools*, P.7. Harvard University Press, Cambridge, Mass. 1970.
7. Ibid., P.8
8. Ibid., P.28.
9. Dietrich Bonhoeffer, *Letters and Papers from Prison*, New Greatly Enlarged Edition, P.369.
10. Ibid., P.369.
11. Ibid., P.370.
12. Eberhard Bethge, *Dietrich Bonhoeffer*, P.758ff. Collins London. 1970.

13. J.A.T. Robinson, *Honest to God*, P.11ff. S.C.M. Press, London. 1963.
14. Ibid., P.75.
15. Harvey Cox, *The Secular City*, P.128.
16. Ibid., P.132.
17. Ibid., P.145 (quoted).
18. J.A.T. Robinson, *The New Reformation*, P.33 (quoted). S.C.M. Press Ltd., London, 1965.
19. Harvey Cox, Op.Cit., P.60
20. Colin Williams, *Faith in a Secular Age*, P.21f. Harper Chapelbooks, New York. 1966.
21. Peter Berger, *A Rumor of Angels*, P.28. Doubleday & Company, Inco., Garden City, New York. 1969.
22. John MacQuarrie, *God and Secularity*, P.58.
23. A.M. Ramsey, *God, Christ and the World*, P.25. S.C.M. Press, London. 1969.
24. W.O. Fennell, *New Theology*, No. 2, P.28ff. The MacMillan Co., New York. 1965.
25. Leslie Newbigin, *Honest Religion for Secular Man*, P.38. The Westminster Press, Philadelphia. 1965.
26. Langdon Gilkey, *Naming the Whirlwind: The Renewal of God-Language*, P.155
27. David Cairns, *God Up There?* P.28. The Saint Andrew Press, Edinburgh. 1967.
28. Lewis Mumford, *The Pentagon of Power*, P.413. Secker and Warburg, London. 1970.

X

The Death-Of-God Theology

Bishop Robinson said that our image of God must go. The writers in this Death-of-God school of theology say God himself has gone.

In the previous chapter we considered secular theology and its implications. In the present school of theology which is so closely related to the former school, we have secular theology carried to its ultimate extreme which is the total rejection of the transcendent in favor of a completely secular view of life and the world.

Christianity has always faced critics and enemies from outside the church—the sceptics, the atheists and the humanists. But in the school of theology we are now to consider we have an attack on the basic tenets of the christian faith from inside the church. This is a new phenomenon in the history of Christianity.

We are told by several writers that the term, death-of-God, is used in our time in at least three senses: there are those who have become real atheists, denying the existence of any Higher Power than man. Then there is the cultural denial of God in our day, meaning that our culture is more and more reflecting a no-God point of view. Others say that the term "god" is so ambiguous we should change it, or drop it from our vocabulary. It means so many different things to different people. However, it is largely the first two meanings of this term "god" that we will consider.

The origin of this death-of-God movement goes back into the thinking of some men in the nineteenth century. The scepticism of Kant who told us we could only know phenomena, that only empirical knowledge was valid; the rationalism of Hegel and others who affirmed that the real god was human reason; the teaching of Feuerbach who reduced all theology to anthropology; the ravings of Nietzsche about superman in his attack on Christianity—these writers and others have led the way in producing the death-of-God syndrome of our time.

In the twentieth century some extreme forms of liberalism, which were largely humanistic, as well as the historical scepticism of some existentialists who hold that there is little factual basis for the christian faith; the rise of science which has led man to believe in his self-sufficiency have also been influential in the development of the God-is-dead theology.

There are four main leaders in this movement in the United States who tell us that the God-is-dead theology is almost altogether an American[1] school of theology. These men are: Gabrial Vahanian who, while he is a believer, writes of the death-of-God in our culture; Thomas J.J. Altizer, William Hamilton and Paul Van Buren. We shall refer to the writings of these men as we analyze this trend in theology.

The following points are to be noted in the teachings of this school of theology.

A Mood in Western Culture

The death-of-God **expresses a mood** in our western culture. Thomas W. Ogletree says that the writers in this school "have taken what can properly be viewed only as a cultural event and turned it into a theological platform. Such a procedure is nothing less than a capitulation to the immanental frame of thought characteristic of the times."[2]

There is a retreat of faith in our culture which is reflected in the writers of this school, and not here alone. The sacred became lost in the fog of secularism. This is the 'waste-land' era of belief, according to many writers. Dannie Abse reflects this mood in a poem:

"Dear God! in the end you had to go.
Dismissing you, Your absence made us sane.

We keep the bread and wine for show. . . .

And still our dark declensions sorrow.
That grape is but grape and grain is grain.
We keep the bread and wine for show."[3]

Gabrial Vahanian calls this culture post-Christian and Paul
Ramsey, [4] in the preface to Vahanian's book, *The Death of
God*, says that "in the post-Christian phase of 'the death of
God', western man is post-Christian culturally as well as
theologically. Atheism is not only a theoretical claim made
by exceptional rebels; it is now also a practical possibility
for countless men. . . . Find yourself and you will not need
God; accomplish something in culture and evidently God is
superfluous." This appears to be the temper of the times
culturally. This is why Bishop Robinson tells us that there
are "three thrusts of modern atheism . . . . three motives
which have impelled men . . . . to question the God of their
upbringing and ours." These are:

"God is intellectually superfluous: God is emotionally
dispensable; God is morally intolerable."[5]

Professor Vahanian claims that faith in our time has
become the victim of what Richard Niebuhr describes as
the "acculturation of Christianity". In America, he says
Christianity has been rationalized and equated with
democracy, progress and "the American dream". On the
European continent it has become "identified with the
superiority of European culture and its surreptitious
imperialism".[6] The acids of secularism have destroyed the
prophetic thrust of the gospel and "Christianity has become
so this-worldly that, perhaps, it has lost heaven and this
world, too."[7] The gospel is being offered to men in a diluted
form at best: the tragedy is that all too often it is mistaken
for the real thing. We have produced a 'technological' and
syncretistic religiosity, claims Vahanian, which is a
substitute for biblical faith. "One of the premises of
technological or do-it-yourself religion is that it makes no
difference what kind of faith it is. Religion thus loses its
nerve."[8]

Vahanian claims that in modern culture secularism has been made into a form of religiosity in which "the present and the immanent are invested with the attributes of the eternal and the transcendent."[9] In some circles democracy, sex and the classless society have been deified. Faith has been equated with success and religion with stability. God for many has become a "Cosmic Pal". Not only has radical immanentism taken over in the realm of faith but pragmatism has perverted the gospel and become a new gospel for many souls. "Religion is good, or faith is a good thing, because it works." Vahanian quotes Norman Vincent Peale in this regard. "Today any successful and competent businessman will employ the latest and best-tested methods in production, distribution and administration, and many are discovering that one of the greatest of all efficiency methods is prayer power." Dr. Vahanian adds: "Prayer is money."[10]

The reading of Professor Vahanian's book is a depressing experience. The picture he presents of American culture with respect to religion is one-sided, for there are other aspects of this culture he has ignored. Nevertheless, we must not treat what he has written about the secularization and religiosity of this culture in a light-hearted manner. It must be taken seriously. For in very truth the mood that has come upon our culture is not the sort that would support, or be concerned with, the tenets of the christian faith. Insofar as this is so, we must give attention to those aspects of American civilization that have brought about the God-is-dead movement which lies back of and supports the God-is-dead theology.

Desire for Emancipation

The God-is-dead theology expresses the **desire for emancipation**. Religion is a binding element in human life. It sets forth truths, principles and commandments which many people today find irksome, restricting man's freedom and constraining him to follow paths that otherwise he would not travel. Modern man rebels against any sort of authority, including that of religion. "The dissolution of authority is one of the main characteristics of this post-Christian age." [11]

Paul Ramsey and others look to Nietzsche as the progenitor of this emancipated type of living. This philosopher said that God had to die in order that man might be free. "If there were a God," wrote Nietzsche, "I could not endure not being he." [12] "Man cannot be while God lives." God stands in the way of man's liberation, so God must go. Paul Van Buren, in discussing the life of Jesus, substitutes the term freedom for faith in connection with Jesus' teachings and action. He considers that Jesus could only be free for his neighbour as he was first free from anxiety and had found his own identity. [13] He regards the whole ministry of Jesus as one that can be summed up in this word freedom, even freedom from God.

This modern love of emancipation which the death-of-God movement reflects discounts the place of discipline in its search for the abundant life. Self-expression is the slogan of the day. As the slang expression has it, "Anything goes". Social standards of conduct are to a large extent regarded as tabus to be cast aside. "Every way of man is right in his own eyes" (Prov. 21:2).

Pure Secularism

The death-of-God theology is a **message of pure secularism**. Transcendence has been completely erased in the teaching of this school. In the preface to his book, *The Secular Meaning of the Gospel*, Dr. Van Buren asks, "How may a Christian who is himself a secular man understand the gospel in a secular way?" [14] A question of similar intent was asked by Bonhoeffer in one of his letters from prison, though his answer is very different from that of Van Buren. Van Buren desires to express the gospel without any reference to God—a titanic intellectual task, one would think. In a conversation with Ved Mehta, Van Buren said, "I am trying to raise a more important issue: whether or not Christianity is fundamentally about God or about man . . . I am trying to argue that it is fundamentally about man, that its language about God is one way—a dated way, among a number of ways—of saying what it is Christianity wants to say about man and human life and human history." [15]

In the fashion of Feuerbach and others, Van Buren is saying that Christianity is a persepctive on man, one way among many of viewing the human situation and condition with the "contagious freedom" of Jesus in our minds. There is no belief in a risen and living Lord to help us on our way, for Van Buren believes that what happened to the early disciples following the first Easter was that "they apparently found themselves caught up in something like the freedom of Jesus himself, having become men who were free to face even death without fear." All of which is completely anthropocentric, earth-bound and totally sec- ular-oriented in its outlook.

William Hamilton takes pretty much the same point of view regarding the life of a Christian in the modern world. He confesses that he has lost God in his experience, especially the God who is "a need-fulfiller and problem- solver." Man is on his own and must solve his own problems and meet his need without recourse to God.

How, then, does a Christian live? He replies: "As the Lord identified himself with me without reserve, as he stood beside men offering for their free and uncoerced choice a particular way, as he did this for their own sakes and not for the sake of his movement or career—so the Christian must do in the secular world." [16]

To live as Jesus lived but without Jesus' God is the way of life for William Hamilton. This is pure secularism, an attempt to follow the central aspect of the Christian ethic without any reference to the source of this ethic or its sustaining truth and power which is to be found only in religious faith. The Jesus Hamilton writes about seems to be someone other than the Jesus of the gospels.

Jesus the Hero

Another emphasis of this group might be authorized under the heading "the hero, Jesus of Nazareth". The Death-of-God writers agree that God is no longer present. God died on Calvary, according to Altizer, in his interpretation of the kenosis passage of Philippians 2:5-11. So Altizer writes about "The Self-Annihilation of God". [17] He even regards the death of God as "a christian confession of faith." God has negated himself in "his own revelatory and redemptive acts."

Altizer is not so interested in Jesus as an historical person, though he writes a good deal about the incarnate word in the midst of secular life, this word being interpreted in oriental mystical fashion or in the symbolism of William Blake and others. But Hamilton and Van Buren make much of the historical person, Jesus. In spite of the questioning of many scholars about what we may know about the real, historical Jesus, these two men accept the basic picture of Jesus in the gospels. But on one conditon: that we "de-divinize" Jesus. [18] In so doing, they find they are left with a hero-example to follow.

For instance, William Hamilton says we should be obedient to Jesus, as he was obedient. Yet he does not ask, to whom was Jesus obedient? He states his attitude to Jesus in this way: "Jesus is the one to whom I repair, the one before whom I stand, the one whose way with others is also to be my way because there is something there, in his words, his life, his way with others, his death, that I do not find elsewhere. I am drawn, and I have given my allegiance." [19] Jesus is made into a model in such a picture, a model from whom the writer derives inspiration for the journey of life.

In chapter VI of his book, *The Secular Meaning of the Gospel*, Dr. Van Buren sees the importance of the Jesus of

137

history in terms of Jesus as the man of freedom which we have referred to above. He is to be distinguished from other men who have had a liberating effect on persons. He believes that men have been liberated by hearing the apostolic message about Jesus and freedom. Those who have been liberated by Jesus find in him "the man who defines for them what it means to be a man and as the point of orientation for their lives."[20] Or again: "He who says, 'Jesus is Lord', says that Jesus' freedom has been contagious and has become the criterion for his life, public and private. As Jesus was led, because of his freedom, into the midst of social and political conflict, so it is with one who shares his freedom."[21] If this is not hero worship it is at least hero adulation.

Disavowals

In addition to these positive emphases of this school, we must also consider the things they disavow. These disavowals are three in number. First, there is a disavowal of tradition. "Being begins in every Now"[22] is a phrase from Nietzsche which is accepted by Altizer to emphasize his contemporary view of Christianity. The past is over and done with, according to this writer. Theology must negate every "past form of the word". The old forms and images of religion are dead. He sees a chasm between the Old and the New Testaments. So he sees a similar discontinuity between the present and tradition with respect to faith. Man must start de novo to build a new faith. The radical theology of all three writers reveals itself as anti-traditional in all respects.

Second, there is a disavowal of morality. This follows from the manner in which some members of this school have interpreted freedom. Commandments and principles find little support among the Death-of-God people. Because God is no longer real, moral standards have no sanction. Because authority has been put out of bounds, we act on our own. "Whirl is king, having driven out Zeus." The only criterion is love which can be interpreted in various ways because the God of love has disappeared from the horizon of members of this school. All acts are relative to the situation in which one finds oneself.

Professor Altizer gives the views of himself and his colleagues in this death-of-God movement when he says that one who rejects God "will sacrifice an established christian meaning and morality." He will abandon "all those moral laws which the christian church has sanctioned," as well as repudiate "an explicitly christian moral judgment." All moral imperatives must be renounced, as well as belief in an absolute moral law. Moral judgments are regarded "as barriers to the full realization of energy and life." Altizer concludes his attack on christian morality with these final words: "The Christian who wagers upon the death of God can be freed from the alien power of all moral law, just as he can be liberated from the threat of an external moral judgment, and released from the burden of a transcendent source of guilt." [23]

Thirdly there is the disavowal of the church. Ved Mehta had a very interesting conversation with Dr. Van Buren, which included discussion of the latter's view concerning his relation to the church of which he was an ordained priest, namely, the Episcopal church. He said that he did not pray. "I am ordained, but when I am asked to preach or to perform services, I usually say I would rather not. I would ask to be defrocked if that could be done in a quiet, inoffensive way, but it can't be. Defrocking requires a lot of fuss." [24]

Nearly all this group of teachers believe that the liturgies the ministries and even the church itself have no place in the new world into which we are entering and in which we are aware of "the absence of the presence of God." For when God goes, "the church soon follows," according to Van Buren's judgment.

Dr. Altizer has no wish to reform the church; rather he seeks to abolish it. He believes that it is because of the church that Christianity has gotten bogged down "in an increasingly archaic ecclesiastical tradition." The church today he regards as irrelevant. Theology must be freed, he claims, from both the seminaries and the churches.

After all the "jaunty iconoclasm" of his book on christian atheism, Dr. Altizer gives us a glimpse of where his scepticism regarding God may lead those who join the death-of-God movement. He writes "The contemporary Christian who bets that God is dead must do so with a full realization that he may very well be embracing a life-destroying nihilism; or, worse yet, he may simply be submitting to the darker currents of our history, passively allowing himself to be the victim of an all-too-human horror. No honest contemporary seeker can ever lose sight of the very real possibility that the willing of the death of God is the way of madness, dehumanization and even the most totalitarian form of society yet realized in history." [25] Comment on such an affirmation seems out of place. It is the strongest condemnation of this movement or school which the writer represents.

Evaluation

Harvey Cox sees in the death-of-God syndrome some lessons for the work of theology. He says that this school "signals the collapse of the static orders and fixed categories by which men have understood themselves in the past. It opens the future in a new and radical way." [26] But we ask: can people truly understand themselves apart from God in whose image they have been created? And can there be any future, even a desire for "He who comes," as Cox says there is, if a major assumption of human thought is that God is dead?

This is not to say that this school of theology has nothing to teach us. In a negative way the God-is-dead theologians have disabused our minds of any naive optimism we may have regarding the religious conditions of North American society. Altizer and his group remind us of the godless aspects of modern thought and culture. They express in words what is to a large degree true in fact, namely, that for a host of people God does not count. Our culture has become so secularized that God, at best, is some vague abstraction, but certainly not a being who has anything to do with our lives.

The God-is-dead theologians ought to make Christians ask themselves some serious questions. Has the God Christianity offered people been a distant God, uninvolved with life? Has the church's moral teaching been too restrictive? Was the worship of God really a worship of idols—of the church, of forms of worship, of ecclesiastical institutions? Perhaps the Death-of-God theology will render the church a real service if it makes us examine ourselves in the light of the gospel.

Worship and prayer have been omitted from the lives of the theologians of this school of theology. Did this omission lead them to experience "the absence of God's presence?" It is likely that when worship and prayer were made optional, or electives, that the reality of God became dim in the experience of these men. The practice of God's presence is an imperative if God is to be real to theologians as well as to other people.

If the church is to make an adequate reply to the Death-of God theologians she must affirm the gospel with the note of authority. In so doing she will have to recover the belief in God's revelation which is supremely given us in Jesus Christ. Here is the foundation of all authority in Christianity. This will also mean a stronger emphasis on scripture than many liberal theologians have been making, for scripture is "the manger in which Christ lies". In scripture we find the record of revelation, the word of God which "is living and active, sharper than any two-edged sword, piercing to the division of soul and spirit, of joints and marrow, and discerning the thoughts and intentions of the heart" (Heb. 4:12). All of which calls the church to continuing reform, renewal and rededication.

Since writing this chapter I have learned that Dr. Van Buren has had a change of mind; that he has had a 'recovery of faith'.

1. T.J.J. Altizer and William Hamilton, *Radical Theology and the Death of God.* P.XIIf. The Bobbs-Merrill Co., New York. 1966
2. Thomas W. Ogletree, *The Death of God Controversy*, P.23. Abingdon Press, New York. 1966
3. Ved Mehta, *The New Theologian*, P.28 (quoted) Harper & Row, New York. 1965.
4. Gabrial Vahanian, *The Death of God*, P.xxi. George Braziller, New York. 1961.
5. J.A.T. Robinson, *The New Reformation?* P.107 S.C.M. Press Ltd. London. 1965.
6. Gabrial Vahanian, Ibid., P.24
7. Ibid., P.48
8. Ibid., P.57
9. Ibid., P.67
10. Ibid., P.195 (quoted)
11. Ibid., P.163
12. Ibid., Preface by Paul Ramsey. P.xvi (quoted).
13. Paul Van Buren, *The Secular Meaning of the Gospel* P.123f. S.C.M. Press, London. 1963.
14. Ibid., P.xiv.
15. Ved Mehta, The New Theologian, P.66 (quoted).
16. William Hamilton, *The New Essence of Christianity*, P.108. The Association Press, New York. 1961.
17. Thomas J.J. Altizer, *The Gospel of Christian Atheism* Chapter 4, P.120ff. The Westminster Press, Philadelphia 1966.
18. Thomas J. Ogletree, Op.Cit., P.27
19. Ibid., P.43 (quoted).
20. Paul Van Buren, *The Secular Meaning of the Gospel*, P.138.
21. Ibid., P.142.
22. Thomas W. Ogletree, Ibid., P.97 (quoted).
23. Thomas J.J. Altizer, Op.Cit., P.147.
24. Ved Mehta, Op.Cit., P.65 (quoted).
    One of the best critiques of Altizer's disavowal of both tradition and the Church is found in Robert McAfee Brown's tranchant review of Altizer's, *The Gospel of Christian Atheism*, in Theology Today, July, 1966. Volume XXIII, Number 2, Pp. 279-290
25. Op. Cit., P.146
26. Harvey Cox, *The Death of God and the Future of Theology*, P.253. In New Theology No. 4, Edited by Martin E. Marty and Dean G. Peerman. The MacMillan Company, New York. 1967.

Note: E.L. Mascall's book, *The Secularisation of Christianity* (Libra Book, Darton, Longmann & Todd, Ltd. London, 1965) is one of the best appraisals of Dr. Van Buren's book, *The Secular Meaning of the Gospel*, of which I am aware. Dr. Mascall also gives in this book a splendid critique of J.A.T. Robinson's, *Honest to God.*

XI

Theology of History

Stirring, challenging and tragic events in recent years have led philosophers and theologians to probe more deeply into the meaning and significance of these events, especially as they relate to the life of man and his place in the vast scheme of things. This has caused thinkers in various schools to ask: What is the meaning of history? Has it any meaning? And christian theologians of many schools have, in one way or another, been constrained to take more seriously than heretofore the relation of the gospel to history.

In this chapter we will take a look at, and evaluate the relation of history to theology as seen through the minds of some noted christian thinkers in the contemporary world. It will be evident to those who have read the previous chapters that this subject of the relation of history to theology is not one that is confined to the writings of those to whom we will refer in this chapter. There is a very real sense in which it is true to say that all christian thinkers have to take history into account when considering the gospel in the life of modern man.

There is a philological distinction in German between 'Historie,' meaning a series of events concerning persons and 'Geschichte' which describes the inner meaning and significance of events. It is in the second sense that we must consider the theology of history. This implies an interpretation of the events that come within our purview. And in saying this we affirm that we believe event and interpretation are two inseparable realities which have a very significant bearing on the understanding of the christian gospel.

History "is the study of man's actions and decisions."[1] It is concerned with people-how they think, emote, act, and respond to a variety of situations. In order to understand these situations and the events involved in them, the historian must do more than record facts. He must endeavour to think himself into the original situation and try to see how people originally thought about what was happening to them and about them. In other words, fact and interpretation cannot be separated. Every historian, then, whether he asserts it or not, must have a subjective view of objective events; that is, a philosophy or theology of history. This would appear to be inescapable for the historian. A truly 'objective' or 'impartial' history cannot be written. If it could be written it would be too prosaic and dull to read, let alone study. It would be a study of events without people, 'warts and all', and this would not be history.

The significance of history in Christianity

The two religions that stem from the faith of ancient Israel, Mohammedanism and Christianity, along with their ancestral religion, place a tremendous importance on history. Later in this chapter we shall have more to say about how this lends importance to the writings of the Old Testament. Let us here, however, confine our remarks to the significance of history in Christianity.

In christian theology the German word 'Heilsgeschichte' has come into prominence and very often no attempt is made to translate it into English because it is really untranslatable. However, it is usually considered as best explained in the words, 'holy history' or 'salvation history'. It is used in two senses: first, it means that the whole of history, secular and religious, is under the control of the sovereign God who is working out his purposes in history in and through people, whether they believe in him or not. Secondly, and of more significance for our study here, Heilsgeschichte refers to those special biblical events that have revelatory meaning for believers and which manifest the whole meaning of history. There is a real sense in which these two interpretations of salvation history are inseparable, even though our chief interest is in the second interpretation.

G. Ernest Wright singles out these chief revelatory events in biblical history which are basic in the gospel: in the Old Testament these events are five in number. (i) The Israelite patriarchs who received promises from God, which are fulfilled in the history of the people. (ii) The exodus from Egypt which is seen to be a special act of God. (iii) The unique wilderness experience and the covenant at Sinai. (iv) The conquest of Canaan which was regarded as God's gift and was accompanied by certain obligations on the part of the people. (v) The government under David which "was regarded as the final fulfilment of the promise of security from enemies and from slavery."[2] The chief 'saving' events in the New Testament are three in number: (i) The real life and teaching of Jesus. (ii) His 'saving' death. (iii) His resurrection. It is on these events as interpreted through the early church, and re-interpreted by the church throughout the centuries, that Christianity has its foundation. And for the church, the central event of all is the person and work of Jesus Christ. "For no other foundation can anyone lay than that which is laid, which is Jesus Christ" (1Cor. 3:11). "The gospel or Kerygma of the early church," writes E.C. Rust, "cannot be separated from the words and deeds, the life, death, and resurrection, the historical actuality of Jesus of Nazareth."[3] This means that the gospel is rooted in actual history. Christianity, in the first instance, is not concerned about something that was thought, but about something that happened—something so momentous that it changed the course of history and the understanding of it, first for the disciples and later for others. Christianity is not based on ideas but on events which were seen to have special meaning. Beliefs were sequential to these events. And central in these events is the person of Jesus Christ. "Christianity recognized no spiritual revelation," writes C.H. Dodd, "which is not directly related to the historical reality of Jesus."[4]

When people de-historicize Christianity then the values which are upheld by this faith of the church are not really inherent in the nature of reality. To deprive values of their rootage in historic fact is to permit the poetry, symbolism and prophetic challenge of the faith to depend on individual experience, not on objective revelation. As H.G. Wood has expressed it:[5] "Idealism in the air, ideas defined with academic precision, and held with academic detachment, do not make history, do not move men. Ideas must be actualized in events, embodied in persons, materialized in institutions, before they effectively shape human lives." It is this embodied, incarnate life in history which is a "stumbling-block" to the Jews and "foolishness" to the Greeks (1 Cor. 1:23), which is the glory of Christianity.

By basing its gospel on certain revelatory historical events Christianity has been accused of "the scandal of particularity". That is, certain particular events loom very large in the christian record so that those who, in philosophical fashion, look for general theories as basic to whatever faith they may find, regard this christian point of view as 'absurd'. What can the birth of a babe nearly two thousand years ago in an obscure land among a people of little significance have to do with the meaning of life for a man in this century, so some might ask? But Christianity affirms that this babe, this person, has everything to do, not merely with the christian system of thought and action, but with the entire meaning of history.

When we are considering the importance of historical events in the gospel it is interesting to note that the content of what has been called the 'first christian sermon', delivered by Peter at Pentecost (Acts 2), is little more than a recitation of a series of historical events in Hebrew history, with promises, which he declared were fulfilled in the coming of Jesus Christ. Stephen's defence (Acts 7) is very much of the same kind. The preaching of Paul in the synagogue at Antioch (Acts 13:14ff) is similar in content.

This Jesus whom they proclaimed was not some mythical figure but a person in history, crucified and risen from the dead. This is the gist of the message of the early church.

The essence of christian discipleship is faith in Jesus Christ as Lord and Saviour. We must not substitute for this, faith in his teaching. His teaching must be integrated with his person. The Sermon on the Mount must not be disassociated from the man of the mount. "In salvation history," writes Dr. Rust, "a unique emphasis falls on Jesus Christ . . . . in the christian faith the person and historic acts of Christ are of primary importance, constituting in themselves the divine self-disclosure. Christianity is not a religion of moral precepts and rational ideas, but one in which the founder himself is the revelation of the eternal order. In him we claim that the living God has entered history and become incarnate."[6]

Christianity and the cyclical view of history

"The dominant conception of the classical world," writes Reinhold Niebuhr, "is the cyclical interpretation of time."[7] According to this view there was nothing new under the sun. Marcus Aurelius could believe that "the rational soul", taking a wide view of life with its "periodic destructions and rebirths", would "see nothing new" and nothing that his ancestors have not seen.[8] This led to a view of history which eliminated the possibility of uniqueness, newness and progress.

This cyclical view of history is one of the theories that Augustine confronted in the days of the dying Roman Empire and the age of the demise of classical culture. In the City of God[9] he refers to this, especially pointing out the strange view of God that lies back of it. If reason will not refute the errors of this view, states Augustine, "faith must deride them. But by God's grace, reason will lay those revolving circles flat enough. For hence is these men's errors. Running rather in a maze than stepping into the right way, they measure the divine, unchangeable power by their human, frail, and weak spirit, in mutability and apprehension." He claims that they are really comparing God to themselves and that is ridiculous. "Cyclicism arises when the finite, human mind, unable to grasp the incomprehensible, tries to force the infinite into its own patterns of thought," states Roger Shinn.[10]

The 'theory of cycles' contradicts the christian message of salvation, that there can be 'a new birth', a transformation of human life, personally and socially, by the grace of God. It denies the creative principle in history.[11] While Christianity states that "in the event of Christ, as it is grasped by faith, the mythical cycle has been broken through, the idea of everlasting recurrence has been eliminated."[12] The 'theory of cycles' and endless recurrence gave men a fatalistic view of life, so that the goddess Fortuna was either blessed or cursed at the games, according to an individual's luck. Gambling became rife. Life was condemned to sterility.

Alan Richardson quotes Paul's letter to the Romans (6:9): "Christ being raised from the dead will never die again. Death no longer has dominion over him." Then he goes on to say: "This is the text that changed the outlook of European man upon history" because Christ's conquest of death gave the final blow to the classical view of history. "The European mind was freed by the proclamation of God's saving act in history from the fatalistic theory of cyclical recurrence."[13]

In contrast to the cyclical view of history, Christianity introduces us to the linear view. In the christian faith history is 'goal-directed'. God has a purpose he is working out in history. Christ manifested this purpose in history and the church carries on his witness in the world. In the present world order the city of earth and the city of God lie 'confusedly together'. But in the end (telos) only the city of God will remain. The city of earth will then be transformed, not eradicated. There will be a new heaven and a new earth—something impossible on the old 'theory of cycles'.

Oscar Cullmann states that "the appearance of Jesus of Nazareth is regarded as a decisive turning point of history ... It asserts that from this mid-point all history is to be understood and judged; it asserts that this fact .... is the final meaning and criterion of all history before and after it." [14] Cullmann divides the christian view of time into a threefold division: before creation; between creation and the parousia; and after the parousia. Mid-point in the second division he places the revelation of God in Jesus Christ which is determinative of the entire history of man for the Christian. [15] Cullman believes that there is a true sense in which we can say the world is saved already. Christ has conquered the demons. He has taken captivity captive The struggle with evil still continues but we know that in the end Christ will be victorious because he has already conquered evil on the cross and on the first Easter. D-day is the promise of V-day. "The revelation consists precisely in the fact of the proclamation that that event on the cross, together with the resurrection which followed, was the already concluded decisive battle." Consequently the Christian carries on the good fight of faith in the confident assurance that Christ will prevail. This, of course, is the message of the last book of the bible. Christ reigns as King of Kings and Lord of Lords.

Christianity's opposition to gnosticism

Gnosticism (from the Greek gnosis, 'knowledge') with its origin in eastern and Hellenic mystery cults, claimed to give knowledge that was superior to either faith or reason. It was based on a radical dualism between God and the world. This world of matter was created by lesser deities that did not know the real God, according to gnosticism. The flesh was the seat of evil and the world of matter had no relationship to spiritual realities. This led to a denigration of man's history because God could have nothing to do with history. Christian doctrines, such as that of God the creator,

149

redeemer and sanctifier were consequently denied. There could be no real incarnation on this basis for the divine could not embody itself in an evil human body. Consequently one of the more prominent forms of gnosticism was docetism (from the Greek, dokeo, 'to seem'), which presented Jesus Christ as a semi-human being, not a real man of flesh and blood. According to docetism Jesus was not really tempted and tried; nor did he suffer and die. It was all a matter of seeming.

It was largely in opposition to gnosticism that the apostles' creed grew in the church out of the old Roman creed. This creed shows something of the battle waged against gnosticism in its docetic form in the early church. God was defined as the maker of heaven and earth. Jesus, truly divine as "God's only son, our Lord," was "born of the virgin Mary, suffered under Pontius Pilate, was crucified, dead, and buried." All these terms concerning Jesus—"born", "suffered", "crucified" "dead", "buried",—were denied by the docetists because their philosophy ruled out beforehand any possibility of a divine person being so humiliated. The whole doctrine of man's redemption was at stake in the anti-historical teachings of the gnostics. Events were of no importance to the gnostics. On the basis of this heretical teaching with its syncretistic and theosophical tendencies, Christianity could offer no witness to the true God before men. Christianity resisted such heresy from the beginning and in all the centuries has proclaimed the truth of salvation in history. C.H. Dodd writes: "The primitive preaching postulates the historical reality of the main facts, and so acted as a preservative of the historical tradition, over against any attempt (such as exhibited itself notably in gnostic heresies) to devaluate the historical element in Christianity." [16]

In our time a theological battle is being waged by many theologians against gnosticism in a new form, namely, the demythologizing teachings of Rudolf Bultmann and the Form critical school of biblical scholars. Bultmann places great emphasis on the Word, and the kerygma of the early church which must be presented today, he claims, without any of the historical trappings and myths in which the kerygma was enshrined in biblical times. In this emphasis Bultmann has much support from the entire existentialist school of theology.

We have noted previously (chapter 8) that Bultmann places no importance on the historical life of Jesus. He denies the resurrection. But he wishes to retain the meaning of the word for contemporary man, apart from its foundation in tradition. "The danger in the movement of Bultmann and his followers," according to E.C. Rust, "is that they should divorce the meaning from the historical actuality, separate Geschichte from Historie, until, for some extremists, it would not appear to matter whether the resurrection was an actual event in world history so long as the church itself would affirm its faith in a risen Lord." [17] Thus the kerygma of the church is separated from its historical basis which theologians such as Rust, Dodd and others believe is contrary to the teaching of scripture. "In the biblical faith, God is known through what he does in history . . . . In salvation history the meaning of history is laid bare and the historical movement of the life of fallen man is redirected to its true goal. It is not just that man is shown the meaning. He is enabled to fulfil the meaning in his own historical existence." [18] On this basis the kerygma of the early church is divorced from any real historical connection with the life and ministry of Jesus. We have, in effect, a new type of Christianity that is anti-historical. "When the process of demythologizing is completed," writes Alan Richardson, "we are left with 'Jesus the word', not to be identified with the Jesus of history. The latter is not kerygma; the gospels are not historical accounts of the life and work of Jesus, but forms under which it was natural to present the kerygma in the Hellenistic age." [19] This means that the church is given some 'other gospel' than that which has been handed on to us from the early apostles. Hence what is at stake in this twentieth century movement which is gnostic in outlook is whether the gospel is founded on historical realities and thus meaningful for man in his historical existence, or whether the kerygma is a theosophical system of human speculation.

No one in this century has contended more forcefully against the Bultmann position in theology than Oscar Cullmann. Nearly all his writings have an anti-existentialist point of view. He believes that the heart of Bultmann's theology is his weak, anti-historical Christology. "The question about Jesus was not answered by early Christianity in terms of a mythology already at hand," writes Cullmann, "but in terms of a series of real facts. These facts were events which happened in the first century of our era. . . . They are the events of the life, work, and death of Jesus of Nazareth, and the experience of his presence and continuing work beyond death within the fellowship of the disciples."[20]

In his more recent book, *Salvation in History*, Dr. Cullman gives us an all-out treatment of this subject of demythologizing the gospel. He points out the close relation between this modern biblical movement and early gnosticism with its anti-historical bias and how it was resisted by the early Church. What was at stake, he believes, was whether Christianity would perish in a general syncretism, or whether it would retain a redemptive message for man involved in history. Cullmann is not opposed to the existentialist call for a decision in faith but he believes that such a decision must be founded on the truth of the gospel which is grounded in historical events. "The question whether the event or the kerygma is decisive for the faith of the witnesses who have given us the biblical salvation history may not be answered in the form of an alternative. . . . Word and event are not separable in the mind of God himself, and, accordingly in the biblical view, the word is an event (dabar), and conversely the event is a word. Nevertheless, from the human point of view, we must acknowledge that the event has priority."[21]

Event and its interpretation are not separated in the kerygma of the early church. This is Cullmann's contention

n his debate with Bultmann. If the latter replies that
tressing event implies an emphasis on the horizontal,
naterial plane of life, practically omitting the vertical
dimension in Christianity, Cullmann replies: "The vertical
ontains the horizontal within it. God's speaking by his Son
in these last days' (Heb. 1:2) is, in fact, of another kind than
his manifold speaking by the prophets. But in its verticality,
his speaking belongs in the horizontal saving process." [22]

Thus, according to Cullmann, faith in the New Testament
hurch was faith in a new divine event that occurred in
history and its saving significance for all mankind. This
event was not instigated by the church. It was an event
which created the church. The church was not involved in
ome sort of self-redemption but it participated in God's
edemptive event in Jesus Christ. The significance of the
heological struggle waged by Cullmann and others against
he de-historicizing of the gospel by modern gnostics is
momentous for the future witness of the church in the
world.

The importance of the Old Testament in salvation history

Philo, the Alexandrian Jewish philosopher of the first
entury A.D., wished to de-historicize the Old Testament.
Marcion desired to banish it from the church. Existential-
sts have de-emphasized its importance. Bultmann finds no
word of God in it for our time. All this is so because the Old
Testament is very largely the record of events surrounding
he people of Israel, together with their leaders, prophets
nd law-givers, a record that is not 'nice' in some of its
historical events but in and through which God was
endeavouring to speak his saving word to his people.

Walther Eichrodt in his *Theology of the Old Testament*,
tresses the covenant relationship given by Yahweh to his
eople, Israel. This covenant, sealed at Sinai, was regarded
s a revelation from God. "The factual nature of the divine
evelation" [23] cannot be gainsaid. "God's disclosure of

himself is not grasped speculatively, not expounded in the form of a lesson; it is as he breaks in on the life of his people in his dealings with them and moulds them according to his will that he grants them knowledge of his being." Eichrodt pursues this matter further when he states that "just as this faith was founded in the first place on a fact of history from which it is continually rekindled, so history provides the field in which it is worked out in practice. It experiences the divine will in the formation of the people's social life; it encounters the divine activity in the fortunes of the nation. In this way history acquires a value which it does not possess in the religions of ancient civilizations."[24]

All this implies that the religion of the Old Testament with all its variety of national and personal experience, is very secular, this-worldly, if you will. The eternal transcendent God who takes up the isles "as a very little thing", is the God who acts in history. "I am the Lord your God, who brought you out of the land of Egypt, out of the house of bondage" (Ex. 20:2).

In salvation history the importance of the Old Testament and its history is to be seen in this: that it contains the books of promise which the New Testament proclaims were fulfilled in Jesus Christ. This is the heart of Peter's sermon at Pentecost (Acts 2:14-36). Luther said that 'the Old Testament was the New Testament concealed; the New Testament was the Old Testament revealed.' There is broadly speaking, much truth in that statement. There is historical continuity between the two Testaments; so much so, that it is practically impossible to understand correctly the message of the one Testament apart from the other. And both Testaments emphasize the facticity of God's self-revelation which finds its culmination in the event of Jesus Christ. He came as 'a burning and a shining light' in Israel, light then enlightens every man that comes into the world. Thus we see the importance of the Old Testament in salvation history.

History and providence

"The doctrine of divine providence," writes E.C. Rust, "is fundamentally the affirmation that God guides and overrules the total process of nature and history and the lives of individual men in order that his purpose may finally be achieved."[25] It is the christian faith that God, who created the world, must also control it in order that his purpose may be finally fulfilled. In his sovereign power, God governs all that he has made. Karl Barth[26] says three things are involved in God's providence: preserving, cooperating and overruling. In other words, God is finally in charge of what takes place in history. The ultimate outcome of any event is in his hands.

It is only by faith that we can understand the meaning of providence. The secular historian sees nothing of a divine creative power in the course of human events. But with our basic faith in God, we are given insight to comprehend his working in all of life. Cyrus of Persia is referred to as God's anointed "to subdue nations before him" (Isa. 45:1). "The nations are like a drop from a bucket" (Isa. 40:15). He clothes the lilies of the field and cares for people individually (Matt. 6:28-32). He acts in what can only be called special providence, such as in the sending of his Son into the world. "When the time had fully come, God sent forth his Son" (Gal. 4:4,5). This was God's own decision, not man's. "God never is before his time and never too late," writes H.G. Wood.[27]

Examples in the bible come to mind when we consider how God overrules events for his own good. We take the example of Joseph, sold into slavery in Egypt by his brethren. But Joseph rose to a place of great authority in Pharaoh's court and befriended his brethren, saying, "as for you, you meant evil against me; but God meant it for good" (Gen. 50:20). This overcoming of evil with good, of making even the wrath of man to praise him, is characteristic of divine providence. When we accept in faith the divine overruling of all events, then we can even think of evil as

serving some divine purpose. God for example, "hardens
Pharaoh's heart (Ex. 7:3). People who appear to oppose Go
may, nevertheless, be used by God, unknown to them, fo
his own glory.

His providence works in judgment and in mercy. Eve
the judgment has a merciful purpose within it to bring me
to repentance and to the knowledge of the truth. God is
righteous judge and his judgment is inescapable. To 'fly i
the face of providence' is to suffer just retributio
eventually. For in the light of providence we cannot final
control the outcome of events. They are in the hands of
higher power. "The hardest strokes of heaven fall in histor
upon those who imagine that they can control things in
sovereign manner, as though they were kings of the earth,
writes Professor Butterfield. "And it is a defect in suc
enthusiasts that they seem unwilling to leave anything t
providence, unwilling even to leave the future flexible, a
one must do." [28]

Rather than the denial of human freedom, it is th
preserving providential grace of God that is the source
freedom. The opposite of freedom is determinism and suc
is not biblical faith, since man is held responsible for h
deeds done in the flesh. Not in some pre-determine
blueprint fashion does God guide our lives, but as one wh
is present in every moment controlling decisions we mak
and the events of history, according to his own goodwill. H
is not a "meddling director", according to Albert Outler, b
"history's Assessor ... He is the first and final judge
human performance, the redeemer who restores meaning
that have been spoiled, the consummator who holds th
future open, against all odds, for the eventual triumph
righteousness." [29]

In this matter of human freedom, what we tend to forg
is that true freedom is found only in relation to God and n
in emancipation from him. God creates man free in love, b
it is this very love which binds him to his Maker. But huma
freedom, can never be absolute. It is always under a high
control and subject to this control. It is this rule

156

providence which makes us responsible creatures, whether in rebellion against God or in faith toward Him.

It is belief in providence which lies at the heart of the teaching regarding election, such as in Romans 8. This chapter as well as others reminds us that in faith we can discern God's providence in the manner in which he supports us. "Nothing shall separate" us from his love in Christ Jesus.

On the wider scene of providence, Dr. Berkhof[30] shows us that in the world at large God is at work. He believes that the very concept of world unity, "the existence of the United Nations", "the humanization of man and the materialization of nature" — all owe their development to the action of the living Christ in history. He claims there is no other way to account for the arrival of these things than by belief in God's providential activity in history. And Dr. Berkhof affirms that the only way in which we can preserve our secularized life from nihilism is by resuming the "proclamation of Christ . . . with unmatched force."[31]

It should be pointed out here that to say that we believe that God rules and overrules all events for his own purpose, does not imply that we can understand or comprehend all his ways. We finite beings need humility here. We are not God. The lesson Job learned should be heard by all of us. As God says to Job, "Where were you when I laid the foundations of the earth? Tell me, if you have understanding" (Job 38:4). Our knowledge at best can only be partial. We can only discern 'the skirts of his ways'. We can believe and we can also keep silence before the mystery of providence because there are many occasions when reticence is becoming to the saints.

Does providence ensure progress? The answer is no! It gives us a task, an opportunity and an openness to life with all its attendant possibility of adventure under God. God's judgment may be pronounced on our vaunted types of progress, which in His eyes are not in accord with his purposes. While it was undoubtedly the christian gospel, with its 'goal-directed' point of view, which laid the ground work for the rise of the idea of progress in recent times, nevertheless there are certain ideas of progress in our culture which are totally secular, horizontal, scientific and technological and which have little, if anything, to do with the progress of righteousness in the world. We often forget that man's freedom to create may also turn out to be his freedom to make mistakes, to sin, or through preoccupation, deny the will of God.

Events in the twentieth century have led many thinkers to raise doubts about the optimism that has been abroad concerning human progress. We have to take stock again of where we are going, or the direction of human affairs. And the man of faith must look to the future in terms of the coming kingdom of God. This sort of progress has been obscured in our technological society. What we must strive for, under God, according to Dr. Baillie, is "nothing less than the progressive embodiment in the life of humanity of the mind that was in Christ and 'a growing up in all things unto him who is the head.' "[32]

History and eschatology

We believe that God is working out his providential purpose in history. Is the end of this purpose, its consummation, in the relativities of history? The christian answer is No! God's purpose will be consummated 'beyond history', in an eternal world which even now is present in ths 'passing age'. "From the beginning the faith of the church was eschatological", writes Roger Shinn.[33] "That is, the christian community believed that history's significance lay not merely in its obvious day-to-day course of events, but in its final destiny under God." Hence talk about history and its consummation are inseparable in the totality of the gospel. We have the promise of fulfilment in the resurrection of Christ and the work of the Holy Spirit. But the reality of that fulfilment lies ahead in the perfected kingdom of God which Christ himself will bring.

158

This does not mean that eschatology calls for a non-historical other-worldliness. On the contrary, "the resurrection of the body" reminds us that history will not be annulled but fulfilled. Eternity will complete, not destroy, the temporal process. There is both continuity and discontinuity in the eternal realm. "If the crucified and resurrected Christ is revealed in history," writes Dr. Berkhof,[34] "then the consummation will mean a radical break with all the forces which hinder his dominion. At the same time the consummation will be the continuation of the resurrection forces which already are active in history." Thus there is a sort of dialectical relation between history and eschatology. History is meaningless without an end, a consummation which eternity provides. Eschatology has little significance for man in history unless it is related inextricably with faith in the world here and now. What God has joined together in his Word, history and eschatology, let not man put asunder.

A contemporary theologian who gives us much food for thought on the relation of history to eschatology is Wolfhart Pannenberg. He is an anti-Bultmannian because he emphasizes the importance of history in Christianity and, unlike Bultmann, he affirms the historicity of the resurrection of Jesus Christ, though the nature of the resurrection is surrounded with mystery.

But to Pannenberg history is open-ended and its meaning can only be known as the end (eschaton), or when history is completed in the kingdom of God. This is why eschatology to this writer is of great significance in the gospel. His whole system of thought is one in which futurity plays a major role. God is "the power of the future". "The power of the future alone makes all things cohere."[35]

The kingdom of God, which plays a large part in Pannenberg's theology, is both a future and present reality. It is not an order of society created by good men. It is God's kingdom. Pannenberg writes: "The kingdom of God must always remain in the kingdom OF GOD. It is not a construction undertaken by extending christian virtue. It is not simply the kingdom of better men."[36]

To Pannenberg the resurrection of Jesus is the key to an understanding of both history and eschatology. In the factual reality of the resurrection he claims that we can see that present and future, as well as the past, are inextricably united. Don H. Olive writes about this matter thus: "The ability to maintain both meaning and openness is given in the resurrection of Jesus. Because the resurrection is depicted as the arrival in the present of an event proper to the future consummation, all history before this consummation has a derived meaning. This is not to say that present history is devoid of meaning altogether. It is rather to say that since Jesus' resurrection breaks through the normal categories of understanding, man must remain open to the still-to-come future of God."[37]

Thus, as A.D. Galloway says, "Pannenberg stakes everything on the resurrection".[38] It is an event that happened in history. It is also an event that has given people a new interpretation of history, one that is contrary to the cyclic view and, in contrast, opens up for man a future filled with gracious expectation because God, who is "the power of the future," will bring in his kingdom in all its fullness and power. Only at the end, when the eschaton has completely arrived, will the fullness or pleroma of the kingdom's reality be realized.

In his *Jesus — God and Man*, in his writing on the kingdom of God, as well as in his essays, Pannenberg brings to our minds these important truths concerning history and eschatology: the centrality of the resurrection of Jesus Christ; the kingdom of God is both realized and still to come; God is not only the God of the past and present, or the lord of history—he is also the God of the future which is as yet largely unrealized. As such he is the foundation of the Christian's hope for the future, he who brought Jesus Christ from the dead. Under God, therefore, man's future is an open one, though the openness depends on man being a servant of the kingdom who responds to the kingdom's call in the everyday life of the present.

Evaluation

The reader of this chapter will be very much aware that the writer is in sympathy with the historical emphasis in theology. He has generally aligned himself with all those who give a large place to the historical basis of the christian gospel.

Among the reasons we give for supporting the theology of history (which is related to, but not identified with, the Heilsgeschichte movement) is that we can see no alternative to an historical basis for the christian faith in the bible. Unless one is nearly a total sceptic, for instance, regarding the historic events recorded in the four gospels respecting the life and ministry of Jesus, he has no alternative but to believe in the historicity of this person, Jesus. This does not mean that the reader of the gospels is uncritical in his view of many events as they are recorded. But he does accept the general historical characteristics of what can be read in these four accounts of Jesus' life.

The ancient 'theory of cycles' as an interpretation of history is not simply a matter of antiquarian interest. It seems to revive in the writings of fatalists, or semi-fatalists in each generation. For instance, Nietzsche and Schopenhauer in the nineteenth century, and O. Spengler, with his biological view of the growth and decay of civilizations, in this century, set forth in different ways the old cyclic view of history. Some writers claim that Arnold Toynbee's interpretation of history in terms of a chariot on wheels, with a charioteer to direct it, has some resemblance to this ancient view. Be that as it may, we should ever be alert to the fact that when belief in a living, providential God wanes there will be those who will come forward to present a cyclic interpretation of the course of human events, with its philosophy of recurrence and its consequential pall of pessimism. Against such a pagan philosophy and interpretation of history the christian theology of history serves to remind people that he "who stretches out the heavens as a curtain . . . and makes the rulers of the earth as nothing"

(Isa. 40:22,23) maintains his sovereign rule over all creation.

Again, it is this historical emphasis which frees Christianity from abstraction and speculation regarding the faith. It makes our religion concrete, an everyday affair, related to human life. The gospel becomes relevant to man in his historical situation, not something of 'pie-in-the-sky'. Man needs salvation in history, not apart from it. It is this which the theology of history affirms unmistakably.

In this theological emphasis on the person of Jesus Christ he emerges more clearly as a real human being about whom transcendent affirmations were made by his disciples and the church. He is not some docetic creature, like Mohammed's coffin suspended halfway between heaven and earth, but a real man among men, one who went to banquets, grew weary, hungry, thirsty, loved friends, and prayed. All of this—and more—brings out the humanity of our Lord.

We also find that the historical point of view in theology is a good antidote to this spiritualising of the gospel which ends in a remote, other-worldly pietism. The gospel must be incarnate. Its truth is sacramentalized, especially in Christ, the supreme sacrament. Spirit is conjoined with matter. The vertical dimension of the faith is linked with the horizontal. All of which is of incalculable value for the life of man in the everyday world.

There are, however, some questions to be raised, if not about the whole theology of history generally, at least regarding some of its specific aspects, or concerning some writers who can be classified in this school of theology. For example. If we speak about God's revelation in his 'mighty deeds' what about his relation to that multitude of deeds that are not mighty? Is he absent from them? If his providence rules over all, how does his providential control relate to the hum-drum affairs of ordinary men? John McIntyre sees a major problem in the relating of Heilsgeschichte to ordinary history. How are ordinary events related to God's mighty acts?[39] Because stress is laid on God's mighty acts, where does man in his freedom relate to these acts? Is his freedom under suspension for a time? Obviously not. But the point we wish to make is that what we ascribe to the doings of God in his mighty acts, or even his lesser acts, cannot exhaust our description of history.

Is there not also in Cullmann's linear theory or interpretation of history from before creation to the consummation, a sort of 'strait-jacket' into which he is attempting to place all history? The mystery of history in relation to providence leaves us with the impression that Cullmann's diagram is too simplistic a pattern into which to try and set the whole of human history.[40]

One thing is certain in the theology of history. The element of mystery, the incomprehensibility of many historical events, is not lessened but increased in this theology. The earthiness of the gospel is accentuated. But so also is the mystery of God's purpose and his eternal kingdom.

Revelation itself is mysterious. Something is unveiled for us in revelation and something remains for us forever veiled and mysterious. We walk by faith, not by sight. Now we know in part. We are finite, limited creatures. Yet we trust in Christ who is the way, the truth and the life. "O the depth of the riches and wisdom and knowledge of God! How unsearchable are his judgments and how inscrutable his ways!" (Rom. 11:33)

1. H. Berkhof, *Christ the Meaning of History*, P.17. S.C.M. Press, London. 1966
2. G. Ernest Wright (with Reginald Fuller), *The Book of the Acts of God*, P.17f. Gerald Duckworth and Co. Ltd., London. 1960.
3. E.C. Rust, *Towards a Theological Understanding of History*, P.67. Oxford University Press, New York. 1963.
4. C.H. Dodd, *History and the Gospel*, P.58. Charles Scribner's Sons, New York. 1938.
5. H.G. Wood, *Christianity and the Nature of History*, P.28. Cambridge Press, London. 1934.
6. E.C. Rust, Op.Cit., P.99.
7. Reinhold Niebuhr, *Faith and History*, P.39. Charles Scribner's Sons, New York. 1949.
8. Ibid., (Quoted), P.41.
9. Saint Augustine, *The City of God*, Book XII, Chapter XVII. Everyman's Library.
10. Roger Shinn, *Christianity and the Problem of History*, P.37. The Bethany Press, St. Louis, Miss. 1964.
11. C.N. Cochrane, *Christianity and Classical Culture*, P.483. Oxford University Press, Toronto. 1944.
12. Roger Shinn, Op.Cit., P.38 (Quoted).
13. A. Richardson, *History: Sacred and Profane*, P.60. S.C.M. Press, London. 1964.
14. O. Cullmann, *Christ and Time*, P.19. S.C.M. Press, London. 1951.
15. O. Cullmann, Ibid., P.82f.
16. C.H. Dodd, Op. Cit., P.77.
17. E.C. Rust, Op. Cit., P.67.
18. E.C. Rust, Ibid., P.67.
19. A. Richardson, Op.Cit., P.144.
20. O. Cullmann, *The Christology of the New Testament*, P.316. The Westminster Press, Philadelphia, 1959.
21. O. Cullmann, *Salvation in History*, P.97 Harper & Row, New York. 1967.
22. O. Cullmann, Ibid., P.100.
23. W. Eichrodt, *Theology of the Old Testament*, Vol. 1, P.37. The Westminster Press, Philadelphia. 1961.
24. W. Eichrodt, Ibid., P.41.
25. E.C. Rust, Op.Cit., P.158.
26. K. Barth, *Dogmatics 111/3*, P.14ff. T. & T. Clark, Edinburgh. 1962.
27. H.G. Wood, Op.Cit., P.80.
28. H. Butterfield, *Christianity and History*, P.104. G. Bell & Sons, London. 1949.
29. Albert Outler, *Who Trusts in God*, P.80. Oxford Press, New York. 1968.
30. H. Berkhof, Op. Cit., P.90
31. H. Berkhof, Ibid., P.98.
32. John Baillie, *The Belief in Progress*, P.235. Oxford University Press, London. 1950.
33. Roger Shinn, Op.Cit., P.30.
34. H. Berkhof, Op.Cit., P.180.
35. Wolfhart Pannenberg, *Theology and the Kingdom of God*, P.25f. Edited by Richard John Neuhaus. The Westminster Press, Philadelphia. 1969.

36. Ibid., P.33. (Quoted).
37. Don H. Olive, *Wolfhart Pannenberg*, P.45f. Word Book, Texas, 1973.
38. A. D. Galloway, *Wolfhart Pannenberg*, P.70. Geo. Allen & Unwin, London. 1973.
39. John McIntyre, *The Christian Doctrine of History*, P.8. Oliver and Boyd, Edinburgh. 1957.
40. Ibid., P.108.

XII

Theology of Hope

A noted psychoanalyst, Erich Fromm, claims that we are facing a mechanized, technological, depersonalized society in which "widespread hopelessness exists with regard to the possibility of changing the course we have taken."[1] He believes that America is at the crossroads. One road leads to a completely mechanized society and the other to "a renaissance of humanism and hope".

From a very different source a well-known theologian begins his book, *Eternal Hope*,[2] with these words: "What oxygen is for the lungs, such is hope for the meaning of human life . . . take hope away and . . . despair supervenes, spelling the paralysis of intellectual and spiritual powers by a feeling of the senselessness and purposelessness of existence." What both of these writers are saying is that without hope the people perish. Without doubt it is the sense of hopelessness and consequent despair which accounts, in part, for the upsurge of the theology of hope in our generation.

W.H. Capps mentions the 'school of hope' which he says might be better referred to as a mood of the contemporary scene. "Hope and the future are in the air"[3] and there are specifically four forces that have helped to create this mood. (i) In this nuclear age there is a great necessity to plan for the future, instead of permitting the future to happen by chance, with its dire possibilities. (ii) It is not only philosophers and theologians, but industrialists and management consultants and people generally who are concerned about man's future, so that men ask, is there hope for humanity? (iii) In theological circles the renewed interest in eschatology has caused theologians to give more attention to what is meant by 'future' and 'hope' from a christian point of view.

(iv) Certain aspects of process theology, especially that which concentrates on 'the future of man,' have led theologians to take into account the theology of hope in a new and more vital way. (v) We can add a fifth force to this list, namely, the Marxist philosophy which issues in some form of Communism and has a temporal eschatology (eschaton or end) in that it looks ahead to the creation of a Marxist utopia. Marxism has undoubtedly made some Christians and non-Christians think more seriously about man's future on earth, not to mention his future beyond death.

It has often been said that where there is hope there is life. The reverse is also true: where there is life there is hope. Unless there is some dynamic, creative vision of the future, life becomes "weary, stale, flat and unprofitable". Hope is the ingredient that makes life real, earnest and purposeful. And the Marxist philosopher, Ernst Bloch, claims that "where there is hope, there is religion."[4] If such a statement appears to many as an exaggeration, we do know that today it is the exponents of religion, among many others, who are giving serious attention to the subject of hope.

There are certain emphases in the theology of hope that are becoming prominent in this school and to which we will direct our attention.

The basis of christian hope

"Hope in God," (Ps. 42:11) said the psalmist. The basis of all hope in biblical religion is the purpose and nature of God. Hope that can be placed in man is uncertain and at best temporal. Real, confident hope is found only in him who is eternal.

Christian hope is based on faith in the God of Israel who has fully revealed himself in Jesus Christ. When Paul gave us the list of the theological virtues, faith, hope and love (1 Cor. 13:13), he placed faith first. Faith is the basis of hope, which in a sense is faith in the future, and this faith in God, manifested in hope in the future, must express itself in love.

Without love, one's faith is 'in vain,' or empty of meaning.

Jurgen Moltmann explains the relation between faith and hope when he writes: "Faith binds man to Christ. Hope sets this faith open to the comprehensive future of Christ. Hope is therefore the 'inseparable companion' of faith." What faith believes, hope anticipates and expects. "Faith believes God to be true, hope awaits the time when this truth shall be manifested . . . faith is the foundation upon which hope rests, hope nourishes and sustains faith . . . Thus in the christian life, faith has the priority, but hope the primacy."[5] Faith gives a Christian the knowledge of Christ and without this knowledge hope would only be an utopian dream. But without hope faith would have no outreach for the future. Faith shows us the road to truth but it is hope that helps us to keep travelling this road.

Hope was one of the characteristic virtues of the early church. Paul writes, "rejoice in hope" (Rom. 12:12), while St. Peter writes about "a living hope" (1 Pet.1:3). The Epistle to the Hebrews refers to hope as "a sure and steadfast anchor of the soul" (Heb. 6:19). In Ephesians we read about some people "having no hope and without God in the world" (Eph. 2:12). Commenting on this verse, J.E. Fison says that the corollary of "godlessness is hopelessness".[6] He states that the early church not only out-lived, out-thought and out-died their pagan contemporaries. They also "out-hoped" them. There is a very real truth in the belief that it was Christianity that made man to hope in the Graeco-Roman world into which Christianity was born.

In the New Testament the basis of the Christian hope, temporal and eternal, is in the fact that God raised Jesus Christ from the dead and "brought life and immortality to light through the gospel" (2 Tim. 1:10). Reference is made in Ephesians to the "great might" or omnipotence of God which can be seen in the super-natural act which God "accomplished in Christ when he raised him from the dead" (Eph. 1:20). J. Moltmann declares that "Christianity stands or falls with the reality of the raising of Jesus from the dead by God. In the New Testament there is no faith that does not start a priori with the resurrection of Jesus."[7]

This writer goes on to quote St. Paul who gives us the basic form of the early Christian confession of faith: "If you confess with your lips that Jesus is Lord and believe in your heart that God raised him from the dead, you will be saved" (Rom 10:9). Moltmann continues: "A christian faith that is not a resurrection faith can, therefore, be neither Christian nor faith."

The noun hope (elpis) in the New Testament is used in the singular and its reference is to Jesus Christ, crucified and risen. The writers of the New Testament have really nothing to say about hopes that have a human foundation. Their one hope, here and hereafter, is in the God who raised Jesus from the dead.

God as the power of the future

When God revealed himself to Moses in a burning bush at Mount Horeb and placed on him the responsibility of going to Pharaoh to request liberty for the children of Israel, Moses asked God to give him his name in order to inform Pharaoh about what God had sent him. The reply Moses received (which has no accurate English translation) was, "I am whom I am . . . Say this . . . I am has sent me to you" (Ex. 3:14). "I am", in a footnote in the New English Bible, is rendered, "I will be". That is, the message Moses received about God's name was simply, "I will be what I will be". Moses will understand who God is as he continues in faithfulness toward him and as he receives further light from God. It is a message that tells Moses that God is really the power of the future. "The christian faith," writes Carl E. Braaten, "is wholly oriented to God as the power of the future which arrives in Jesus of Nazareth under the signs of hope and promise."[8]

Hope that is founded on the character of God and the historic reality of the resurrection of Jesus is always a certainty in biblical religion. Men may have hopes that will never be realized. It is not so with the hope that we have in

Christ. "He *must* reign until he has put all his enemies under his feet" (1 Cor. 15:25). Doubt regarding the issue of christian hope is ruled out beforehand because it is a hope that is related to God and realized proleptically in the person of the risen Lord.

Wolfhart Pannenberg, who refers to God as the power of the future, reminds us that his power is already present. "The future is powerful in the present. It is the power of contradiction to the present, and releases forces to overcome it. Just for this reason is it alone able to rescue and preserve."[9] This power, Pannenberg believes, is personal and opens up for men possibilities of transformation of persons and social conditions. It leaves man discontented with the present because new potentialities of creativity are envisioned in man's future when we think of that future as the power of God. He draws us into that future. He helps us to see that spiritual promises can be realized. As Johannes B. Metz affirms, "the Christ-event gives added stimulus to attempts to shape the future ... The preaching of the resurrection ... is essentially a missionary preaching of promise. In obedience to it the Christian attempts to transform the world in the direction of that new world which is promised to him once and for all in Christ Jesus."[10] Positing this ground of hope that the Christian has in God, he is acknowledging thereby that there is a wonderful source of power and meaning, of possible achievement and creative insight, for good in man's tomorrow. Browning wrote that "Man partly is and wholly hopes to be." This wholeness of man's hopes must be related to God if they are to be realized fully in the eschaton when God will be all in all.

The Teilhard de Chardin Association, following up both the writings and the spirit of this French paleontologist, is concentrating its research and writings on the future of man. In a volume in the Teilhard Study Library (No. 6) Philip Hefner gives us a Teilhardian perspective regarding man's future. Like Teilhard himself, this writer indicates a tremendous trust in the created order, based in part on a sort of evolutionary optimism regarding man's future and the possibility of man, now in the noosphere (the level of mind and thought), going on to a Christosphere in which man is 'taken up' into the realm of Christ. Like Teilhard he believes that this future, with its wide range of possibilities for personal enhancement, will be one in which there will be greater convergence and unification, because God as the power of the future makes for unity.

There will also be progressive personalization which means that "the factors and forces which are apparent in pre-human and non-human energy configurations, as well as in man, which make for personal identity and value constitute a continuum which shall advance toward intensification, in ways that we cannot foresee, but in ways that are not retrogressive." [11] This implies "the worth and reliability of creation", that creation itself is good and we must believe in its goodness in spite of negative, evil factors in the world. All human energies will be activated toward the future in a more unified manner, bringing about the 'new man' through the fulfilment of his destiny in love. There can be no creation of a "usable future" apart from love, the unifying, energizing and creative power in the world.

Many writers in this school of hope, including Hefner, make much of the fact that in this view of hope the future is open, not closed, because God is the power of the future. "A Teilhardian perspective," writes Hefner, "calls attention to the open-ended character of evolution; man and the cosmos are still evolving, and this entails qualitatively new developments." [12] This writer and others make clear that this is not scientific or humanistic optimism regarding man's future but a view of tomorrow whose ultimate horizon of hope is based on a present experience of God who is the Lord of the future. To believe in God, the Lord of creation, is to have hope regarding man and creation.

Teilhard himself believes that this open horizon ahead of us is 'unlimited'. He holds that "the cosmic phenomenon of spiritualization is irreversible" and that man will be drawn toward Omega point by the immanent power of the spirit of God. This will mean the development of a "super humanity" by which he means "the higher biological state that mankind seems destined to attain if, carrying to its extreme limit the process from which it historically emerged, it succeeds in becoming completely totalized upon itself, body and soul." [13] In other words de Chardin believes in the historical reality of "the gradual ascent of mankind" towards the fullness (pleroma) of personhood and community in Jesus Christ. And the task of the church is to help mankind attain this end.

We must not think of de Chardin, Hefner and others of this school as being naive optimists. Hefner tells us that the Teilhardian perspective "is risk and wager as much as it is optimism." [14] But it is a recognition that human destiny which is the final outcome of hope, "is God's future in Jesus Christ" and this God has placed tremendous energies in man's hands for building the temple of tomorrow, both temporal and eternal.

Promise, expectation and hope

The bible is a collection of books with many promises of God to people, beginning with his convenant promises. One of the most influential promises is that of God to Abram (Gen. 12:1-3). He was to be a blessing to others after him. And "he who promised is faithful" (Heb. 10:23).

At Pentecost Peter stated that what was promised by God through the Old Testament prophets, such as Joel, that he would "pour out" his spirit "upon all flesh", has now come to pass in Jesus who, by his resurrection, has shown himself to be the Messiah or the Christ. This is God's fulfilment of his promise to his people Israel and "to all that are afar off, every one whom the Lord our God calls to him" (Acts 2:39). This affirmation is confirmed in the words of Paul that "all the promises of God find their Yes in him (Christ)" (2 Cor. 1:20). This is why the New Testament has been sometimes called the book of fulfilment. "The word of revelation in the Old Testament is not primarily a word of information or even a word of address ... but is rather a word of promise. Its statements are announcements, its preaching is the proclamation of what is to come . . . The principal word of promise points to the future." [15]

But for those who believe, these promises, fulfilled in Christ, who is the Lord of the future, ought to make them a people full of expectation regarding the future. They ought to be those who 'live on tiptoe', in wonder, looking for a new vision of a greater, more spiritual tomorrow. Expectation is really part of faith, "the assurance of things hoped for, the conviction of things not seen" (Heb. 11:1). "Expectation," says Moltmann, "makes life good, for in expectation man can accept his whole present and find joy not only in its joy but also in its sorrow. . . . "Hell is hopelessness." [16] Over the entrance of Dante's hell were inscribed the words: "Abandon hope, all ye who enter here."

Christian expectation, based on God's promises fulfilled in Jesus Christ, looks forward to that ultimate hope of the parousia, the final disclosure of the reigning Christ who will establish a new heaven and a new earth. Promise, expectation and hope must have a consummation and that consummation is the full disclosure that Christ is Lord. Presence and parousia belong together. Through the spirit Christ is present now with his people. But he "will come again" and completely reveal what we today "know in part". "Only those who know the presence can hope for the parousia. Only those who hope for the parousia can know the presence." [17]

If hope has grown dim regarding man and his future it is not because the promises are obscure, because God has spoken and God has come to fulfill his promises in Jesus Christ. Nor can such spiritual dimness be charged to the gospel itself as having no hope. The New Testament informs us of St. Paul appealing in his epistle to the Romans for believers to "abound in hope" through "the power of the holy spirit". Spiritual dimness regarding eternal realities is due in large part to a lack of expectation, which means we have let our faith grow cold. We have not maintained the practice of the presence of God without which the reality of God, who is the God of hope, cannot be maintained. As Francis Thompson wrote:

> "Tis ye, 'tis your estranged faces,
> That miss the many-splendoured thing."

Christians, therefore, should continually pray, "Come, Lord Jesus" (Rev. 22:20).

The significance of eschatology in relation to hope

Carl E. Braaten claims that because of the importance of this doctrine of hope today, theology must start at the end, namely at eschatology. The New Testament has only one gospel and that gospel is basically eschatological; that is, it is oriented toward the future triumph of Christ and the kingdom of God. Braaten quotes the Marxist, Ernst Bloch, "The real genesis is not at the beginning, but at the end." Braaten believes this is a good theological slogan for our day because "eschatalogy is the source of light and life."[18] The entire christian faith is permeated by eschatology. It is not something that is 'added to' this faith, as in the last chapter in textbooks on theology, but it is the perspective in all christian thought which is goal-directed toward the triumph of the kingdom over all evil. Eschatology is "the dimension of the eternal breaking in from above and touching the present moment."[19] Apocalyptic, which is one important form of eschatology, gives us a picture of the final separation of the evil from the good and expresses Christ's victory in terms of the lord who shall reign "for ever and ever". One does not need to accept all that Albert Schweitzer had to say about Jesus and apocalyptic; but one thing this genius did make us see was that apocalyptic had much to do with the message of Jesus, a message that led to much of the kerygma of the early church being formulated in apocalyptic terms. Ernst Kasemann says that "Apocalypticism was the mother of all christian theology."[20] In part this is an exaggeration. But it proves the point of the significance of this form of

174

eschatology in the christian faith.

In this eschatological outlook in which the parousia is central, there are also involved the symbols of the last judgment and the general resurrection. Judgment is now in the earth and this will have a climax (Matt. 25:31ff). The process of judgment will have a culmination at that judgment seat where no mistakes are made. And the resurrection is not merely 'spiritual'. It involves the resurrection of the body", the real person, though not in the flesh. And the final expression of the eschatological gospel is the Johannine teaching of eternal life. "And this is eternal life, that they know thee the only true God, and Jesus Christ whom thou hast sent" (John 17:3).

Hope and freedom

The theology of hope, with its emphasis on openness to the future because God is the power of the future, implies freedom not only for God but also for man. In the following chapter we shall give our attention to what this freedom means for many social revolutionaries in our time who seek for the liberation of groups of people in many parts of the world. Here we shall simply take note of how such an upsurge of liberation movements arises out of the gospel of hope which is not simply hope after death but hope for people here and now.

Teilhard de Chardin sees this super-humanity toward which mankind is striving under God as being "the triumph of freedom".[21] In his writings on the future of man he has much to say on this subject of man being liberated not only from 'the bondage to decay' but from all other sorts of bondage as well. If our hope is ultimately God's hope for humanity, then it must be a future with God that is truly meaningful and creative, fully personal, which means free and responsible. He accepts the fact that there must always be an unpredictable element in all we say about the future. But that God-oriented future for which we strive in faith is one that here and now must lead us to emancipate the hungry, the thirsty, the stranger, the sick and the prisoner, if we are to take seriously the parable of the judgment in Matthew 25. It is as if the son of man will be saying to us at the last judgment, "did you help to liberate people from these shackles? Did you help to set them free?" Our hope hereafter is, therefore, determined by how we act here and now. And if this 'here and now' is to have fullness of life for millions of people in the future on this earth, its realization will depend on how we regard the future. The fact of the matter is that in the christian view of hope we are unable to separate hope that is temporal and hope that is eternal. There is only one hope with two aspects, the hope that we have in the risen Christ who will come again to judge the living and the dead. It is "in this hope" that "we are saved" (Rom. 8:24).

Hope and the conquest of death

"If for this life only we have hoped in Christ, we are of all men most to be pitied" (1 Cor. 15:19). Almost instinctively a person asks the question, "If a man die, shall he live again?" (Job 14:14). It would appear that not even Marxist education in atheism has entirely erased this question from the minds of Marx's disciples. Bishop Newbigin[22] refers to the Polish Marxist philosopher, Adam Schaff, who complained that Marxists had no answer to such questions as the meaning of life and life after death because they tried to deny that the problems which such questions raise really exist. Schaff says that this is like trying to deny the existence of America. He goes on to say that we cannot shrug off questions of "why", and "what for?" He continues, "This applies still more to the compulsive questions which come from reflection upon death—why all this effort to stay alive if we are going to die anyway? It is difficult to avoid the feeling that death is senseless—avoidable, accidental death especially. . . . From the point of view of the progression of nature death is entirely sensible. But from the point of view of a given individual death is senseless and places in doubt everything he does."

The first book of the bible reminds us that we are made of the dust and to the dust we shall return (Gen. 3:19). But the message of the New Testament is that Christ has conquered death for every man who believes in him. "Christ has been raised from the dead, the first fruits of those who have fallen asleep. . . . The last enemy to be destroyed is death" (1 Cor. 15:20,26).

Plato said that all philosophy was a meditation on death. Death is "the last enemy" because unless we have something with which to meet it and overcome it, all our promises, expectations and achievements amount to nothing. And the christian hope, based on the faith of the New Testament, is an "anticipated practice of death."

But the God who is the ground of our hope is not the God of the dead but the God of the living. And this living God includes the conquest of death within the compass of his promise and glory. So our christian expectation regarding the future should not be limited to the boundary line of death. This boundary line in the light of Christ's resurrection, must now be shifted beyond death because God is the God of both the living and the dead. Our hope is in him who brought Jesus Christ from the dead. "Thanks be to God, who gives us the victory through our Lord Jesus Christ," exclaims St. Paul. "Therefore, my beloved brethren, be steadfast, immovable, always abounding in the work of the Lord, knowing that in the Lord your labor is not in vain" (1 Cor. 15:57, 58). Thus the final hope of man, in this world and in the world to come, is in the Easter fact that Christ is risen and in the Easter faith that Christ is alive forevermore.

Evaluation

A theology of hope presents secular man with a very timely message for a world of change. This theology accepts change, sees the creative possibilities regarding change because it is oriented toward the future. Consequently there is likely to be less "future shock" for theologians of hope who anticipate many changes in the world of tomorrow.

A theology of hope also presents us with a dynamic view of God as opposed to former static views. In this it has a kinship with process theology, though it differs from such theology in many other ways. Man needs a concept of the living God to match the living present and future.

It is apparent that the theology of hope signals a return to central issues in the christian gospel by stressing the importance of Jesus Christ, crucified and risen, whose parousia (second coming) Christians await in expectation and faith. Eschatology is therefore given a major emphasis in this school of theology, an emphasis that is long overdue. This theology shows us that Jesus Christ is more than a moral teacher or a superior man; He is the Lord, who died and rose again and is the living saviour of those who believe in him.

Thus hope with an eschatological foundation discloses in contrast the weakness of mere secular theology and religion which has no eternal ground on which to stand and from which it takes its bearing for action in the everyday world. A this-worldly theology, with only a horizontal perspective on life, is lacking in that dynamic motivation which can come from faith in a transcendent God who has revealed himself in Christ who is our transcendent hope for both time and eternity.

Finally, the theology of hope serves to tell us that we have here no abiding city but we seek one to come. Man is a traveller, a pilgrim on the earth, seeking for an eternal city which is the city of the living God. Man is an amphibian; he is a spiritual creature living in a material world in a material body. But God, who is a spirit, is man's true home. As he regards his own life, and that of the world sacramentally, man will use material things for spiritual ends and find eternal life even in the midst of time. Death for such a one is not the end but only a transition to a larger life in that temple not made with hands, eternal in the heavens.

On the other hand we find certain emphases, if not in the theology of hope generally at least in the writings of some members of this school, which we believe are open to criticism. For example, we believe that Teilhard de Chardin, who belongs more to the school of process theologians as we have noted (Chapter 7), is far too optimistic about man's future, even when we think of that future as being under God. The problem of man's rebellion against God seems not to have been taken as seriously as we think it should be. The impression left after reading *The Future of Man* is that man will be carried along on the swelling tide of evolution to participate in the Christogenesis of some distant future. De Chardin's thought here seems too vague, too speculative and too visionary.

A criticism made of J. Moltmann's *Theology of Hope*, in which we concur, is that his concept of hope is far too eschatological. The same might be said regarding Carl E. Braaten's point of view. We can accept the truth that the writings of the New Testament present us with the figure and teaching of Jesus Christ as an eschatological being, with a hope that reaches into the future. But surely some of the teaching of Jesus, including the parables of the kingdom, is matter-of-fact teaching about man's relationship to man and to God for everyday life with little thought of the far-off divine event toward which the whole of creation is said to be moving. In the background of Jesus' teaching this belief in the God ahead of us, the God of hope and the eschaton, is there. But we do not think it necessary to link the great commandment of love to God and neighbor to some message of hope in order to have people obey this command now in the daily round and common task.

Cannot this emphasis on eschatology turn into another form of escapist theology? At the time when the Evanston Assembly of the World Council of Churches was held, the theme was, "Jesus Christ, the hope of the world". Eschatology was brought to the forefront of christian thinking at this assembly, beginning with Dr. Edmund

Schlink's opening address. Some commentators said then that far too many churchmen were escaping down their "eschatological rabbit holes" in order to avoid the strong winds of change and the challenges facing the church in the social milieu of the time. This is still a matter which eschatologists must take seriously in our time if the theology of hope is to have relevance in this era of rapid change.

Then, too, is the picture of God as the power of the future, God ahead of us, not 'up there', adequate as one that is true to the nature of God? Of course God is concerned about the future. His spirit is always ahead of us. But God also is a rock and refuge, a high tower and a place of comfort. What people in any school of theology should learn is that there is no one picture or analogy concerning God which can describe him in all his glory. He is too great for our small, finite minds to comprehend. Therefore, why not acknowledge from the beginning that any analogy of God we present is only partial at best. God 'ahead of us,' God 'the power of the future,' or God 'up there,' or 'down there'—all tell us something about God, but they do not, because they cannot, tell us all that there is to say about the nature of God. The element of mystery, which includes God's unfathomableness, will always remain.

This serves to remind us of the truth of God's freedom, brought home to us by Calvin and others in the days of the Reformation, and by Karl Barth in our time. Man must not endeavour to hem God in by his human concepts. We must not restrict him in his being or in his actions by the measure of our thought. It is arrogant presumption to limit the Holy One of Israel. Even speaking of God as only "the power of the future" is placing a limitation on the Almighty.

The writer of the fortieth chapter of Isaiah, setting forth the greatness of God over his creation, also makes us aware that in comparison to God, man's power is puny and weak. Humility before God is, therefore, becoming to the saints.

"Have you not known? Have you not heard?
The Lord is the everlasting God,

the creator of the ends of the earth.
He does not faint or grow weary,
his understanding is unsearchable" (Is. 40:28).

1. Erich Fromm, *The Revolution of Hope*, P.5. Bantam Books, Harper & Row, New York. 1968.
2. Emil Brunner, *Eternal Hope*, P.7. The Westminster Press, Philadelphia. 1954.
3. W.H. Capps, editor, *The Future of Hope*, P.4ff. Fortress Press, Philadelphia. 1970.
4. Carl E. Braaten, *The Future of God*, P.33 (Quoted). Harper & Row, New York. 1969.
5. Jurgen Moltmann, *Theology of Hope*, P.20 S.C.M. Press, London. 1965.
6. J.E. Fison, *The Christian Hope*, P.80. Longmans, Green & Co., London. 1954.
7. J. Moltmann, Op.Cit., P.165f.
8. Carl E. Braaten, Op.Cit., P.17.
9. Wolfhart Pannenberg, *Basic Questions in Theology*, Vol. 2, P.243. Fortress Press, Philadelphia. 1971.
10. Johannes B. Metz, *Creative Hope in New Theology*, No.5, P.135. The MacMillan Company, New York. 1968.
11. Philip Hefner, *The Future of our Future: A Teilhardian Perspective, in Hope and the Future of Man*, ed. E.H. Cousins, P.27. Garnstone Press, London, 1973.
12. Ibid., P.28
13. Teilhard de Chardin, *Science and Christ*, P.152. Collins, London. 1965.
14. P. Hefner, Ibid., P.38.
15. Johannes B. Metz, Op. Cit., P.133.
16. J. Moltmann, Op. Cit., P.32
17. J.E. Fison, Op.Cit., P.70.
18. Carl E. Braaten, Op.Cit., P.18.
19. Carl E. Braaten, Op.Cit., P.19.
20. Carl E. Braaten, Op. Cit., P.21 (Quoted).
21. T. de Chardin, *The Future of Man*, P.183ff. Collins, London, 1964.
22. Leslie Newbigin, *Honest Religion For Secular Man*, P.39f. The Westminster Press, Philadelphia. 1966.

XIII

Theology of Revolution

A Francisan nun, Maurina Borges de Silveira, was arrested and tortured in a Brazil prison. "She was made to strip, then was beaten and given electric shocks. She was told to stop praying and to abjure Christ and the bible, for no one could help her . . . . what crime did this woman commit? . . . . she allowed a group of young people to meet at the orphanage she ran. They discussed politics, and they left behind documents, which Sister Maurina, finding that they were of a 'subversive' nature, burned. Sometime later the group was arrested. Sister Maurina was accused of suppressing evidence and was in turn arrested and tortured. So far as is known, she had no connections whatever with any 'subversive' group." [1]

Brazil is ruled by a military dictatorship. It is a regime that upholds the power of the landholders and continues the suppression of the poor and ignorant peasant. According to M.M. Alves "torture, murder, violation of every article of the U.N. Declaration of Human Rights, an economic system that breeds injustice by concentrating more and more wealth in the hands of the very few and accumulates capital through monstrous exploitation of labor, an incredibly high rate of adult illiteracy and child mortality, economic occupation by foreigners (especially Americans), a regime that views every citizen as a suspect—such is the situation in Brazil today." [2] Mr. Alves believes that because this regime is maintained by force it can only be changed by force.

These references simply serve to point up a condition of social life that is prevalent in many countries of the world, especially in the third or developing world. It is a condition that makes plain the dire need for change if millions of people are to be emancipated from misery, poverty, ignorance and race prejudice. As the "Declaration of Recife", drafted by Archbishop Helder Camara of Brazil and Dr. Ralph Abernathy of the Southern Christian Leadership Conference on the occasion of the latter's visit to Brazil, stated: "We affirm together our common dedication to the liberation of the poor peoples of the world from the scourges of war, misery and racism. We believe this can and must be done through a worldwide campaign to awaken the conscience of all people of the world to the great human cost of poverty, racism and war."[3]

The theology of revolution is related to the revolution of "rising expectations" in many parts of the world. People in poverty and under oppression are coming to realize that the good life is passing them by; that ideas of change and forces of change are in the air; and they should no longer tolerate the inhuman conditions under which they have been forced to live. Thus the theology of revolution turns out to be really a theology of liberation. Its slogan is "Freedom Now"! Its marching song is "We shall overcome someday"!

In our consideration of the theology of revolution we purpose to look first at the teaching of scripture that lends support to this theology, followed by a brief survey of some of the oppressive features on the world scene from which people must be liberated. It can easily be seen that the things that will concern us in this chapter are intimately related to some aspects of the theology of hope that we discussed in chapter twelve.

What biblical teaching lends support to the theology of revolution? Thinkers in this school have a relatively easy task in finding such support for the revolutionary measures they propose. They turn to the liberation movement under Moses who went to Pharaoh and requested, in the name of Yahweh, the emancipation of the children of Israel from slavery in Egypt. "Let my people go" was his demand. The God of Israel is one who will "deliver the needy when he calls, and the poor and him who has no helper" (Ps. 72:12). The message of the prophets tells of God's concern for the poor and his judgment of the rich for oppressing the poor. Amos speaks of God's judgment coming upon the nation because the rich "sell the righteous for silver, and the needy for a pair of shoes—they that trample the head of the poor into the dust of the earth, and turn aside the way of the afflicted" (Amos 2:7). Isaiah's counsel is, "seek justice, correct oppression, defend the fatherless, plead for the widow" (Is. 1:17).

Leaders in the theology of revolution also find support in the teaching and ministry of Jesus. At the beginning of his ministry, Jesus went into the synagogue at Nazareth and read from Isaiah, chapter 61:

> "The Spirit of the Lord is upon me,
> because he has anointed me to preach good
> news to the poor.
> He has sent me to proclaim release to the
> captives and recovering of sight to the blind,
> to set at liberty those who are oppressed,
> to proclaim the acceptable year of the Lord."

Then he stated that "today this scripture has been fulfilled in your hearing" (Luke 4:18, 19, 21).

"Jesus' work is essentially one of liberation," writes James H. Cone.[4] He believes that Jesus "was always kind to traitors, adulterers, and sinners." He praised the deeds of the good Samaritan. He condemned the religious arrogance of the Pharisees (Matt. 21:31). "The kingdom is for the poor and not the rich because the former has nothing to expect from the world while the latter's entire existence is grounded in his commitment to worldly things ... It is not that poverty is a precondition for entrance into the kingdom. But those who recognize their utter dependence on God and wait on him despite the miserable absurdity of life are typically the poor, according to Jesus."[5] After quoting several other New Testament references to show that Jesus is on the side of the oppressed, Dr. Cone states that "Black power and Christianity have this in common: the liberation of man!"[6]

It is apparent from the selections of Jesus' teachings made by Dr. Cone and others who could be mentioned, that Jesus

is regarded as the great liberator. And it is in this sense of
liberation that they would define revolution. In the words of
the sixteen Bishops of the Third World in their 1967
Declaration, following Pope Paul VI's encyclical Populorum
Progressio, a revolution is "a break with some system that
no longer ensured the common good, and the establishment
of a new order more likely to bring it about."[7] They affirm
that all revolutions are not necessarily good but that there
are times when they are necessary.

Racism

Racism is one of the major problems confronting mankind
today and it finds a place of great importance in the theology
of revolution.

Let the late Martin Luther King, Jr., describe a typical
situation where racism was prominent—Birmingham,
Alabama: "You would be born (as a Negro) in a jim-crow
hospital to parents who probably lived in a ghetto. You
would attend a jim-crow school (The city fathers opposed the
Supreme Court's ruling on school-desegregation). You would
spend your childhood playing mainly in streets because the
'colored' parks were abysmally inadequate. . . . If you went
shopping with your father and mother, you would trudge
along as they purchased at every counter, except one, in the
large or small stores. If you were hungry or thirsty you
would have to forget about it until you got back into the
Negro section of the town. . . . If your family attended
church, you would go to a negro church. If you wanted to visit
a church attended by white people, you would not be
welcome. . . . If you wanted a job in this city . . . . you had
better settle on doing menial work as a porter or laborer."[8]

This picture of racism and the injustice it upholds can be
duplicated, with even worse forms of oppression, in many
countries of the world. Jurgen Moltmann writes that "racism
is not limited to particular countries today. It is a world
problem. White racism in former colonial countries, where

slaves used to be kept, is certainly not the only variety. There is also colored racism in India, Indonesia and Africa, as there is xenophobia to be found everywhere."[9] He goes on to point out that racism is used as an instrument of domination in order to secure political, social and economic privileges for whites in some instances and to regard blacks or coloreds as second-class citizens. In this connection it should be pointed out that, according to Dr. Cone, black power is necessary in order to assist the blacks to gain their dignity and freedom as persons, not necessarily by force, but by asserting their rights in society. And black theology is for black people to help them to know their rights under God, to become sensitive to injustice and to make the blacks believe that they, too, can enter in the inheritance of the children of God. "The goal of black theology," writes Dr. Cone, "is to prepare the minds of the blacks for freedom so that they will be ready to give all for it. Black theology must speak to and for black people as they seek to remove the structures of white power which hover over their being, stripping it of its blackness."[10]

To this black theologian reconciliation cannot be on the white man's terms. This may mean simply accepting injustice, being silent, agreeing with 'tokenism', and the laws and actions which are an affront to his human dignity. Because of this fact he must often oppose the established 'law and order' syndrome set up by white people for their own domination. "White oppressors are incompetent to dictate the terms of reconciliation", writes Dr. Cone, "because they are enslaved by their own racism and will inevitably seek to base the terms on their right to play God in human relationships . . . . and since practically all white people in this country (U.S.A.) are taught from birth to treat blacks as things, black theology must counsel black people to be suspicious of all whites who want to be 'friends of black people . . . .' The problem of reconciliation is the oppressor's problem."[11] Therefore it is useless, according to this writer, to speak about reconciliation until full emancipation has been achieved by the blacks. "Black theology believes that the biblical doctrine of reconciliation can be made a reality only when white people are prepared to address black men as BLACK men and not as some grease-painted form of white humanity."[12] To be black, Dr. Cone believes, is ultimately not a matter of skin color, but of the heart; that is, that 'your heart, your soul, your mind, and your body are where the dispossessed are."[13] Whiteness to him "is a symbol of man's depravity."

The strong language of Dr. Cone against racism, which can be duplicated by many other writers, shows clearly that we in the church especially and in the world at large have a problem of major proportions to overcome in order to usher in a society of justice and true brotherhood.

Poverty

Barbara Ward says that "a small number of states, equaling some twenty per cent of the world's population, controls eighty per cent of the world's wealth .... the gap between this wealthy group of states and the rest of mankind can perhaps be most vividly illustrated by comparing their sixty billion dollar annual increase with the total income of other areas. The combined national incomes of all the states in Latin America is not much above sixty billion. The national income of India (with 500 million people) is only two-thirds of that sum. The national income of Africa is lower still. In other words, the affluent world, largely concentrated round the north Atlantic, adds each year to its existing wealth all and more of the entire income available to other continents."[14] It is simply a case of the rich getting richer and the poor getting poorer in our contemporary world.

The imbalance in incomes within as well as between nations is striking indeed. Glaring inequality is to be seen in many countries. For instance, "in Jamaica, with its tourist boom and its bauxite exports, sixty per cent of the population receives nineteen per cent of the national income. In Columbia, the richest twenty per cent receive sixty-eight per cent of the national income with the top five per cent getting over forty per cent." [15]

In this situation where almost two-thirds of the world's population is underfed, or nearly so, where poverty robs people of their true personhood and dignity, we have the seeds of violent revolution and war. For poverty spells not only undernourishment but also lack of educational facilities, poor health, a high death rate, especially among children, illiteracy, poor housing and in many cases a lack of the will to live. This condition of human affairs is a challenge to the church as well as to governments, especially in the affluent nations.

Freedom

We have noted that the purpose of revolution, according to those who propound a theology of revolution, is that of liberation. Man must be emancipated from his condition of misery, destitution, racism and poverty. This calls for a new or renewed struggle to obtain freedom for millions. What is freedom within the context of the theology of revolution? Dr. Cone gives a reply. "A man is free," he writes, "when he sees clearly the fulfilment of his being and is thus capable of making the envisioned self a reality." [16] God made man to be free—and responsible to him and all mankind.

What has to be realized is that with the problem of white racism, for instance, the white person is, to some degree, robbed of his true freedom as well as the black man. It has been said that you can't keep a man down in the ditch without staying there with him. So it is in this matter of racism.

It was this ringing call for freedom for all that Martin Luther King, Jr. stressed in his famous speech in front of the Lincoln Memorial in Washington in August, 1963. "I have a dream," he said, "that one day every valley shall be exalted, every hill and mountain shall be made low .... With this faith we will be able to hew out of the mountains of despair the stone of hope. With this faith we will be able to work together, to pray together, to struggle together, to go to jail together, to stand up for freedom together, knowing we will be free one day. This will be the day when all God's children will be able to sing with new meaning, 'Let freedom ring' .... When we allow freedom to ring from every town and every hamlet, from every state and every city, we will be able to speed up that day when all of God's children, black men and white men, Jews and Gentiles, Protestants and Catholics, will be able to join hands and sing in the words of the old Negro spiritual, 'Free at last! Free at last! Great God Almighty, we are free at last!' "[17]

Ruben A. Alves considers freedom under the term humanization. By that he means man taking responsibility for his own life in the full dignity of his manhood. There is a humanistic type of humanization, he claims, which concentrates only on human resources. But there are also he believes, other types of humanization and they give to freedom a "vocation". One type is political which means "the negation of the inhuman in the present, its openness to hope, its concern for the transformation of negation and hope into history through political action" and thus is a kind of politics that leads to a greater human liberation.[18]

The other type of humanization that Alves propounds, and which is bound up with the thrust of politics, is messianic humanism which brings in a transcendent power. "When it pronounces the name 'God' it is referring to the power for humanization that remains determined to make man historically free even when all objective and subjective possibilities immanent in history have been exhausted .... The beginning, middle and end of God's activity is the liberation of man."[19] In other words, this writer believes there is a grace in life, bestowed on all who will accept it, which makes for freedom. It is this grace, issuing from God himself, which is working in, with, and for man to give him the liberty of the sons of God.

Violence

In the stride toward freedom a great deal is being written and discussed about whether or not force can be justified by Christians and the church. Can freedom be promoted by the use of violent means? This debatable question has been brought into prominence recently by the World Council of Churches making an original grant of two hundred thousand dollars to the freedom fighters of southern Africa through its program to combat racism.

There are those people who point out that we do not have to decide whether or not to use violence, for violence is here already. We live in a violent world. Shootings, lynchings, murders, stabbings take place daily where racism, poverty and oppression are to be found. To meet this violence with violent means seems, according to some, the only way to act in the situation. And even though the World Council grant was to be specifically used for humanitarian and educational purposes, the fact is that it would give aid to the freedom fighters and so, even indirectly, it may have abetted their use of violent means to overthrow their oppressors.

On the other hand, we have people like Martin Luther King, Jr., who took up Gandhi's method of non-violence to attain the goal of freedom. To meet hate with hate, force with force, did not solve the real problem, according to King. "The use of violence in our struggle," states Dr. King, "would be both impractical and immoral. To meet hate with retaliatory hate would do nothing but intensify the existence of evil in the universe. . . . We must meet the forces of hate with the power of love; we must meet physical force with soul force. Our aim must never be to defeat or humiliate the white man, but to win his friendship and understanding." [20] The stress here is on friendship, even toward those one must oppose, in order that a new climate of understanding may be brought into the situation when the time comes for cessation of resistance to racism.

The question will be asked at once: will non-violent means win victories for justice on the international field? It is one thing for Gandhi to use non-violent means against the British in India who believe in a large measure of freedom of action, and for Dr. King to take similar action and make some progress toward racial equality in the United States where liberty, in large measure, is the hallmark of nationhood. But is it not a very different thing to ask whether non-violence will be able to do any good between nations, many of whom have very little experience with liberty as we know it?

Dr. King replies in the affirmative. He believes that the next stage in the movement of non-violence "is to become international. National movements within the developed countries must help to make it politically feasible for their governments to undertake the kind of massive aid that the developing countries need if they are to break the chains of poverty."[21] He believes that within his own country leaders should strive to quicken the conscience of people to the exploitation that American companies are carrying on against the poor people, for instance in Latin American countries.

So Dr. King concludes with a statement of his faith in non-violence in these words: "In a world facing the revolt of ragged and hungry masses of God's children; in a world torn between the tensions of East and West, white and coloured, individualists and collectivists; in a world whose cultural and spiritual power lags so far behind her technological capabilities that we live each day on the verge of nuclear co-annihilation; in this world, non-violence is no longer an option for intellectual analysis, it is an imperative for action."[22]

Even those who do not accept the non-violent approach to our social problems, especially oppression by a minority of a majority, believe nevertheless that violence and force should only be used as a last resort. Only when no other means of resisting injustice seems open to people—only then should they resort to force.

The 1966 World Conference on Church and Society, held at Geneva,[23] wrestled with this problem of christian action to promote justice. We select some sentences from the final document of this conference as indicative of what many Christians would accept as a good statement concerning the problem of violence. The conference said, in part: "Violence is very much a reality in our world, both the overt use of force to oppress and the invisible violence perpetrated on people who by the millions have been or still are the victims of oppression and unjust social systems. Therefore the question often emerges today whether the violence which sheds blood in planned revolutions may not be a lesser evil than violence which, though bloodless, condemns whole populations to perennial despair . . . . It cannot be said that the only possible position for the Christian is one of absolute nonviolence. There are situations where Christians may become involved in violence. Whenever it is used, however, it must be seen as an 'ultimate recourse' which is justified only in extreme situations. The use of violence requires a rigorous definition of the needs for which it is used and a clear recognition of the evils which are inherent in it, and it should always be tempered by mercy." The statement goes on to say that we can never tell beforehand what the results of violent revolution will be. However, there appear to be situations where it is deemed necessary to promote justice. It is only in the actual situation that a decision whether or not to use violence can be made. This cannot be adequately accomplished merely on the ground of general principles decided beforehand as to whether or not it is right to use force in every situation.

Evaluation

The christian theology of revolution is timely and challenging, activating many movements for social and ecclesiastical reform and as such it is a power with which we must reckon in the modern world. It gives a spur to the conscience of man, urging him to take seriously the inhuman conditions under which so many fellow humans live from day to day. It can serve as a gadfly to church people to arouse them from their slumbers in the comfortable pew and to join the march to the city of God.

Revolution is here in our midst. Change, some of it violent, is all around us. What the church must do is offer resources, material and spiritual, to a host of christian people, especially youth, to get on with the business of change in a constructive and creative manner. In this way the church will become involved in the revolution and give it direction toward a goal that is in line with christian truth.

If the revolution, as we believe, is here, can the church produce the type of character that is positive, courageous, highly motivated, unselfish and sacrificial to carry through the revolution in a christian manner, combatting racism, poverty, illiteracy and misery in many forms? When we read about the cultural revolution that has taken place in China, and the changes that have been brought about, we have to ask seriously whether the modern church can motivate people, with christian constraint and love, to be equal to the challenge of the christian revolution? We believe that the theology of revolution is putting this question to the church now and in so doing is rendering a good service to the church.

Again, if revolution is here, the carrying through with the revolution in a christian manner cannot be left to a few pioneering souls. The whole church must become involved. Here is where the church must be God's avant-garde, leading the way to the kingdom instead of lagging behind and being prodded into doing the right thing by social forces outside the church. The danger that the church faces is that of social conscience outrunning religion.

The church, in order to be a witness for Christ in these days of revolution must not only speak the prophetic word. It must also live according to its precepts and principles. Love of neighbor must be seen by men in action as well as in words. For example, in speaking about freedom, do men outside the church see that there is freedom within its walls for people to act and speak in a responsible manner? Or are the church leaders so involved with the institution that they cannot see their way open to permit change? Change for the sake of change is of little value. But change to promote the christian revolution, to give enhancement of life, spiritual and physical, to others, is surely part and parcel of the life of the church as Christ would wish it to be.

Another service the theology of revolution performs is that of preventing the church and christian people from accommodating themselves to the status quo, from domesticating themselves in things as they are and so avoiding the challenge of the prophetic word of God. Complacency can lay its deadening hand on the church and on the individual and Christians need to give heed to the revolutionary message that comes from this school of theology in order to arouse themselves from their dogmatic, or undogmatic, slumbers, or their unholy fascination with liturgical frills, and make themselves aware of the call of God in our generation.

Of course there are dangers in the theology of revolution. There are defects in its virtues, beginning with the defects of some of its extremists. Every movement that is for something worthwhile always has to contend with "enemies" within its own camp, that is those who, unwisely, or over-zealously, say and do things which bring the movement into disrepute, or whose actions give comfort to the real enemies of revolution—the racists and the capitalists and the union leaders and others "whose god is their belly" or their pocket book and who are unconcerned about the plight of their fellow-men. Alertness on the part of those who are leaders in the revolution of rising expectations will make certain that its spokesmen are wise as well as dedicated.

There is also a tendency for those in the theology and work of revolution to polarize points of view—the left against the right, the black against the white, the good against the bad. This permits no middle ground for constructive compromise so that people who are concerned with the aims of the revolution can get on with the job. For instance, the manner in which Dr. James H. Cone, in his book to which we have frequently referred in this chapter, sees all that is black as good and all that is white as evil, will not really be helpful in

194

combatting racism. And even if by using these terms black and white he is referring to the heart, not to skin color, the very fact that he uses these terms in the manner that he does, immediately tends to 'turn off' some people from being his colleagues in the revolution he desires to promote.

Then, again, in order to foster the christian revolution attention must be given not only to the immediate situation where oppression and misery are to be seen with their consequent injustice and despair, but perhaps even more to those forces, maybe thousands of miles distant from the situation, which produces poverty. For example, it is not enough to change the economic situation in Central America without changing the motives and actions of industrialists in North America, some of whom control so much of the economics and politics of Central America. The same can be said regarding the economics and politics of South America. The base of so many of Brazil's social problems, for example, is not to be found in Brazil but in the headquarters and offices of companies in New York, Chicago or Toronto where decisions are made to bring in higher profits at the expense of laborers in Brazil. Thus the revolutionary attack on the modern form of chattel slavery must be concentrated not on the situation where poverty prevails but on our own affluent society where men have an easy conscience about the exploitation of the worker whom they do not know or see.

The theology of revolution for the most part emphasizes the needs of the 'outer man', the need for freedom in society, the need for food and a better standard of living. This emphasis is thoroughly Christian. But there are also the needs of the 'inner man', and this means the whole man. Man as body and soul is one man and we must avoid helping people in only one aspect of their life. To feed a man's stomach and give him nothing for his mind, is to starve him of that which is necessary for the enrichment of his total life.

One writer who is himself involved in a revolutionary situation in Latin America, Gustavo Gutierrez, is a person who sees that liberation must be total if it is to meet the needs of people. In his book, *A Theology of Liberation*, which

195

is one of the best books on this subject that has come to this writer's attention and is worthy of much greater comment than we can make here, points out that "modern man's aspirations include not only liberation from *exterior* pressures which prevent his fulfilment as a member of a certain social class, country, or society. He seeks likewise an *interior* liberation, in an individual and intimate dimension; he seeks liberation not only on a social plane but also on a psychological."[24] This writer points out that the center of all our trouble is human sin, with personal and social dimensions. And it is "Christ the Saviour (who) liberates man from sin, which is the ultimate root of all disruption of friendship and of all injustice and oppression. Christ makes man truly free."[25]

Father Gutierrez's book makes disturbing reading to those who are "at ease in Zion." But the book is disturbing in the right sense in that it confronts us with the challenge of the christian message in this day when liberation in all its forms is an imperative for millions of people. He claims that the church has been strong in the past on orthodoxy and to a large extent has left the orthopraxis to nonbelievers. This dualism between belief and practice must be erased by Christians who must from now on not only believe in God but do his holy will.

In the conclusion to his book, Father Gutierrez calls for a faith "based on commitment to abolish injustice and to build a new society." This commitment will involve a person in "active, effective participation in the struggle which the exploited social classes have undertaken against their oppressors."[26] This means deeds more than words.

So he ends his book by paraphrasing some words of Pascal: "All the political theologies, the theologies of hope, of revolution, and of liberation, are not worth one act of genuine solidarity with exploited social classes. They are not worth one act of faith, love, and hope, committed—in one way or another—in active participation to liberate man from everything that dehumanizes him and prevents him from living according to the will of the Father."[27]

Perhaps in this area what we need is not comment on the theology of liberation or revolution as much as to heed the biblical injunction "Go and do likewise" (Luke 10:37).

1.   M.M. Alves, *The Christian Century*, June 10, 1970 P.726f.
2.   M.M. Alves, Ibid., P.727
3.   Brady Tyson, *The Christian Century* June 10, 1970 P.722.
4.   James H. Cone, *Black Theology and Black Power*, P.35. The Seabury Press, New York. 1969
5.   Ibid, P.36F
6.   Ibid., P.39
7.   Martin E. Marty and Dean G. Peerman, Ed., *New Theology*, No. 6, P.245. The MacMillan Company, Toronto. 1969.
8.   Martin Luther King, Jr. *Why We Can't Wait*, P.39ff. Harper & Row, New York. 1963.
9.   J. Moltmann, *Racism and the Right to Resist*, P.2 Study Encounter, Vol. VIII, No. 1, 1972. The World Council of Churches.
10. James H. Cone, Op.Cit., P.118.
11. James H. Cone, Op.Cit., P.145.
12. James H. Cone, Op.Cit., P.147.
13. James H. Cone, Op.Cit., P.151.
14. Barbara Ward, *The Lopsided World*, P.11f. W.W. Norton & Co., New York. 1968.
15. Charles Elliott, *Poverty 2000*, P.2, Study Encounter, Vol. VII, No. 3. 1971. World Council of Churches.
16. James H. Cone, Op.Cit., P.39
17. Coretta Scott King, *My Life with Martin Luther King, Jr.*, P.253f(Quoted). Hodder & Stoughton, London. 1969.
18. Ruben A. Alves, *The Theology of Human Hope*, P.75. Abbey Press, Indiana. 1972.
19. Ibid., P.99
20. New Theology, No. 6, P.182 (Quoted).
21. Martin Luther King, Jr., *The Trumpet of Conscience*, P.75. Hodder & Stoughton, London. 1967.
22. Ibid., P.77
23. *Violence, Nonviolence and the Struggle for Social Justice*, Study Encounter, Vol. VII, No. 3., P.2. (Quoted). 1971.
24. Gustavo Gutierrez, *A Theology of Liberation*, P.30. Orbis Books, New York. 1973.
25. Ibid., P.37
26. Ibid., P.307
27. Ibid., P.308.

XIV

Theology in Ecumenical Perspective

The rise of the ecumenical movement has been one of the most significant features of church life in recent decades. Its effects have been world wide and its influence has been seen in both spiritual and material aspects of life in the church and in the world.

The word ecumenical is derived from the Greek oikoumene (oikos, house), which originally meant the whole inhabited world. Whereas the word 'international' takes for granted many separate nations, the term 'ecumenical' regards as axiomatic the oneness of mankind. Originally ecumenical was a secular word but in the course of history it became applied to church life.

Theologically, ecumenism deals with those issues which churches encounter in their search for a greater unity. It accepts the fact that there is now a certain degree of unity among the churches because of their common faith in Jesus Christ as Lord and Saviour. Ecumenism, therefore, endeavours to make more manifest this given unity and by co-operation, conversation and reunion[1] to move toward a larger expression of that unity which we have in Jesus Christ. "The unity of the church," stated William Temple, "on which our faith and hope is set, is grounded in the unity of God and the uniqueness of his redeeming act in Jesus Christ. . . . The unity of the church of God is a perpetual fact; our task is not to create it but to exhibit it."[2]

We believe that the ecumenical movement, which has many organizations in community, national and international life, the most prominent being the World Council of Churches, is primarily a movement, not a static structure. Its spirit can be promoted and exhibited both within and apart from organizations. Wherever Christians make a witness for unity in the church and among men there the spirit of ecumenicity is to be found. This is in accord with the purpose of God which is expressed by St. Paul in Ephesians: "He has made known to us his hidden purpose—such was his will and pleasure determined beforehand in Christ—to be put into effect when the time was ripe: namely, that the universe, all in heaven and on earth, might be brought into a unity in Christ"(1:9,10). So the chief purpose of the ecumenical movement is to make known to the world that the church believes "there is one body and one Spirit, as there is also one hope held out in God's call to you; one lord, one faith, one baptism; one God and Father of all, who is over all and through all and in all. . . . So shall we all at last attain to the unity inherent in our faith and our knowledge of the son of God—to mature manhood, measured by nothing less than the full stature of Christ" (Eph. 4:4-6, 13. N.E.B.). All of which is in accord with our Lord's prayer for his church, "may they all be one: as thou, Father, art in me, and I in thee, so also may they be one in us, that the world may believe that thou didst send me" (John 17:21. N.E.B.). Unity in God the Father through our lord Jesus Christ and by the power of the Holy Spirit—this is the aim and goal of the ecumenical movement.

In this chapter our purpose is not to deal with the history of the ecumenical movement but to consider christian theology in our time in the light of this movement. In other words, we will take a look at theology from an ecumenical perspective and try to see what this means for theological thought today and tomorrow.

Does this mean a search for a consensus of theology, or the bringing together in one school all the variety of emphases in theology? The answer is in the negative. Rather, seeing theology in ecumenical perspective implies dialogue and sympathetic confrontation of schools of theology with each other with a view to achieving greater understanding, lessening theological diatribe and polemic, promoting the ultimate reconciliation of differing points of view, and giving a better witness to the christian faith to every creature in all the world. Room must always be left for diversity in theology as in the expression of the christian life. But diversity and unity in theology, as elsewhere, are not necessarily antithetical but complementary.[3]

A change of climate

Since the calling of Vatican Council II by Pope John XXIII in 1959 there has been a "change of climate" between Roman Catholics and Protestants, as well as between Roman Catholics and the Orthodox churches. It is represented by what Robert McAfee Brown describes as "deliverance from diatribe" into dialogue,[4] with a desire to confer, to discuss, to co-operate where possible and to seek, under God, for more and better ways to express that unity which is given to the church by Jesus Christ.

The decree on ecumenism of Vatican Council II marks a step forward in relations between Roman Catholics and other christian churches. This decree affirms that "without doubt, . . . discord openly contradicts the will of Christ, provides a stumbling block to the world, and inflicts damage on the most holy cause of proclaiming the good news to every creature."[5] The decree states that Christ "is the principle of the church's unity," that all "who believe in Christ and have been properly baptized are brought into a certain, though imperfect, communion with the catholic church." All Roman Catholics are "exhorted" . . . "to participate skilfully in the work of ecumenism", to dialogue with their "separated brethren", to pray together with them, "to acknowledge and esteem the truly christian endowments from our common heritage which are to be found among our separated brethren" and to carry on theological training in an ecumenical setting. On this latter point the decree states: "Instruction in sacred theology and other branches of knowledge, especially those of a historical nature, must also be presented from an ecumenical point of view, so that at every point they may more accurately correspond with the facts of the case."[6] All this is for the purpose of professing before the world our faith in the triune God who will unite us in worship and work, to the end that all peoples will believe and find newness of life.

This 'change of climate' has also taken place between several Protestant and Anglican-Orthodox churches because the influence of Pope John's pontificate and Vatican Council II have been universal. This 'change of climate' has made it possible for Christians to discuss together their various differences in theology as well as to plan to do those things together which their conscience permits them to do.

In the theological field Christians belonging to different churches now confer together about doctrinal matters. Theological and biblical scholarship, such as is seen in the Faith and Order Commission of the World Council of Churches, embraces thinkers from all the major branches of the christian church. It would appear to be unthinkable any longer for Protestant scholars to do theology on their own, or Roman Catholic scholars to carry on their work in isolation from scholars in other churches. We have begun to take all this for granted today. But in comparison with a couple of decades ago, this matter of conferring together as brother Christians in theology is revolutionary. All this has made for better understanding between Christians, even when they do not agree. And it has been doctrinally fruitful for the work of theology.

Renewal

The Decree on Ecumenism of Vatican II declares, "There can be no ecumenism worthy of the name without a change of heart. . . . Let all Christ's faithful remember that the more purely they strive to live according to the gospel, the more they are fostering and even practising christian unity."[7]

This 'change of heart' is at the center of christian renewal which is the prerequisite of ecumenism. We cannot move forward together as Christ's people unless we are united in faith, hope and love toward Christ and our fellowmen. There must be humility, a willingness to learn from each other and a generosity of spirit which can only come from a reliance on divine grace. Prayer, both private and corporate, will be seen as the very heart of all church renewal. For it is through prayer that we open our minds to the Holy Spirit who is "the Lord and giver of life", and who is the real source and inspirer of ecumenical thought and practice.

Father Gregory Baum points out that in calling the Second Vatican Council, Pope John had in mind "a quest for her own renewal", that is of the Catholic church. The fact is that "we discover some areas where purification through gospel and liturgy is necessary, others where elaboration and expansion are imperative. Striving for unity, we learn that we ourselves must change."[8]

This change will mean a renewed study of the bible, better opportunities for fellowship across denominational lines, more common worship, a deeper appreciation of each other's ecclesiastical traditions and heritage, and a common desire to declare the truth of Christ to the world.

The phrase, 'ecclesia semper reformanda', which means that there must be a continuing reformation within the church, has an appeal today for both Roman Catholics and Protestants. It makes us aware that ecumenism is not an establishment but a movement, a movement under the Holy Spirit who will not permit us to be content and complacent about things as they are in the church or in the world. The spirit moves us on to greater unity and service for God and man. "The reform of the church," however, "is not simply innovation, and not simply response, however ingenious, to the challenges of the time. It is renewal of the body of Christ by the grace of God received in faith. It is renewal which must go on all the time, and from which no aspect of the church is exempt."[9]

While ecumenism has as its aim the greater unity of the

church, which we will consider shortly at some length, we must not think of unity for the sake of unity. It must be unity for the sake of the church's witness in the world. Archbishop Ramsey has said that "it is a mistake to be chiefly at discussing unity as such. . . . Why not make renewal prior to unity as a theme? The agenda therefore should be what we can do to make our own respective churches better serve God today in their life, their witness, their holiness."[10]

The term 'new' in the New Testament (Eg. Eph.2:15) does not mean new in the sense of something that has not appeared previously. Rather, it means new in terms of quality, of depth of spiritual reality, of fellowship with God and man. It is newness in this sense that is implied in the term renewal. Such renewal is the work of the Holy Spirit in the life of the church.

In this renewal Christians will receive new insights into christian fellowship, service and outreach. They will be given new ideas about how to make their witness count in the world, or how to express their love for others and make Christ real to people. Christian renewal will also give a new spur or stimulus to both worship and work, making these responses to God's grace more meaningful in daily life. Renewal will also give a new outlook and perspective to theological thinking, not only to theologians but to the ordinary Christian who takes seriously his discipleship to Christ.

Renewal in the way we have described it may, and probably will lead to changes in church structures and organization. But such changes are not of primary importance. They should only come as a result of a 'change of heart', a new way to make known to men by structural means the spiritual reality of which we have become aware through new knowledge. Structural change should be sequential to this 'change of heart'.

The same must be said about theological change. New insights regarding the christian gospel we should expect to be given us from time to time as we study, think and rely on the grace of God for guidance. But a new theological stance is not one that is given simply to be different but rather to show to the world a fresh perspective of gospel truth in a new situation and with a deeper meaning than was heretofore known.

Unity

"Our search for unity rests upon a necessity inherent in the very nature of the christian gospel," according to the Oberlin Faith and Order Conference.[11] The oneness of God whom we worship and oneness of his redemption of the world in Jesus Christ urges the church to manifest this oneness in the world. "God has made man for community and unity. . . . and yet the tragedy of man's life. . . . is that man has separated himself from God and his fellowman by his sin. . . . Thus the search for unity is basically a search for salvation,"[12] for the restoration of that unity among people which is according to God's will. "Unity rests primarily on what God has done, is doing, and will do. By his act of creation he has made us for unity. By his redemptive action in Jesus Christ, he has made us one. And by the continual activity of his spirit he renews our life in order that we may manifest our unity. Unity is not an option which we may take or leave; rather, if we are faithful to the gospel which we have received and in which we stand, we must acknowledge that it is God's gift, God's demand, and God's promise. Christian faith means receiving this gift, obeying this demand and hoping in this promise."[13]

The criticism is often made of ecumenists that their search for unity will mean the slurring over of theological differences, or the search for a least common denominator in doctrine. In responsible ecumenical circles we do not believe this to be true. There can be diversity in unity which will make us realize how great is the truth of the gospel which we affirm. Ecumenicity, according to Hans Kung, "does not mean playing down the truth, soft-pedalling our differences, making false syntheses and easy compromises, but self-searching, self-criticism, self-reform —in the light of the gospel of Jesus Christ." [14] He claims that "it is only in faith that the church must have unity, not in theology." [15] He goes on to quote Pope John XXIII, from his inaugural encyclical on reunion, to support his statement that we can have unity in the church and at the same time diversity in theological views. Pope John said "there are many points which the church leaves to the discussion of theologians, in that there is no absolute certainty about them. . . . controversies do not disrupt the church's unity; rather they contribute greatly to a deeper and better understanding of her dogmas. These very differences shed in effect a new light on the church's teaching, and pave and fortify the way to the attainment of unity." [16] Then the Pope goes on to quote the saying, "Unity in essentials, freedom in uncertainties, in all things charity."

There are two broad understandings of the church which must ultimately be reconciled, even though varying emphases may be maintained. The concept of the church as the fellowship of the faithful, or the people of God, and the concept of the church as a divinely ordered structure which sustains a fellowship in Christ. In the former view of the church, the fellowship has institutions and structures, but these are not primary in importance. In the latter view, the hierarchical structure is of paramount importance. This division of the two broad views of the church, Protestant and Catholic, was noted by the First Assembly of the World Council of Churches at Amsterdam in 1948.

The question may be asked: are these two views of the church, the Protestant and the Catholic, with all their varieties in actual church life, mutually exclusive? Vatican II did not seem to think so. The Dogmatic Constitution of the church (Lumen Gentium) sets forth the view of the church as both "the people of God" (chapter two) and as a body with a "hierarchical structure" (chapter three). It should be noted that the hierarchy is thought of not primarily in terms of authority but in terms of service.

Vatican II has a good deal to say about the important place of the laity in church life and the idea of conciliarity in the church among the bishops, clergy and laity. It also gave emphasis to the necessity of the bishops and Pope acting together in important matters. These were very prominent features of the documents of this council.

A methodist theologian, John Deschner, sees that one of the "Developments in the Field of Church Unity" is that of conciliarity, though it is different in many respects from that which has been promulgated by Vatican II because of the different structures in church life in Protestantism. He quotes the Louvain Conference of the Faith and Order Commission (1971) as follows: "Conciliarity has been, in some form or degree, characteristic of the life of the christian church in all ages and at various levels. By conciliarity we mean the coming together of Christians— locally, regionally and globally—for common prayer, counsel and decision, in the belief that the Holy Spirit can use such meetings for his own purpose of reconciling, renewing and reforming the church by guiding it towards the fulness of truth and love. Conciliarity can find different expressions at different times and places." [17]

Such a view of conciliarity will be acceptable to all. Dr. Deschner goes on to state that conciliarity directs our attention to an ecumenical goal which can be fruitful for the whole church. It is comprehensive, it points to a "pluriform ecumenical goal," as well as a goal that is attainable because it moves "toward the fulness of worship: in the one eucharist."

All of this is very positive and it reveals a common approach to unity. We believe, however, that Roman Catholics would desire to add to this view of conciliarity the place of the pontiff as the supreme head of the church. Conciliarity, according to the documents of Vatican II, can only be found in its fulness when Christians are related in faith and doctrine to the successor to St. Peter in Rome. This presents the churches with a problem for ecumenical dialogue. Whether there can be reconciliation of these differing views of the church in the future, we cannot say at this juncture in history. The very idea of a hierarchy in the church other than that of Jesus Christ, the Lord, is anathema to many Protestants. But that Christ's authority as well as his call to service must find expression in the church no Protestant can deny. All of which makes it clear that ecumenical discussion is an imperative in the church if there is to be a happy issue out of these theological differences.

It is on this subject of the nature of the church that our deepest differences are to be found and this is basic for all the other theological differences between Roman Catholics and Protestants. The search for church unity, therefore, takes on a serious dimension for it is concerned with matters that pertain to the very roots of the christian faith. Ecumenical discussion, worship and action can thus be seen as the path to ecclesiastical reconciliation. Theology in an ecumenical perspective is a necessity for the good of the church and its mission in the world. We believe that God wills it.

Mission

The Montreal Conference on Faith and Order (1963) stated that "If the unity which is 'God's will and his gift to his church' is to be made visible, it is essential that local churches accept the missionary obligation which God has given to his whole church."[18] This obligation is to share the life which we have in Jesus Christ, in word and act, among the peoples of the world.

The Report of the New Delhi Assembly of the World Council of Churches (1961) states that "the missionary task is not finished. It is rather entering upon a new and more challenging phase. All our concerns with one another must not cause us to forget the fact that two-thirds of the human race are without the knowledge of Christ as the light of the world. We owe them that knowledge. We have no better claim to Christ than they have. Nothing else that we can offer them is a discharge of that debt."[19]

Within the last few years there has been a tremendous change in the concept of mission. The old idea of sending and receiving churches has gone. The world is one big mission field at home and abroad. The fast methods of communication have turned the earth into a 'global village'. Peoples of other religions meet us daily and we have to re-think our christian relationship to them and to their views of God and man. Then, too, the crying need in many impoverished lands for material help has led churches to concentrate on mission in terms of technological and material assistance. All of this has meant that we have had to have a reappraisal of mission outlook and strategy.

Does this reappraisal mean that we must soften our proclamation of the gospel to men of other faiths or no faith? Bishop Neill replies: "The age of missions is at an end; the age of mission has begun . . . The end of missions means not the end of mission but its transformation; there has never been a time at which the obligation to proclaim the gospel has been more seriously and pressingly laid on the church."[20] For the mission of the church is the mission of God to the world through Jesus Christ. God's purpose is to indwell humanity and the gospel makes this purpose plain to the church. We must be faithful to our christian responsibility to 'go into all the world' with the good news that God has visited and redeemed his people in the person of Jesus Christ.

St. Paul has expressed the missionary obligation given to the church in these words: "God was in Christ reconciling the world to himself, not counting their trespasses against them, and entrusting to us the message of reconciliation. So we are ambassadors for Christ, God making his appeal through us. We beseech you on behalf of Christ, be reconciled to God" (2 Cor. 5:19,20). All this leaves the church with no other choice than that of proclaiming the gospel to all men. "Missionary obligation is the life-blood of the Christian faith," according to J.S. Thomson. "It began

208

with the mission of Jesus who accepted his vocation as a decisive fulfilment of the father's search for his lost children. This was the work God had given him to do and from him it passed to his followers ... united in a community called the church, which regarded itself as the first fruit of the divine mission of Jesus Christ."[21] Our God is a missionary God who sent his Son on a mission in the world. The church is under obligation to carry on God's mission under the Lordship of Christ and by the power of the Holy Spirit.

It is in this perspective of the missionary obligation laid on the church that we must see this call for unity. The ecumenical movement is not an end in itself but a means to a greater end, namely, that of furthering the gospel in the world. Unity is for mission. "We must say bluntly," declares Bishop Newbigin, "that when the church ceases to be a mission, then it ceases to have any right to the titles by which she is adorned in the New Testament."[22] All discussion regarding the nature of the church must be carried on in this context of the mission of the church for nature and mission are inseparable. Dr. J. C. McLelland states that in our talk about church unity we have given too much attention to church polity. What we need instead is "preoccupation with mission, to meet the demand of the future".[23] He believes that polity should be ordered by mission. While Dr. McLelland is critical of some plans for church union, nevertheless in a true ecumenical spirit he says that "Christians should will unity in order to participate in God's mission to and in the world."[24] Ecumenism, he affirms, should be concerned with shalom (peace), the wholeness of life in the kingdom of God which is offered to people in the gospel. This is the church's chief concern to which union and unity are predicate, not subject. Dr. McLelland's emphasis on mission is the correct one for the church today and tomorrow.

Bishop Stephen Neill in his Bampton Lectures for 1964 lays stress on the mission of the church as being involved in its unity and its total life. He shows, for example, how the sacraments of the church from the beginning were missionary sacraments. "The sacramental practice of the church grew up in a period in which missionary witness was its main activity, and sacraments were understood in relation to the missionary dimension."[25] He points out that "the baptism of an infant speaks of the missionary task of the church in relation to the future. The baptism of an adult speaks of the missionary dimension of the life of the church in a post-Christian world."[26] Bishop Neill follows through with the claim of the missionary dimension of the eucharist. "The significance of the eucharist," he states, "lies not in itself but in what happens when it is over, when the worshippers go out into that cold and hostile world which is awaiting them outside the doors of the place of worship. The eucharist has significance primarily as the missionary sacrament of a missionary church."[27]

The fact is that the truth of the gospel of Christ is not a privilege to be enjoyed by the faithful for their own advantage. It is a gift to be held in trust for the whole of humanity. For, as stated in Ephesians, the great ecumenical epistle, and elsewhere, it is the destiny of the whole of humanity to be brought together in unity with Christ. All things in heaven and earth are to be "summed up" in him. To proclaim this truth is the responsibility of Christ's church. This means the church is on a mission. To deny this responsibility is to forfeit the name church according to the New Testament. Unity is for mission. Mission demands unity. Mission and unity, therefore, must be inextricably involved in all ecumenical discussion, planning and theological thought.

The call to mission and unity demands more theological thought in an ecumenical perspective. We see the truth of this statement when we consider the social problems of the time—poverty, racism, injustice and war. There is no denominational answer to these problems. Christians together must wrestle with these ugly facts of our social life. In our relations with people of other religions we must dialogue with them first as Christians, not as Protestants,

Anglicans or Roman Catholics.

Then, too, there is the call of unity and mission in relation to the culture of our modern world, art, drama, the media of communication, not to mention family life, religion and education, the field of labour and management relations and the arena of entertainment and recreation. Truly "the field is the world". A denominational approach to these areas of human life is partial at best. Only an ecumenical approach will be satisfactory, even if only partially successful. The one church must present the one gospel to the one world. Theological thought, which should give direction to this ecumenical approach to life, must be carried on in ecumenical perspective.

What seems to be lacking in the church is both the will to unity and to mission. Like the church at Laodicea, we have become lukewarm in our discipleship. Therefore we conclude as we began by saying that it is total renewal of the church which is necessary if unity and mssion are to be given priority in ecclesiastical circles in our time.

Evaluation

In the strict sense of the word 'school' the thought of this chapter has not presented a school of theology that has a different emphasis from some other schools. Rather, 'theology in ecumenical perspective' refers to a dimension of theology in which many schools should be involved. Therefore it is not our purpose here to make an evaluation as we have previously of schools of theology but to offer some suggestions respecting theology in its relation to the ecumenical movement today.

Conservative evangelicals shy away from, or are critical of, the ecumenical movement. This, we believe, means that we are, regrettably, not dealing in the ecumenical movement with representatives of this branch of the church which has its own particular contribution to make to contemporary theological thought and church activity. This is to be deplored. It spells isolation for the conservative evangelicals as well as for the ecumenical movement. Efforts, therefore, should continue to be made to bring together for dialogue and discussion theologians from among the conservative evangelicals and some in the ecumenical movement in order to see the wholeness of the truth which is found in the gospel. Each has a contribution to make to the catholicity of the church as well as its apostolicity.

This will mean that both conservative evangelicals and ecumenical thinkers must concentrate on that which is central in our faith, Jesus Christ, and his meaning and message for the church today. Christology is the fundamental doctrine of the church and it is in and through faith in Christ that we will find that we can be both evangelical and ecumenical. "He is our peace" in theology as elsewhere, peace meaning wholeness and health for theology and for the church.

Ecumenical thinking about the faith will also be on its guard to see that the missionary emphasis has a biblical basis, that the rationale of mission is not merely social motivation but the whole truth of the gospel that God has sent his Son to redeem the world and that the church, his body, must also be a redemptive power. This means that the grace of God must be the fundamental causative factor if the church's missionary strategy and social action are to become truly effective.

Theology can make a further significant contribution to the ecumenical movement if it reminds the church that there must be a growing together of the denominations in unity. Co-operation in worship and work would seem to be a pre-requisite to unity. Plans for organic union must also be seen as instruments of co-operation leading to union. A spirit of fellowship must be created, a thinking together about the gospel and the mission of the church in the world.

Theologians who carry on their thinking in an ecumenical perspective will do a great service for the church by keeping before christian people the goal of the ecumenical movement which is to proclaim and make known to all men the glorious reality of the kingdom of God. This is the heart of the gospel, and the church, following her Lord, must say, "repent, and believe in the gospel" (Mark 1:15). In the one fellowship which Christ has created and in the one mission to which we are called we should discover that unity which the spirit imparts. In the bonds of peace which the spirit sustains we shall find our salvation.

1. W.A. Visser 't Hooft, *A Handbook of Christian Theology*, P.90ff. Meridian Books, New York. 1958.
2. William Temple, *Faith and Order*, Edinburgh, 1937. The MacMillan Company, New York. 1938.
3. W. M. Horton, *Christian Theology: An Ecumenical Approach*, Pp.1-10. Harper and Brothers, New York. 1955.
4. Robert McAfee Brown, *The Ecumenical Revolution*, Pp.3,4. Doubleday and Company, New York. 1967.
5. *The Documents of Vatican II*, Walter M. Abbott, S.J. Editor, P.336ff. Guild Press, New York. 1966.
6. Ibid., P.353.
7. *The Documents of Vatican II*, Ibid., P.351.
8. W.S. Morris, Ed., *The Unity We Seek*, "The Necessity of Protestant-Catholic Dialogue,"Gregory Baum, P.12. The Ryerson Press, Toronto. 1962.
9. Lewis Mudge, *One Church: Catholic and Reformed*, P.53. Lutterworth Press, London. 1963.
10. The Ecumenical Review, October, 1972. *"From Impatience to Humility in our Commitment to Fellowship,"* P.432 (Quoted). World Council of Churches, Geneva.
11. *The Nature of the Unity We Seek*, Report of the Oberlin Conference on Faith and Order, 1957. P.176. The Bethany Press, St. Louis, 1958.
12. Ibid., P.176.
13. Ibid., P.179f.
14. Hans Kung, *The Council and Reunion*, P.144, Sheed & Ward, New York. 1961.
15. Ibid., P.172
16. Ibid., P.173 (Quoted).
17. *The Ecumenical Review*, Op.Cit., P.456f.
18. *Report of the Fourth World Conference on Faith and Order*, Montreal, 1963. P.87. Edited by P.C. Rodger & L. Vischer. S.C.M. Press, London. 1964.
19. The New Delhi Report, S.C.M. Press, London, 1962. P.250.
20. Stephen Neill, *A History of Christian Missions*, P.572f. Penguin Books Limited, Middlesex, 1964.

21. J.S. Thomson, *The Divine Mission*, P.2. The United Church Publishing House, Toronto. 1957.
22. Stephen Neill, *The Church and Christian Union*, P.330f (Quoted). Oxford University Press, London. 1968.
23. J.C. McLelland, *Toward a Radical Church*, P.137. The Ryerson Press, Toronto. 1967.
24. Ibid., P.141.
25. Stephen Neill, *The Church and Christian Union*, P.192. Oxford University Press, New York. 1968.
26. Ibid., P.205.
27. Ibid., P.219.

XV

"The Happy Science"

Karl Barth has written that "Evangelical theology is concerned with Immanuel, God with us!. Having this God for its object, it can be nothing else but the most thankful and happy science."[1]

Today, however, some would say tht theology is anything but 'happy'. The schools of theology referred to in the previous chapters indicate not simply variety, which to some degree is not necessarily to be deplored, but also confusion regarding both the object and task of theology. Contemporary theology has been described as undergoing a "transition" (from what and to what is not defined), or a "radical disorientation", or a "renewal". Even when we hear it said that we live in a "theological age," however, the statement carries with it very often a tone of pessimism regarding the value and purpose of theology. "'The Queen of the Sciences' was deposed very long ago," writes David H.C. Read, "and in recent years has hovered like a poor relation round the doorways of the palace."[2] This writer goes on to say that to many people theology seems to deal with what is "not only obscure but purely speculative". One thing is certain: if theology is to recover its authority in the modern world and render its needful service to man, it must re-examine and restate its basic criterion, motive and purpose in relation to both the church and the world.

If theology is not too 'happy' today, can it still be called a science? Karl Barth, who was a happy theologian, thought so. "(1) Like all other so-called sciences, it is a human effort after a definite object of knowledge. (2) Like all other sciences, it follows a definite self-consistent path of knowledge. (3) Like all other sciences, it is in the position of being accountable for this path to itself and to every one—every one who is capable of effort after this object and therefore of following this path."[3] Like all sciences, theology has a language of its own which does not necessarily mean that it must be obscure to the uninitiated, though obfuscation of meaning instead of clarity appears to be the hallmark of some theologians. Theology deals with the language of the church and the significance and meaning of this language for the life of believers.

Theology and revelation

Divine self-revelation is the ultimate criterion of the christian faith. It is because God has acted and God has spoken that the church is able to proclaim the reconciling word. "Is there any word from the Lord?" Christianity replies in the affirmative. "When in former times God spoke to our forefathers he spoke in fragmentary and varied fashion through the prophets. But in this the final age he has spoken to us in the Son whom he has made heir to the whole universe" (Heb. 1:1, 2, N.E.B.). Christ in his life, death, resurrection and ascension is the culmination, the climax of God's self-revelation.

Theology is concerned with the Word (logos) of God. This Word is recorded in holy scripture. It was revealed to us supremely in the person of Jesus Christ, the Word made flesh, who "dwelt among us, full of grace and truth" (John 1:14). The task of theology, therefore, is to use human language in such a way as to make clear to people the meaning of the divine Word for their lives. This implies that doctrinal forms must be employed to set forth the truth of God's revelation in a manner that will convey the saving content of this revelation.

The correlate of God's self-revelation is faith which is also God's gift to men. Revelation is the objective aspect while faith is the subjective pole of christian experience. Faith means trust, belief and obedience to the word of God. Its centre and focus is Jesus Christ, who lived and is living, the

216

Lord of all life.

Faith must not be taken to be opposed to reason. Reason is the handmaid of faith, the means whereby we express our faith in language that people can understand. Through faith reason is given a firm foundation in the word of God. It is the rationalistic, autonomous or self-sufficient use of reason to which Christianity is opposed because this is simply a form of religion without God and his grace. The rationalistic use of reason is humanistic and has no place for God's disclosure in his word. All depends on man 'finding' God by rational means; not God finding man in the first place. The Christian point of view is that men "should seek God, in the hope that they might feel him and find him" (Acts 17:27) because we "live and move and have our being" in God who has first found us. The words Pascal puts into the mouth of Christ are relevent here: "You would not have sought me if I had not already found you."

Theology must make clear to people the truth that God revealed himself not simply to give men illumination concerning life, its problems and its mystery. It was to save that He came. Revelation brings to us the message that God in Christ "has visited and redeemed his people . . . to give knowledge of salvation to his people in the forgiveness of their sins, through the tender mercy of our God" (Luke 1:68,77,78). Divine salvation is no narrow term confined to the individual. It stands for wholeness and completeness for groups and nations as well as for persons. God's salvation gives liberation from the fetters that bind men to the slavery of systems, forms and traditions which nullify the word of God. It gives newness of life to all who receive Christ by faith (2 Cor. 5:17).

Christian doctrine is important but we are not saved by doctrine. William Temple has written that "doctrine is of an importance too great to be exaggerated, but its place is secondary, not primary . . . What is offered to man's apprehension in any specific Revelation is not truth concerning God but the living God himself."[4] And it is God himself, who has revealed himself in Jesus Christ and who

217

"bears the very stamp of his nature", whom we receive by faith.

Paul Tillich affirms that theology must endeavour to answer the questions raised by man in the culture of the time in which he lives. In other words, the theologian must 'listen to the world'. We do not believe that this matter of the world and its problems is to be forgotten. But we believe it is of primary importance for theology to listen to the Word and bring to bear upon man's culture the meaning and message of that Word. Theology itself will raise deeper questions about man's condition than any culture will ask. For it is the Christ, who knew what was in man as no other has known, who is able to show man his true condition and his need under God. Contrary to Tillich, therefore, theology should first seek to correlate its task with the Word of God before, or along with, the bringing of its message to the world. This is affirmed in the oft-quoted statement attributed to Karl Barth that two things are necessary for an intelligible christian witness today: the bible and the daily newspaper—and in that order.

We are only able to speak of God's self-revelation in his Word because we have the record of this revelation in the bible which is "the royal law" which sets before us "the lively oracles of God". God speaks to us in and through the written word as well as the Word made flesh, Jesus Christ. The preached or proclaimed Word must be based on and arise out of the truth of the written Word of which Christ himself is Lord. The heart and core of the message of scripture is Jesus Christ and essentially it is he whom the church declares to men as God's truth, God's message and God's salvation. And while the bible itself tells us that God has revealed himself in creation, in his acts in history and in the heart of man, it also affirms in a manner that is unmistakable that the fulness of his self-disclosure is in Jesus Christ, his only son and our Lord. Theology, therefore, must have a biblical base, orientation and proclamation.

Theology and the church

A primary task of theology is to clarify and make explicit the language of the church. But in our time a gulf has arisen separating theology from the church, or the church from theology. Many reasons for this separation may be given: the secularism of our age, the preoccupation with science, the fascination of technology and other causes may be offered why the "Queen of the Sciences" has forsaken her palace.

But there are deeper and stronger reasons for this divorce of theology and the church. Theology has become "too contemporary", following the latest fads in doctrine, escaping from the great traditions instead of re-thinking them and their import for our time. The history of christian thought has much to teach theologians today and such history must be given its rightful place in theological discourse in the church.

Then, too, much theology is confined to the seminary, so that its relation to the church as a living organism of the spirit of God is overlooked or by-passed. And at the same time, seminaries too often overstress the 'practical' subjects, the means and methods of doing things in the church and society. There is insufficient emphasis on the basic, foundational courses such as bible, church history and christian thought, historical and contemporary. Pragmatism, utilitarianism and methodology are given priority in many seminaries so that the word of God, if not bound, is at least somewhat restricted in the very place where it ought to be given priority.

One reason why the conservative churches are growing is that their pulpits declare an authoritative word from the Lord based on scripture in contrast to many other pulpits whose chief word is "it seems to me", or it is "my opinion that" and the like. We may not always agree with some of the conservative interpretations of scripture. But if the mainline churches in their pulpit messages and christian education programmes do not give primacy to biblical teaching they are less than Christian and their appeal will not be made in the power of the Holy Spirit who makes the words of scripture come alive in the hearts of believers. Preaching that is based very largely on the daily newspaper, the latest public event, the most recent sensational happening, is not christian preaching. The proclamation from a christian pulpit must be based on and arise out of the Word of God which has a word for every human event and the common life of mankind in all conditions.

The church today has become very 'activist'. It is deeply involved in social affairs. Social service is the hallmark of its mission in the world. Love is the word that takes over in church life. Salvation by works has become a substitute for salvation by faith in Jesus Christ.

It is not our desire to cast aspersions on christian service as the expression of christian love. Over the years we have been very much involved in service of various kinds. But we believe that service without a deep religious faith is a frustrating affair. Love for others is the fruit of love for God, who is love. To divorce the two parts of the great commandment, love to God and love to the neighbour, is to dishonour God and to forget that the neighbour is one whom God loves and for whom Christ died. Faith is the foundation of service. Among the great theological virtues St. Paul mentions in 1 Corinthians 13, faith comes first. Hope and love,—these are the outreach of faith. It is true that "faith without works is dead" (James 2:20). But it is also true that works without faith may end in disillusionment and despair.

Theology and worship

The most important task of the church is to call people to the worship of almighty God. All else that the church does is derivative and secondary, as well as dependent on this responsibility of worship. This may sound rather out of date in an activist age but its truth is of primary significance in any age. The church is called to worship God.

The rationale of worship is to be found in the grace of God and the gratitude his grace elicits from the hearts of the faithful. He is our creator and redeemer and our only boast must be in him who has called us into his church through Jesus Christ by the power of his spirit.

This implies that worship must have a theological foundation. It is not psychology or aesthetics or social conformity which determine the worship of God but theology. And it must be a theology of grace, the divine condescension for "us men and our salvation", the initiative of the Almighty coming to us in mercy and in judgment to redeem us and to unite us in love with Himself. And the centre of this grace, the focal point of Christian worship, is God's Word written in scripture, proclaimed in sacrament and sermon and made manifest in the person of the living Lord Jesus Christ. In Him who is both God and man in the unity of His person, humanity is lifted up to God and God is with us, Immanuel! Therefore our worship, which is total in its reference to life, is 'in Christ'. "This crucified, risen and reigning Christ," writes Dr. James I. McCord, "is the only mediator between God and man. He has effected the great reconciliation and he alone makes true worship possible. We worship in him and through him. Through Christ the inner life of the triune God is extended to include human nature."[5]

Within the context of worship we are to see the place of preaching and sacrament. The preaching of the Word is the proclamation or heralding of God's message to men that they may hear and believe unto salvation. The sacraments are God's 'visible Word', the word of God in another form, making plain to us that God's word is embodied in the life of mankind. They declare, as does scripture and preaching, the truth of Jesus Christ and they set forth the truth that the church is the family of God or the people of God whom he has called out of the world to serve the world. Sacraments not only signify the presence of the word of

God; they also convey it to believing people, for Christ is present in his sacraments. He is the host. We are his invited guests.

The sacraments play a vital part in worship in setting forth the objectivity of God's grace which is primary in worship. A fog of subjectivism has settled over much of christian worship today and this leads to all sorts of experiments, weird and wonderful to behold, which depart from the christian theological base of worship in the Word of God. This catering to the subjective whims of people, this pandering after the latest nicety in order to make worship more attractive, is nothing less than the paganizing of christian worship, for it has little or nothing to do with theology.

Christian worship will lead to obedience, for the worship of God is also the service of God. If there is a slackening in the church's mission in the world, confusion about the church's priorities, the cause is likely to be found in this denigration of worship. Our best hope for the recovery of a sense of true mission, of christian witness and of vital communion with God is through the restoration of the Word of God to its central place in worship, to the end that God will be glorified and the life of man edified.

Theology and evangelism

Evangelism is interpreted by many today as proselytising, as a form of religious triumphialism or imperialism, as the use of methods to cajole people into discipleship, robbing them of their freedom to decide before God. This has meant that the term evangelism is in disrepute in many Christian circles.

Evangelism is derived from the word 'evangel' or gospel and means simply the proclamation of the gospel to people. There are many means by which the gospel can be proclaimed: a christian life; a christian deed, a congregational witness, acts of love. But none of these means should supplant the proclamation of Christ as Lord by means of the spoken word to friends, in groups, from the pulpit, to audiences large and small as well as by use of the modern media of newspaper, magazine, television and radio. Jesus came preaching and his ambassadors—who may be lay as well as clerical Christians—must do likewise. "And how are they to hear without a preacher"? (Rom. 10:14)

Evangelism ought to be at the very heart of the church's witness. The evangel is the good news of God, and the church cannot keep this good news to herself. She must pass it on to others. The God of Christians is not a national deity, or a racial deity. He is the God of the whole earth with whom all men have to do, whether they know it or not. To declare the reality, nature and truth of this God revealed in Christ is what evangelism is all about. It may be done by a teacher in Sunday school, by a parent in the home, by a friend at work—in myriad ways. But evangelism is nothing less than telling others that Christ is Lord.

Neither the church nor individual Christians can convert anyone to the gospel. Conversion in its true sense is the work of the Holy Spirit in a person's heart. But the Spirit must have agents, people through whom he can declare the truth of Christ. The church and its believers are such agents, or ambassadors for Christ. Through them, the Holy Spirit presents people with the need for decision regarding Christ. This is not simply a human affair. It is the work of God, using his people as vehicles of his message, and saying to men, "be reconciled to God" (2 Cor. 5:20).

We must not set in contrast a personal gospel (evangelism) and a social gospel (service). There is only one gospel which is at one and the same time fully personal and fully social. Persons are not found in isolation but in society and as persons influence society, so also society and its culture influence individuals. While the evangelistic appeal is personal its outreach must be social if it is to lead men into obedience to Jesus Christ who is Lord. An evangelism that ends with the individual ends. A gospel that is only social lacks personal warmth and vitality. What God has joined together, the personal and the social, must not be rent asunder by the work of men.

"No evangelistic outburst of the church will have creative power unless it is informed with a living and vital theology, while at the same time. ... theology becomes only a speculative pastime unless it is given expression through the processes and work of evangelism. Neither a shallow nor an unevangelical theology can produce profound spiritual changes in the life of a people. A sincere evangelism and a Christ-centered theology will alone equip a church for her God-given task."[6]

That was written thirty years ago. We would underscore its truth for today. If a church is weak in evangelism we had better look well to its cause which will likely be found in its weakness in theology. "First the lightened mind; then the burning heart." There will be no passion to tell the good news of God unless the reality of God is afire in the believer's heart. This means that the believer is convinced of the theological and saving truth of the gospel which he is to declare.

There are those within the church today who are confused about the christian message and as to whether we are called to proclaim it to others. They tell us that there are good people who are unbelievers, that there are truths in other religions, that many ideologies and cults have their strong points, that people of great faith are found outside of Christianity. All of which is true. Nor is it altogether a modern situation, though today because the world is a 'global village,' these questions seem less remote than in former times.

But what these questions do is make us aware that we must re-think our theology in a new setting. Basically we are confronted with a theological task that is immense in its range, for all the great problems and questions are problems that concern christian doctrine because they ultimately are related to God and his way with men, whether we acknowledge God or not. All the penultimate matters are related to the ultimate, though we sometimes become so preoccupied with the penultimate that we forget the ultimate.

What is required of theologians today is the firm resolve to revise and revitalize theology for this new age with its gadgets and its gas, its sputniks and its spacemen, its drop-outs and its cop-outs. It must be a theology which takes into serious consideration the place of Christ and his significance in this space-age, in relation to other religions, and in view of the secularizing processes in our world. This is not an easy task but it is a very necessary one if evangelism in our time is not to be dismissed as irrelevant, or allowed to evaporate in emotional froth or bland admonitions and exhortations.

Theology must involve the work of scholars, but there is a real sense in which every Christian is a theologian, one who is ready to give a reason for the faith that he holds. But theology should not be an academic subject, cold and impersonal. Its matter is the truth of the living God whose Word "is living and active, sharper than any two-edged sword, piercing to the division of soul and spirit, of joints and marrow, and discerning the thoughts and intentions of the heart" (Heb.4:12). And if theologians are those who have to do with the truth of the living God they themselves must be seized with this truth in the depths of their souls. When this truth really takes hold of those who do theological thinking, when it really becomes vital in their own minds, they will give to evangelism a new thrust and a new vitality which seems to be lacking at the present time.

The prelude to theology

In the last chapter of his book, *Evangelical Theology: An Introduction*, Barth classifies "theological work" as consisting of four basic acts: prayer, study, service and love.[7] We will consider these four acts as the preparation for doing theology.

(A) *Prayer.*

Dr. George S. Hendry[8] refers to prayer as "the life line of theology." He writes: "For some time I have employed a simple device in forming a judgment on the systematic writings of theologians, new and old. I read what they have to say about prayer. It provides a significant clue." In this connection Dr. Hendry says he wants to see how much space a theologian devotes to prayer, what he has to say about prayer as an individual act and also what he says about petition. Dr. Hendry singles out Karl Barth and Karl Rahner, one a Protestant and the other a Roman Catholic, as two theologians who give priority to prayer in their theology. According to Hendry, "prayer is the authentic expression of faith in Christ" and without it "theology will founder on the rocks." One might ask: is this why theology is foundering today?

"Theological work," writes Barth, "takes place in a realm which not only has open windows facing the surrounding life of the church and world, but also and above all has a skylight. ... theological work is opened by heaven and God's work and word, but it is also open towards heaven."[9]

Theology is not simply a human task. Doing theology must be inspired and guided by heavenly wisdom, by the reality of the spirit at work in the theologian's mind and heart. The practice of the presence of God, communion with him who is the source and ground of theology, would seem to be a prerequisite for all who work in theology. Because God is the object of theology the theologian must turn to God in prayer from time to time if God is to be real in his mind. Only thus can his theology be clarified, vivified and sanctified.

Theological work is, in part, listening to what God says to us in his Word. He is the one who addresses us, who speaks to us through his spirit and to whom we are to respond in faith and work. Such a response means prayer in which petition and intercession must have a very distincitive part. "Any theology which would not even consider the necessity

to respond to God personally could only be false theology,"
states Barth. [10] In his exposition of the Lord's prayer [11] and
in his Dogmatics [12] Barth gives a detailed treatment of the
subject of prayer and its relation to theology.

The life and work of any Christian is an offering to God.
How much more true this must be for the work of a
theologian! He uses God language, he treats of God's Word,
he tries to express God's truth to men. To work thus
without personal reference to God in prayer would seem to
be a 'striving after the wind'. 'Come, Creator Spirit' should
be at the very heart of the theologian's petitionary prayer
for without an openness to the spirit's coming, directing and
indwelling, theological work becomes purely academic,
having little relevance to the life of man in the light of God.

(B)   Study.

"Prayer without study would be empty," writes Barth. [13]
"Study without prayer would be blind." Like prayer, study
is a discipline that has to be learned.

The chief theologians of the church are the members of
the clergy. They have the opportunity week by week of
giving theological direction to the people who come to
worship God. Unless they have acquired the discipline of
theological study they will likely be "blind mouths" to
whom "the hungry sheep look up, and are not fed".

Preoccupation and busyness are the twin obstacles in the
way of many clergy who would otherwise become good
students of the Word of God. Their lives are so full of a
number of things which they believe they have to do that
they have little time for thought about their chief task of
breaking the bread of life to hungry souls. But we cannot
stress too much that if there is to be a theological
renaissance that will eventually have an influence on the
whole church, and not simply in seminaries, it must come by
way of the clergy who have mastered the art of study and
who feed the flock committed to their charge.

This is not the place to go into details about how to

acquire a study discipline or what to study, except to say that a concerted study of the scriptures would seem to be of primary importance if one is to proclaim the Word of God. This means something more than devotional reading of the scriptures, important as that is. It means also more than an historical-critical examination of scripture passages, though this has its place. It means studying scripture theologically, trying to see what God's living word has to say to people now, in judgment and in mercy.

But such a study of the scriptures will be linked with other studies such as history, both church and secular, books on theology, the great field of literature, past and present, the drama, art and music of the ages. All life and its culture can provide the preacher with material which can be made the servant of the word of God by illuminating the word and by bringing it into the context of man's everyday living.

(C) Service.

The theologian is the servant of the Word of God. The goal of all his work is to serve God and serve mankind. His exemplar and Lord, Jesus Christ, came as a servant and he must follow in the footsteps of him who gave his life "a ransom for many". Nor must this vicarious aspect of the work of a theologian be forgotten. There will be travail of soul on many occasions in his work of conveying the truth to people.

As servants of the Word of God theologians are accountable to that Word. The Word can never become their 'property', as if they own it. Rather, the Word owns them. The true theologian will feel like Jeremiah: "There is in my heart as it were a burning fire shut up in my bones, and I am weary of holding it in, and I cannot" (Jer. 20:9). God's Word must possess the theologian in such a manner that he cannot refrain from placing himself, through his theological thinking, at the service of God.

Theology is concerned about truth and it is the duty of

theologians of the Word to proclaim this truth "whether they hear or refuse to hear" (Ezekiel 2:5). In proclaiming the Word the theologian and preacher has a responsibility to the community as well as to the church family. For the Word must not be declared in a vacuum or by means of vague abstract language but, as Bonhoeffer never tired of saying, we must proclaim the concrete word of God for our age.

(D) Love.

"Theological work is a good work when it is permitted to be done in love," writes Barth. [14] Though the theologian speaks with the tongues of men or of angels and has no love, it profits nothing. Love builds up good theology as well as the good life, for theology to be valuable must be related to life.

We have read that Luther's friend, Melanchthon, prayed that in the next life he would be delivered from the fury of the theologians. A study of church history brings home to us the fact that very often theologians have carried on their work in diatribe, not in love. It is no wonder, then, that so much of theology has been and is being discredited. Its truth was not declared with love.

One thing that is commendable among the results of Vatican II, thanks in part to the benign influence of Pope John XXIII, is that the documents of Vatican II are set forth not in a polemical manner but in a way that calls for discussion in the spirit of charity at many points where there are differences between Roman Catholics and others, whether Christians or non-Christians. These documents call on people to seek the truth in love.

The First Epistle General of John says that "God is love, and he who abides in love abides in God, and God abides in him" (1 John 4:16). It would, therefore, seem logical that the christian theologian who attempts to give expression to the Word of God in words of men should himself be a person who so abides in God that God's love shines forth in all his

229

work, for his work is the service of love.

We quoted Barth at the beginning of this chapter as stating that theology was both a "thankful" and a "happy" science. It is a thankful science because it is a grace, an undeserved and unmerited gift from God to be able in some humble way to offer God's truth to people. Theology is about God, of God, from God and for God. It is an offering, howsoever inadequate, that we make to God who has redeemed us through Jesus Christ by the power of his spirit. All we have and all we are we owe to him. We are not our own for we have been bought with a price. Gratitude must therefore be the first mark of a Christian and even more especially of a christian theologian whose responsibility is that of helping men and women to know this wondrous grace of God for themselves and thereby find fulness of life.

Theology is also the happy science, in spite of unhappy, gloomy theologians. Barth writes of these "woeful theologians who go around with faces that are eternally troubled or even embittered, always in a rush to bring forward their critical reservations and negations."[15] The reason? They have not found or come to realize that their sufficiency or satisfaction is of God, not of themselves. A Christian is a person who knows that around and underneath all life are God's everlasting arms to sustain him. That is why he does not fear what life will do to him. And it is the christian theologian who ought to understand this truth supremely. He is the one who informs people that, in spite of the evil in the world, God's providence rules over all. He is the one who proclaims that God is able to make the evil that men do turn to good under his sovereign grace, even as he brought life out of death on the first Easter. The theologian must be happy in his work because his basic theological book is the New Testament which begins with the angels singing at Christ's birth and ends with the church, under persecution, hearing the triumphant hallelujah chorus, telling us that Christ reigns as King of Kings and Lord of Lords. Deep within the heart of every true theologian, even in the midst of tragedy, there must be a song of praise to God. God lives, Christ reigns. The Spirit sanctifies. This is the triune truth which christian theology affirms and it is this truth that makes it the happy science.

"Praise God from whom all blessings flows."

1. Karl Barth, *Evangelical Theology: An Introduction*, P.12 Holt, Rinehart and Winston, New York. 1963.
2. David H.C. Read, *Christian Ethics*, P.24 Hodder & Stoughton, London. 1968.
3. Karl Barth, *Church Dogmatics*, Vol. 1, Part 1, P.7. T. & T. Clark, Edinburgh. 1936.
4. William Temple, *Nature, Man and God*, P.322. MacMillan & Co. Ltd., London, 1951.
5. James I. McCord, *The Reformed World*, June, 1973. *"Worship in the Reformed Churches"*, P.247. World Alliance of Reformed Churches, Geneva.
6. R.C. Chalmers, *See The Christ Stand*, P.220f. The Ryerson Press, Toronto. 1945.
7. Karl Barth, *Evangelical Theology: An Introduction*, Chapter 4, P.157ff.
8. George S. Hendry, *The Princeton Seminary Bulletin, "The Life Line of Theology"*, December, 1972. P.22ff.
9. Karl Barth, Op.Cit., P.161.
10. Karl Barth, Ibid., P.165
11. Karl Barth, *Prayer and Preaching*, S.C.M. Press, London. 1964.
12. Karl Barth, *Church Dogmatics*, Vol. III, Part 4, Pp.87ff. T. & T. Clark, Edinburgh. 1961.
13. Karl Barth, *Evangelical Theology: An Introduction*, P.171.
14. Karl Barth, Ibid., P.196
15. Karl Barth, Ibid., P.94

BIBLIOGRAPHY

General

Bowden, J., and J. Richmond — A Reader in Contemporary Theology

Hastings, A.W., & E. Hastings, (Ed) — Theologians of our Time

Hordern, William — A Layman's Guide to Protestant Theology

Hordern, William — New Directions in Theology Today — Vol. 1 Introduction

Hughes, Philip E., (Ed) — Creative Minds in Contemporary Theology

Mackintosh, H.R. — Types of Modern Theology

MacQuarrie, John — 20th Century Religious Thought

Marty, Martin E., and Dean G. Peerman, (Ed) — A Handbook of Christian Theologians

Nicholls, William — The Pelican Guide to Modern Theology, Vol. 1 (Systematic and Philosophical Theology)

Reinisch, Leonhard, (Ed) — Theologians of Our Time

Richardson, Alan, (Ed) — A Dictionary of Christian Theology

Williams, Daniel Day — What Present Day Theologians Are Thinking

Chapter One

Barth, K. — From Rousseau to Ritschl

Griffith, G.O. — Interpreters of Man

MacGregor, Geddes — Introduction to Religious Philosophy

Roberts, David E. — Existentialism and Religious Belief

Russell, Bertrand — A History of Western Philosophy

Tillich, Paul — Perspectives on 19th and 20th Century Protestant Theology

Van Dusen, H.P. — The Vindication of Liberal Theology

Chapter Two

Baillie, D.M. — God Was in Christ
Coe, G.A. — What is Christian Education?
DeWolf, L. Harold — The Case for Liberal Theology
Horton, Walter M. — Christian Theology: An Ecumenical
                        Approach
Niebuhr, Reinhold — Faith and History
Roberts, D.E., and H.P. Van Dusen — Liberal Theology:
                        An Appraisal
Van Dusen, H.P. — The Vindication of Liberal Theology

Chapter Three

Barth, Karl — Dogmatics 1/1, 1/2
Barth, Karl — Dogmatics in Outline
Barth, Karl — The Humanity of God
Barth, Karl — The Word of God and the Word of Man
Brunner, Emil — The Divine-Human Encounter
Hordern, William — A New Reformation Theology
Niebuhr, Reinhold — The Nature and Destiny of Man —
                        Vol. 1
Niebuhr, Richard H. — The Meaning of Revelation
Ramsdell, E.T. — The Christian Perspective

Chapter Four

Baillie, D.M. — God Was in Christ
Baillie, John — Christian Devotion
Baillie, John — Our Knowledge of God
Baillie, John — The Sense of the Presence of God
Baillie, John — What is Christian Civilization?
Dillistone, F.W. — The Christian Understanding of
                        Atonement
Hazelton, Roger — Christ and Ourselves
Hodgson, Leonard — For Faith and Freedom, Vol 2:
                        Christian Theology
Hordern, William — A New Reformation Theology

McIntyre, John — On the Love of God

Chapter Five

Carnell, E.J. — The Case for Orthodox Theology
Hammond, T.C. — In Understanding Be Men (Revised by
        D.F. Wright)
Henry, Carl F.H. (Ed) — Jesus of Nazareth, F.F. Bruce
        and others.
Packer, J.I. — Evangelism and the Sovereignty of God

Chapter Six

Abbott, Walter J., (Ed) — The Documents of Vatican II
Adam, Karl — The Spirit of Catholicism
Aubrey, E.E. — Present Theological Tendencies
Dulles, Avery, — Revelation and the Quest for Unity
Gilson, E. — The Christian Philosophy of
        St. Thomas Aquinas
Gilson, E. — The Spirit of Medieval Philosophy
Gilson, E. — The Unity of Philosophical Experience
Maritain, Jacques — True Humanism
Rahner, Karl — Nature and Grace
Schillebeeckx, Edward, O.P. — God and the Future of Man
von Balthasar, Hans Urs — A Theology of History

Chapter Seven

Bonhoeffer, D. — Letters and Papers from Prison
Birch, L. Charles — Nature and God
Cobb, John B. Jr. — A Christian Natural Theology
Coulson, C.A. — Science and Christian Belief
de Lubac, Henri — The Religion of Teilhard de Chardin
Farley, Edward — The Transcendence of God
Hartshorne, Charles — Man's Vision of God
Pittenger, Norman — God in Process
Robinson, J.A.T. — Exploration Into God
Teilhard de Chardin, Pierre — Hymn of the Universe

Teilhard de Chardin, Pierre — Le Milieu Divin
Teilhard de Chardin, Pierre — Science and Christ
Teilhard de Chardin, Pierre — The Phenomenon of Man
Temple, William — Nature, Man and God
Whitehead, A.N. — Adventures of Ideas
Whitehead, A.N. — Process and Reality
Whitehead, A.N. — Religion in the Making
Whitehead, A.N. — Science and the Modern World

Chapter Eight

Berdyaev, Nicholas — Freedom and the Spirit
Berdyaev, Nicholas — Slavery and Freedom
Buber, Martin — I and Thou
Bultmann, Rudolph — Faith and Understanding
Cobb, John B., Jr., — Living Options in Protestant
    Theology
MacQuarrie, John — An Existentialist Theology
Roberts, David E. — Existentialism and Religious Belief
Tillich, Paul — Systematic Theology, Vol. 1
Tillich, Paul — The Courage to Be
Tillich, Paul — The New Being

Chapter Nine

Abbott, Walter J. (Ed.) — The Documents of Vatican II
Berger, Peter — A Rumor of Angels
Bethge, Eberhard — Dietrich Bonhoeffer
Bonhoeffer, Dietrich — Letters and Papers From Prison
Cairns, D.S. — God Up There?
Cox, Harvey — The Feast of Fools
Cox, Harvey — The Secular City
Fennell, W.O. — New Theology No. 2
Gilkey, Langdon — Naming the Whirlwind: The Renewal of
    God-Language
MacQuarrie, John — New Directions in Theology Today,
    Vol. III God and Secularity
Mumford, Lewis — The Pentagon of Power

Newbigin, Leslie — Honest Religion for Secular Man
Ramsey, A.M. — God, Christ and the World
Robinson, J.A.T. — Honest to God
Robinson, J.A.T. — The New Reformation?
Toffler, Alvin — Future Shock
Williams, Colin — Faith in a Secular Age

Chapter Ten

Altizer, T.J.J. — The Gospel of Christian Atheism
Altizer, T.J.J., and William Hamilton — Radical Theology
       and the Death of God
Cox, Harvey — New Theology No. 4, The Death of God and
      the Future of Theology
Hamilton, William — The New Essence of Christianity
Mehta, Vad — The New Theologian
Ogletree, T.W. — The Death of God Controversy
Robinson, J.A.T. — The New Reformation?
Vahanian, Gabrial — The Death of God
Van Buren, Paul — The Secular Meaning of the Gospel

Chapter Eleven

St. Augustine — The City of God
Baillie, John — The Belief in Progress
Barth, Karl — Church Dogmatics 111/3
Berkhof, H. — Christ the Meaning of History
Butterfield, H. — Christianity and History
Cochrane, C.N. — Christianity and Classical Culture
Cullmann, O. — Christ and Time
Cullmann, O. — The Christology of the New Testament
Cullmann, O. — Salvation in History
Dodd, C.H. — History and the Gospel
Eichrodt, W. — Theology of the Old Testament, Vol. 1
Galloway, A.D. — Wolfhart Pannenberg
McIntyre, John — The Christian Doctrine of History
Niebuhr, Reinhold — Faith and History
Olive, Don H. — Wolfhart Pannenberg

Outler, Albert — Who Trusts in God
Pannenberg, Wolfhart — Theology and the Kingdom
Richardson, Alan — History: Sacred and Profane
Rust, E.C. — Towards a Theological Understanding of
          History
Shinn, Roger — Christianity and the Problem of History
Wood, H.G. — Christianity and the Nature of History
Wright, G. Ernest (with R. Fuller) — The Book of the Acts
                                        of God

Chapter Twelve

Braaten, Carl E. — The Future of God
Brunner, Emil — Eternal Hope
Fison, J.E. — The Christian Hope
Fromm, Erich — The Revolution of Hope
Hefner, Philip — The Future of Our Future: A Teilhardian
                   Perspective in Hope and the Future of
                   Man, (Ed. E.H. Cousins)
Metz, Johannes B. — Creative Hope — New Theology No. 5
Moltmann, Jurgen — Theology of Hope
Newbigin, Leslie — Honest Religion for Secular Man
Pannenberg, Wolfhart — Basic Questions in Theology,
          Vol. 2
Teilhard de Chardin — The Future of Man
Teilhard de Chardin — Science and Christ

Chapter Thirteen

Alves, Ruben A. — The Theology of Human Hope
Cone, James H. — Black Theology and Black Power
Elliott, Charles — Study Encounter, Vol. VIII, No. 3, 1971
Gutierrez, Gustavo — A Theology of Liberation
King, Coretta Scott — My Life with Martin Luther King, Jr.
King, Martin Luther, Jr. — The Trumpet of Conscience
King, Martin Luther, Jr. — Why We Can't Wait
Marty, Martin E., and Dean G. Peerman — New Theology
                                          No. 6

Moltmann, Jurgen — Study Encounter, Vol. VIII,
          No. 1 1972
Ward, Barbara — The Lopsided World

Chapter Fourteen

Abbott, Walter J. (Ed) — The Documents of Vatican II
Baum, Gregory — The Necessity of Protestant-Catholic
          Dialogue in the Unity We Seek
          (Ed. W.S. Morris)
Brown, Robert McAfee — The Ecumenical Revolution
Horton, Walter M. — Christian Theology: An Ecumenical
          Approach
Kung, Hans — The Council and Reunion
McLelland, Joseph C. — Toward a Radical Church
Montreal Conference Report on Faith and Order, 1963
Mudge, Lewis — One Church: Catholic and Reformed
Neill, Stephen — A History of Christian Missions
New Delhi Conference Report, 1961
Oberlin Conference Report on Faith and Order, 1957
Temple, William — Faith and Order Conference,
          Edinburgh, 1937
Thomson, J.S. — The Divine Mission

Chapter Fifteen

Barth, Karl — Evangelical Theology: An Introduction
Barth, Karl — Church Dogmatics 1/1
Barth, Karl — Church Dogmatics 111/4
Barth, Karl — Prayer and Preaching
Chalmers, R.C. — See the Christ Stand
Hendry, George S. — The Life Line of Theology, Princeton
          Seminary Bulletin, December, 1972
McCord, James I. — Worship in the Reformed Churches,
          The Reformed World, June, 1973
Read, David H.C. — Christian Ethics
Temple, William — Nature, Man and God

ADDITIONAL BOOKS OF REFERENCE

General

Finegan, Jack — Christian Theology

Kaufman, Gordon D. — Systematic Theology: A Historicist
    Perspective

Loetscher, Lefferts A. Editor-in-Chief — 20th Century
    Encyclopedia of Religious Knowledge

Marty, Martin E. and Peerman, Dean, Editors — New
    Theology, Volumes 1 to 10

New Catechism, A — Catholic Faith for Adults (Dutch
    Catechism)

Pelikan, Jaroslav, Editor — Twentieth Century Theology in
    the Making
        Vol. 1 — Themes of Biblical Theology
        Vol.II — The Theological Dialogue:
            Issues and Resources.

Shaw, J.M — Christian Doctrine

Sykes, S.W. — Christian Theology Today

Whale, John S. — Christian Doctrine

Chapter One

Cunliffe-Jones, H. — Christian Thought Since 1600

Heick, Otto W. — A History of Christian Thought, Vol. II

Joad, C.E.M. — Guide to Philosophy

Kierkegaard, S. — Fear and Trembling & Sickness
    Unto Death

Pelikan, Jaroslav — Historical Theology

Randall, John Herman, Jr., — The Making of the Modern
    Mind

Welch, Claude — Protestant Thought in the Nineteenth
    Century

Chapter Two

DeWolf, L. Harold — A Theology of the Living Church

Ferre, Nels F.S. — The Christian Understanding of God
Fletcher, Joseph — Situation Ethics

Chapter Three

Brunner, Emil — The Christian Doctrine of God.
                Dogmatics, Vol. 1
Camfield, F.W., Editor — Reformation Old and New
Hartwell, Herbert— The Theology of Karl Barth.
                An Introduction
Smart, James D. — The Divided Mind of Modern Theology
Von Balthasar, Hans Urs — The Theology of Karl Barth

Chapter Four

Forsyth, P.T. — The Person and Place of Jesus Christ
McIntyre, John — The Shape of Christology

Chapter Five

Bruce, F.F. — The New Testament Documents: Are They
                Reliable?
Bruce, F.F. — The Apostolic Defence of the Gospel
Ford, Leighton — The Christian Persuader
Henry, Carl F.H., Editor — Revelation and the Bible
Henry, Carl F.H. & W. Stanley Mooneyham Editors
                One Race, One Gospel, One Task
                (World Congress on Evangelism)
Machen, J. Gresham — Christianity and Liberalism
Marshall, I. Howard — Christian Beliefs
Packer, James I. — Fundamentalism and the Word of God
Stott, John R.W. — Basic Christianity

Chapter Six

Chenu, M.D. — Nature, Man and Society in the Twelfth
                Century
Gaffe, Claude, Editor — Humanism and Christianity

Lonergan, Bernard J. — Method in Theology
Newman, John Henry Cardinal — An Essay on the
    Development of Christian Doctrine
Rahner, Karl — The Trinity

Chapter Seven

Morrison, J.M. — Honesty and God
Ogden, Schubert M. — The Reality of God
Robinson, John A.T. — The Human Face of God

Chapter Eight

Collins, James — The Existentialists: A Critical Study
Heinemann, F.H. — Existentialism and the Modern
    Predicament
Herberg, Will — Four Existentialist Theologians
MacQuarrie, John — Studies in Christian Existentialism

Chapter Nine

Barbour, Ian G. — Issues in Science and Religion
Nicholls, William. Editor — Conflicting Images of Man
Van Leeuwen, Arend T., — Christianity in World History

Chapter Ten

Baum, Gregory — The Future of Belief Debate
Dewart, Leslie — The Future of Belief
Hordern, William — Speaking of God
Mascall, E.L. — The Christian Universe
Mascall, E.L. — The Secularization of Christianity
Ramsey, Ian T. — Religious Language

Chapter Eleven

Buttrick, G.A. — Christ and History
Pannenberg, Wolfhart — Revelation as History

Robinson, James M. & Cobb, John B. Jr., Editors
    Theology as History

Chapter Twelve

Cousins, E.H., Editor — Hope and the Future of Man
McKeating, Henry — God and the Future
Minear, Paul S. — Christian Hope and the Second Coming
Thomson, James S. — The Hope of the Gospel
Schillebeeckx, Edward, O.P. — God and the Future of Man

Chapter Thirteen

Morris-Colin — Unyoung, Uncoloured, Unpoor
Raines, John C. & Dean, Thomas, Editors — Marxism
        and Radical Religion
Ward, Barbara — Faith and Freedom

Chapter Fourteen

Baillie, D.M. & John Marsh, Editors — Intercommunion
Fey, Harold E., Editor — The Ecumenical Advance
        A History of the Ecumenical Movement,
        Volume 2.
Goodall, Norman — The Ecumenical Movement : What It
        Is and What It does
Goodall, Norman — Ecumenical Progress, 1961-71.
Lawrence, John — The Hard Facts of Unity
MacKay, John A. — Ecumenism: The Science of the
        Church Universal
Newbigin, Leslie — The Reunion of the Church
Outler, Albert — The Christian Tradition and the
        Unity We Seek
Rouse, Edith & Neill, S.C. Editors — A History of
        the Ecumenical Movement, 1517-1948
Whale, John S. — Christian Reunion
Visser 't Hooft, W.A. — Memoirs

William, Colin W. — New Directions in Theology Today
     Volume IV. The Church

Chapter Fifteen

Barry, F.R. — To Recover Confidence
Bonhoeffer, Dietrich — The Way to Freedom
Ramsey, Michael and Suenens, Leon-Joseph Cardinal
          The Future of the Christian Church
Smith, Ronald Gregor, Editor — World Come of Age
Webb, Pauline — Salvation Today

Dr. Chalmers is also the author of:

    See The Christ Stand
    The Pure Celestial Fire
    The Protestant Spirit
    Our Living Faith
    A Gospel to Proclaim
    Project World (New Curriculum Series)

Editor and contributor to:
    The Minister's Handbook
    The Heritage of Western Culture

Editor and contributor, with J.A. Irving, to:
    Challenge and Response
    The Light and the Flame
    The Meaning of Life in Five Great Religions

62